CW01460033

The archaeology of the uplands: a rapid assessment of archaeological knowledge and practice

by Timothy Darvill
for the Countryside
Committee of the Council
for British Archaeology

with contributions by:
Barry Cunliffe, Keith Falconer,
Stafford Linsley, Frances Lynch,
Paul Mellars, Stephen Moorhouse,
Richard Morris, Harold Mytum,
and Malcolm Todd

Foreword by Tom Hassall
Preface by
Charles Thomas
Chairman of the CBA
Countryside Committee

1986
Published by
Royal Commission on the
Historical Monuments of England
and
The Council for British Archaeology

Published 1986 by the Council for British Archaeology
112 Kennington Road, London SE11 6RE

Copyright © 1986 the Council for British Archaeology
all rights reserved

British Library Cataloguing in Publication Data

The Archaeology of the uplands : a rapid
    assessment of archaeological knowledge and
    practice.
    1. Archaeology — England   2. England —
    Antiquities
    I. Darvill, T.C.   II. Cunliffe, Barry
    III. Royal Commission on the Historical
    Monuments of England IV. Council for British
    Archaeology, *Countryside Committee*
    936.2   DA90

    ISBN 0-906780-63-2

Typeset from disc, printed and made in England by
Derry & Sons Ltd, Canal St, Nottingham

Front:

Llech Idris standing stone (Gwynedd), looking north-east along the Afon Gain valley. The stone is 3.2m (10.5 ft) high (photo Mick Sharp)

Contents

Acknowledgments

The preparation of this report was much assisted by the many people who took the trouble to complete and return the questionnaires, and those who participated in the seminars. The following deserve special thanks: Mike Griffiths, John Williams, Pat Phillips, Tom Clare, Philip Mayes, Stephen Briggs, John Manley, Chris Musson, Alan Saville, Richard McDonnell, Tom Greeves, Richard White and Peter Rose for the seminar papers they presented; Frances Lynch and Barri Jones for chairing the Newtown and Leeds seminars, respectively; Richard Morris, Chris Arnold and Mick Aston for arranging the seminars at Leeds, Newtown and Bristol; John Manley, Nick Johnson, Steve Dickinson, Jeff Haynes, Barbara Bender, Mike Mills, Richard Hodges, Pauline Beswick, Peter Crew, Peter Waltham, Stephen Briggs, Roger Mercer, Chris Houlder, John Latham, Clare Fell, Guy Somerset, D Stratham, Peter Drewett, G Wimble, Jane Hill-Kann, Frances Lynch, Roy Canham, Garreth Dowdell, Alan Saville, Alison Allden and the Devon Archaeological Society, all of whom furnished comments upon aspects of upland archaeology; Charles Thomas, Henry Cleere, Tom Greeves, Chris Musson, Don Benson, Mike Griffiths, Mike Feist, Desmond Bonney, Bill Startin and Tim Gates, who read and commented upon early drafts of this report; Terry Betts of the RCHME Aerial Photographic Unit, who assisted by sorting out photographs, and Mick Sharp who took his cameras into the uplands during winter to take pictures especially for this report. Peter Spencer of RCHME prepared the final drawings.

Contributors

Barry Cunliffe, Institute of Archaeology, 36 Beaumont St, Oxford OX1 2PG
Timothy Darvill, 209 Seymour Rd, Gloucester GL1 5HR
Keith Falconer, RCHM(E), Rougemont, Rougemont Close, Salisbury SP1 1LY
Stafford Linsley, Dept of Adult Education, Windsor Terrace, Jesmond, Newcastle upon Tyne
Frances Lynch, Dept of History, University College of North Wales, Bangor, Gwynedd LL57 2DG
Paul Mellars, Dept of Archaeology, Downing St, Cambridge CB2 3DZ
Stephen Moorhouse, 27 Moorside Terr, Drighlington, Bradford BD11 1HX
Harold Mytum, Dept of Archaeology, University of York, Heslington, York YO1 5DD
Malcolm Todd, Dept of Archaeology, The University, Exeter

Illustrations

Foreword

Tom Hassall

Secretary of the Royal Commission on the Historical Monuments of England

In 1984 a programme of action in the uplands of England and Wales was urged upon the government by the Countryside Commission in its report *A better future for the uplands*. That report concentrated on social, economic, recreational and environmental needs, and emphasized the importance of striking a balance between them. The existence of an archaeological dimension in the environment was fully appreciated, but not examined in any detail.

In discussions between the Countryside Commission and the Council for British Archaeology it was agreed that a study dealing specifically with archaeological aspects of the uplands would form a useful adjunct to the Countryside Commission's report. What is the extent of the archaeological resource in the uplands? Why is it important? What is happening to it? And how may the management, conservation, and interpretation of archaeological monuments and landscapes in our uplands be bettered?

It was to answer such questions that the Royal Commission on the Historical Monuments of England agreed to cooperate with the CBA by funding their appointment of a Project Officer, Dr Tim Darvill, for six months. Work began in October 1984, and the first draft of this report was delivered at the end of March 1985. Because of its size and technicality the CBA went on to commission a shorter, more popular report, to bring the main findings to a wider audience.

Half a year is too short a time in which to evaluate an archaeological resource which may fairly be described as immense. Inevitably, therefore, this book is in the nature of an outline statement, a sketch. It is also only a summary of the *current* position: a tool for use today, to inform and advise owners and managers of land, together with those who exercise duties of control and care over upland landscapes.

For its part, in recent years the Royal Commission has turned its attention increasingly to the field archaeology of the uplands. A full survey of Bodmin Moor has been completed in collaboration with the Cornwall Committee for Rescue Archaeology and English Heritage. Work is in hand on selected areas of the Cheviots and the Peak District, and a project on Exmoor is planned. Since 1983, when it assumed responsibility for archaeology within the Ordnance Survey, the Royal Commission has undertaken map revision work in some upland areas. A survey of archaeological remains of all periods on Dartmoor, based entirely on air photography, has also been carried out in conjunction with English Heritage.

Preface

Charles Thomas
Chairman of the CBA Countryside Committee, 1982–5

It may not be clear precisely what the writer of Psalm 121, verse 1 meant to imply; but anyone who has experienced the Lake District or Scotland's Trossachs over a public holiday will know that thousands still need to "lift up their eyes unto the hills", for a sense of renewal they would regard as part of their rightful heritage. Our neighbours the Dutch, proud as they may be of their neat and fertile flatlands, place especial store on their only mountainous enclave, that tiny finger of elevated country around Valkenburg.

We British – strangely, for a nation that claims to have shown the Swiss what to do with very much higher mountains – have occasionally been blamed for neglecting our own uplands. We like to accuse ourselves, too, of making the very surface of Britain, that most precious and least readily replaced of all our resources, subservient to short-term needs. Whether such action be manifest in mineral extraction, superfluous afforestation, land clearances that produce yet more agricultural surplus, or simply a creeping rash of insensitive buildings, our national consciousness has at least been stirred. Mass travel has encouraged awkward questions upon return – travel to France with its various *Parcs Naturels* (or *Regionals*), perhaps even to the vast and splendidly-conceived reservations of the United States. What is the point (we ask) of a "National Park" here at home, if yet another reservoir or motorway is permitted to infringe it?

Yet this new feeling that stalks abroad is both fostered and reflected by appropriate agencies. And the Countryside Commission, in its recent hard look at Britain's uplands, as to both their present state and possible future, may (unintentionally) have done a real service to the British field archaeology lobby. It is nobody's particular fault that one such professional organization, pursuing its remit to examine the interactions between everyday life, the nation's leisure, and economic realities as these exist above the 800 ft contour, failed to include the historical dimension within its first summary. Nobody asked for, and nobody supplied, this – the collated thoughts of another, also professional, group of workers. Rather may this all have pointed up the annoying compartmentalism of our society. It would, however, rapidly become the fault of the archaeologists if, encouraged as they have been to supply this extra input, they now failed to quantify and to qualify the necessary information; or, further, failed to produce it within a reasonable time.

When archaeologists boast, as they often do, that the whole of Britain is one great archaeological site, this is arguably shorthand for a much longer, and supportable, claim. It might be set out on these lines. "The outcome of our cumulative researches, particularly through aerial photography and field surveys, is the demonstration that (with negligible exceptions) the face of Britain has been modified by man continuously during the last five millennia, and in that respect almost any given portion of it has to rank as a potential archaeological site." Now this in itself is an important, and to many people a novel, conclusion, and it is also one apparently unaffected by differences in vertical height. Therefore the Countryside Commission's request for detailed information becomes important to archaeologists, not least because of the stimulus given by such a challenge.

The conclusion is, of course, also a generalization. As such it nevertheless overrides a series of earlier and lesser generalizations. These, inherent in physical and historical geography, and economic history, as well as in archaeological theory, are too numerous and diffuse to be recapitulated here. Some of them involved notions, in their day sensible because they rested on available data and seemingly conclusive observations, that tended to rule out areas of upland Britain as suitable past habitats – save perhaps for helpless peasants and the odd Wuthering Heights eccentric chieftain. Earlier men, Saxons or Britons or figures from prehistory, were credited with a remarkable empirical knowledge about the grades of land, as subsequently clarified for their descendants by the Soil Survey of Great Britain. Errors were compounded because of uncertainties about the extent and locations of former woodlands, or the sequence of types of ploughs, or economic models of wool production. In hindsight, much of this can be sympathetically understood because (by contemporary standards) there was so very little in the way of field data.

We must be fair to the present, as to the past. Our advance in perception, our readiness to proceed from collected data to models of prehistoric land-use in these allegedly least favoured sectors of our landscape, are not completely due either to straight archaeological method or to the cleverness of today's archaeologists. As the chapters contributed below will say, there are dozens of factors to be taken into account, and many of them were inapplicable until quite recently. Aerial photography is one such. The holistic reconstruction by botanists, entomologists, and other natural scientists of the physical past in detail, or the sphere of palaeoenvironmental study, are others. We begin to draw upon reconstructions of past phases of climate, on a local scale. The story inherent in a stratified sequence of soils can be the history of the use of that piece of landscape.

Also, we have learnt to look outwards, to seek insights from contemporary societies in Europe, for here the archaeological potential of Britain's "upland" past, however defined, comes into focus with so many ideas and suggestions (some happily coincident with independent British conclusions) that one hardly knows which to pick out. Certain of the French limestone plateaus, virtually relief maps of landscape archaeology, remind us that our Peak District would not only have possessed a different character under different past climatic conditions but may also have supported both intensive farming and very precise rotative grazing. What we know of medieval France could suggest that food production, and consumption of that produce, occurred at widely separate localities. Again, old – sometimes, very old – upland roads and tracks lose none of their significance just because we may be obliged to realize that they never were "roads" in the conventional sense, or were only used on rare occasions perhaps during transhumance. In the Cevennes and the Massif Central, the droveways – engineered, buttressed, elaborately repaired, and now forgotten – conveyed millions of sheep, not humans.

And more, in a few areas of Switzerland there is at least one economy involving terraces, hillside fields, stone buildings other than homesteads, long up-and-down roads for animal transport, a seasonal harvest, and even an archaeologically undetectable range of harvest festivals and processions. This economy is based not on barley or wheat, but on hay. Its function is to support an ancient and specialized dairy cattle industry (Netting 1981).

The catalogue cannot end with agriculture. There are other and separate archaeologies of Britain's uplands. There is a military archaeology, because over three and a half centuries the Roman administration and the legions made very light indeed of Britain's puny mountains. The imperial power thought nothing of driving roads, quarrying out hillsides, and constructing manned forts in places where now only the curlew cries and the solitary rambler plots past. Pre-Roman hillforts – citadels? cattle-refuges? expensive symbols of authority? – occur in wildly unlikely high spots. The archaeology of mining is something that extends in time almost to the present day. We continue to be surprised, even at home; the archaeology of a whole medieval tin-mining and tin-streaming industry on Dartmoor has only very lately been recognized and plotted. And, looking much further back, Neolithic men quarried particular rocks for their stone axes high up in the fells and pikes of the Lake District; in places where admittedly no-one seems to have chosen to live, then, or now, but where a great many Original Britons chose to work.

These are no more than hints and glimpses. The unifying theme is imposed by the context of this report. In one sense, then, "uplands" may appear to lack real meaning within British archaeology, simply because the traces of most past activities upon dry land exhibit overall distributions that ignore the 244m (800ft) (or any other) contour. However, the concept acquires meaning if we accept that our own uplands, for non-archaeological reasons, now make up one of the principal reservoirs of archaeological evidence.

Archaeologists, who are as concerned as any other band of citizens about each and every aspect of the national heritage, are going a little beyond the mere suggestion that the future of our uplands should include consideration of visible history. They want to make public what has been discovered, and shown to exist in factual reality. The past historical dimension is already there, as a great tapestry of archaeological remains, the property of us all. Relative isolation, depopulation patterns, and the vagaries of economic land-use have in their varying ways preserved a surprisingly extensive resource. Its Lowland counterpart has, over the last 30 or 40 years, taken the most fearful and destructive punishment. Three cheers for the hilltops, the heather, the hawks, and the humming-bird hawk moths and long may they bring delight to all who work or live or find recreation within our uplands. But any future for this total resource will be that much fuller if we now take the step of admitting nationally that it has long held no less rich an archaeology: something that our descendants, archaeologists or not, must be allowed to explore and to enjoy in their own times.

1 Introduction

1.1 Background to the study

The uplands of England and Wales have been used by people for at least 10,000 years. During that time men and women have collected and produced food, exploited natural resources, made homes and communities, established ritual centres, and buried their dead. The uplands are extremely rich in archaeological remains relating to all of these activities, and because of their relative isolation and exclusion from intensive land-use in recent centuries visible remains have often survived. Their continued survival, management, and exploitation in the face of changing lifestyles and increasing pressure on the use of land forms the theme of this report.

Economic, social, and land-use changes in upland areas have been well documented by the various government departments and agencies which have commissioned surveys and appraisals within the last decade. The results of these studies are easily available (see Countryside Commission 1984b for references) and will not be repeated here. Archaeological matters have often been touched upon in existing reports, but only rarely have they been elaborated or given the attention they deserve. Indeed, it was only at the end of 1984 that the Historic Buildings and Monuments Commission announced its intention to produce a full statement on countryside issues.

Within the National Parks, which collectively account for a little under 60% of the uplands in England and Wales, greater emphasis than elsewhere has been given to the importance of the archaeological heritage. Much earlier work concerning the importance and potential of historic landscape conservation within National Parks is conveniently summarized by Haynes (1983a), while Wager (1981) provides a useful case study by detailing the implications of positive management policies for historic landscapes within the Peak District National Park. Both reports recognize the finite and non-renewable nature of the archaeological resource, and emphasize the fact that in upland areas the quality of preservation is so high that in many places relatively complete prehistoric or historic landscapes survive on a scale unknown elsewhere in Britain (Fig 1).

The Council for British Archaeology has long maintained an interest in upland archaeology. The need to investigate and record archaeological remains in upland areas was a recurrent theme in its *Survey and policy of field research* (CBA 1948), and occurs regularly in subsequent Annual Reports. This study represents an intensification of that interest, and is offered as a contribution to the debate which has been stimulated by the Countryside Commission's report (1984a) *A better future for the uplands*.

Fig 1 Prehistoric enclosed settlement on Brent Moor, Dartmoor. Circular huts and compounds are clearly visible within the enclosure, and other features are visible round about (photo National Monuments Record, Crown copyright reserved)

1.2 Aims and methods

As many varied interests seek to shape future government policy towards the uplands, the need for a detailed and wide-ranging assessment of the present state of archaeological knowledge is obvious. Accordingly, the Archaeology of the Uplands Project was established under the aegis of the CBA's Countryside Committee, in conjunction with the Royal Commission on the Historical Monuments of England and the Countryside Commission. A steering committee drawing members from each of the three participating bodies monitored the progress of the project, which was undertaken between October 1984 and March 1985.

The brief was to focus solely upon archaeological issues connected with the uplands. Social and economic matters, like the controversial subject of agricultural grant structures which has been fully dealt with elsewhere (MacEwen & Sinclair 1983; Countryside Commission 1984a) are therefore considered only when they impinge directly upon archaeology.

The Project had six specific aims:

1 to assess existing knowledge of the archaeology of the uplands

2 to determine the nature and extent of the recorded archaeological resource

3 to document current and likely future threats to archaeological remains, pointing out where and how damage may occur

4 to assess the manpower and resources available to cope with threats to upland archaeology

5 to review the place of upland archaeology as a resource in academic, educational, environmental, and recreational pursuits

6 to summarize the main issues involved in effective resource management, and to set out policy options for conservation, preservation, and exploitation

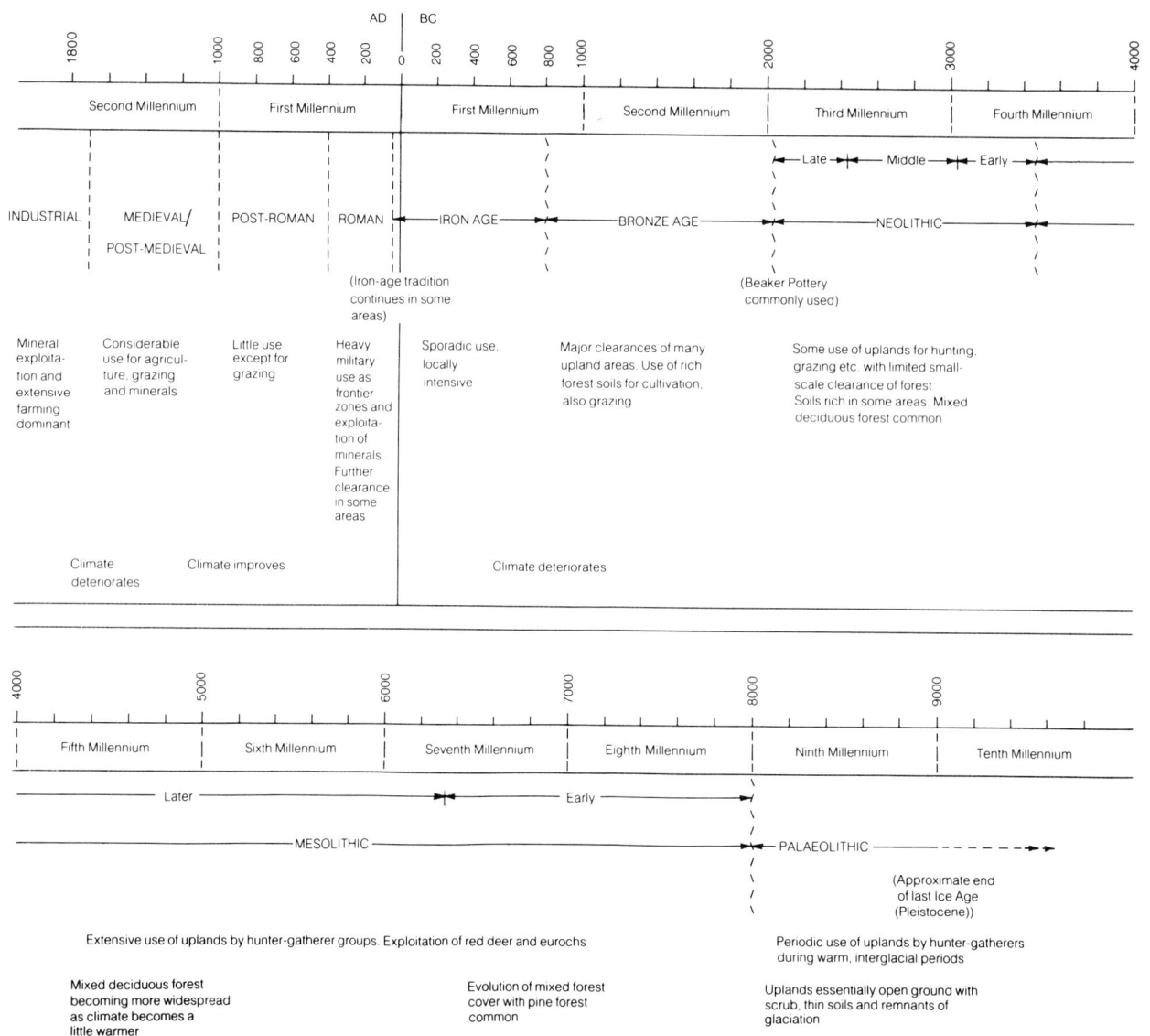

Fig 2   Simplified time-chart showing the main chronological subdivisions of occupation in upland areas (see ch 4 for detailed discussion of evidence). Note: dates AD are in calendar years but dates BC are in radiocarbon years

3

A

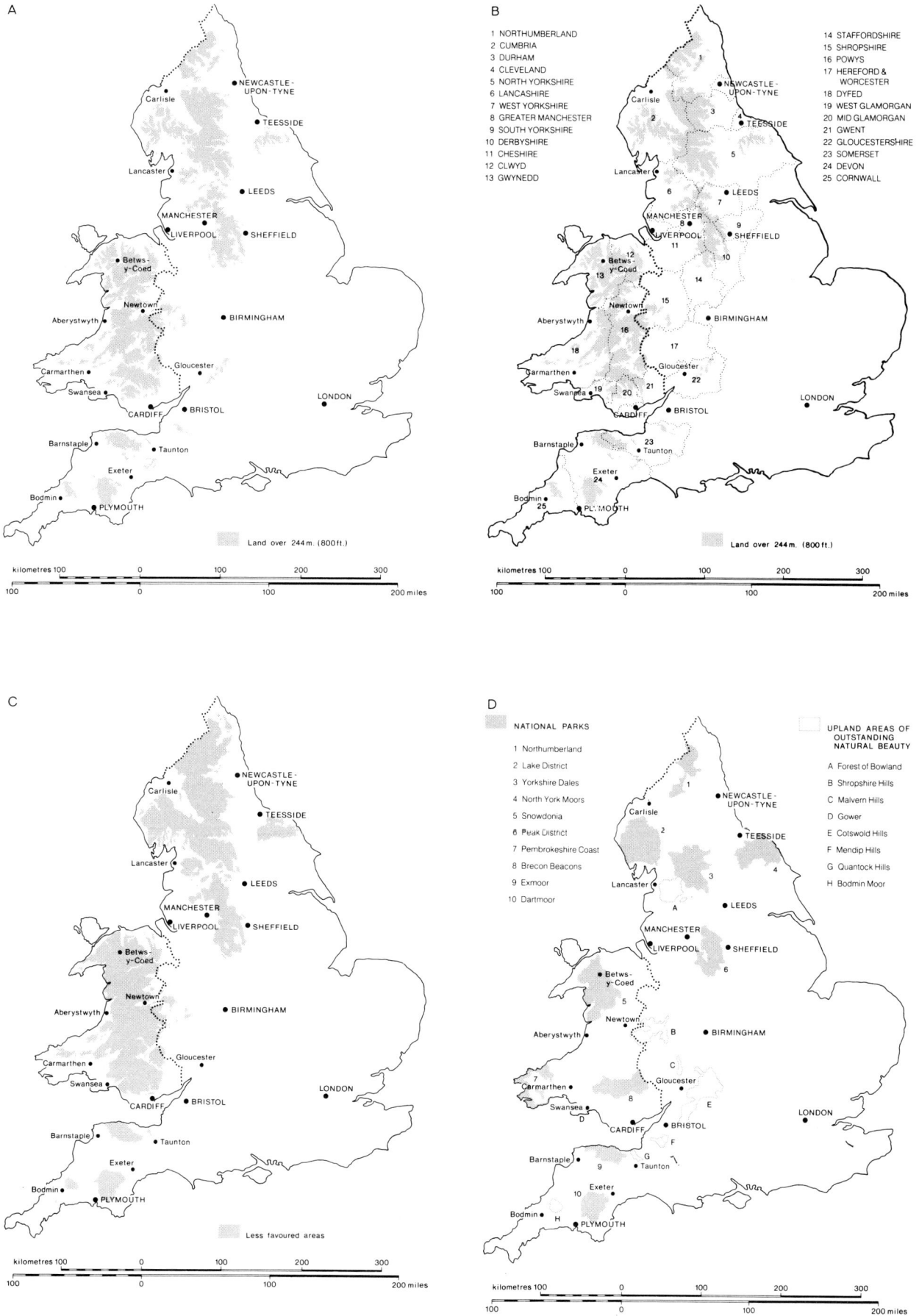

1 NORTHUMBERLAND		14 STAFFORDSHIRE
2 CUMBRIA		15 SHROPSHIRE
3 DURHAM		16 POWYS
4 CLEVELAND		17 HEREFORD & WORCESTER
5 NORTH YORKSHIRE		18 DYFED
6 LANCASHIRE		19 WEST GLAMORGAN
7 WEST YORKSHIRE		20 MID GLAMORGAN
8 GREATER MANCHESTER		21 GWENT
9 SOUTH YORKSHIRE		22 GLOUCESTERSHIRE
10 DERBYSHIRE		23 SOMERSET
11 CHESHIRE		24 DEVON
12 CLWYD		25 CORNWALL
13 GWYNEDD		

Land over 244 m. (800 ft.)

NATIONAL PARKS

1 Northumberland
2 Lake District
3 Yorkshire Dales
4 North York Moors
5 Snowdonia
6 Peak District
7 Pembrokeshire Coast
8 Brecon Beacons
9 Exmoor
10 Dartmoor

UPLAND AREAS OF OUTSTANDING NATURAL BEAUTY

A Forest of Bowland
B Shropshire Hills
C Malvern Hills
D Gower
E Cotswold Hills
F Mendip Hills
G Quantock Hills
H Bodmin Moor

Less favoured areas

Fig 3   General location maps showing: (A) land above 244m (800 ft) OD; (B) Counties with upland areas; (C) designated Less Favoured Areas; (D) National Parks and upland AONBs

4

In order to obtain up-to-date information a series of questionnaires was circulated and a leaflet outlining the scope of the project, and inviting comments, was widely distributed. In addition, three seminars were organized, in Leeds, Newtown (Powys), and Bristol. Appendix A gives full details of the consultation procedure. The response to the questionnaires was good (c 86% returned), but the results of the project must of course be seen in the light of its short duration.

Archaeology is broadly defined as the study of past human societies through their material remains, from early prehistoric times to the modern era (see Fig 2 for chronological summary and terminology). Inhabited dwellings were, however, excluded from the study. The term "site" is used here to refer to any part of, or point within, the landscape exhibiting traces of past human activity. The Glossary at the end of this report explains terms and concepts which may be unfamiliar to some readers.

1.3 Defining the uplands

The uplands discussed here are those in England and Wales only. Following principles established by the Department of the Environment and the Institute of Terrestrial Ecology (Countryside Commission 1978a), the uplands are defined as areas which mostly lie above the 244 m (800 ft) contour.

Thus defined, the uplands cover approximately 2 million hectares (4.9 million acres), representing 13% of the land area of England and Wales, 9% of England and 39% of Wales. Some 60% of the uplands lie within National Parks, or areas formally designated as being of Outstanding Natural Beauty (AONB). All ten National Parks, and 25 out of 53 counties (47%) in England and Wales, contain areas of upland (see Fig 3).

Within the uplands there is considerable variety of land type. Large areas are enclosed farmland, but more notable are the tracts of rough grazing, moorland, blanket bog, and forest. Most of the uplands are classified as "poor" in agricultural terms. The uplands include most of the areas within England and Wales defined as Less Favoured Areas (LFAs) under European Economic Community Directives 75/268 and 75/276, amended by 76/685.

It is important that the uplands are not confused with the familiar archaeological concept of the Highland Zone which includes uplands, lowlands, and coastlands in much of the west and north of Britain (Fox 1932; and see below, ch 2).

The singling out of the uplands for special study follows 20th century practice in subdividing the landscape according to economic, social, and physiographical criteria. Archaeologically, such subdivision is justified as a way to approach issues concerned with the preservation, recovery, and analysis of archaeological remains. This is no different from focusing on urban archaeology, the wetlands, or the coastlands, and it does not conflict with the axiom that upland societies in the past were inextricably linked with those of other areas within the wider landscape.

In addition to those areas above the 244 m (800 ft) contour, there are a few parts of the country – for example West Penwith (Cornwall) and portions of Northumberland – which many would consider to be of upland character despite their exclusion on the strict definition applied here. The conclusions of this report naturally have implications for these areas and, indeed, aspects of the present study have relevance for a much larger part of England and Wales, and for Scotland.

1.4 Upland landscapes

For many people, mention of the uplands conjures up a picture of wild, dramatic landscapes with a harsh climate, rugged terrain, poor soils, semi-wild vegetation, and scattered settlement. But the uplands vary a good deal.

Structurally, the uplands are full of contrasts. Lower Palaeozoic slates, sandstones, and tough limestones, interrupted by intrusive granites and metamorphic rocks, dominate Dartmoor, Bodmin Moor, north and central Wales, and the Lake District. Upper Palaeozoic rocks, including limestones and sandstones, characterize Exmoor, the Quantocks, south Wales, the Pennines, and much of Northumberland. Younger, generally soft, limestones are present in the Cotswolds and North York Moors. The appearance of the landscape has been considerably modified by successive glaciations. Naturally, the soils derived from, and the drift deposits that in places clothe these rocks have also changed. Indeed, so too have the patterns of vegetation.

Turning to climate, rain shadows, proximity to the sea, altitude, and the degree of exposure to wind all create micro-climates of varying character (Taylor 1976). In general the rainfall is higher and the temperature lower than the national averages, but within each upland block the south-western sides tend to be warmer and wetter than their north-eastern counterparts. While the absolute values of climatic factors have changed, the relative effects of topography on climate will have remained fairly constant.

Present day land-use is varied (Table 1) and multiple land-use common (Allaby 1983, 29; Countryside Commission 1978a). Again usages have changed through the ages. Environment acts as a major determinant of land-use, and the constraints imposed may be subdivided into three sets of factors:

Table 1 Land use in upland areas*

Land use	Approximate % of total
Rough grazing (incl common land)	50.00
Forestry	25.00
Agriculture	13.50
Ministry of Defence	3.75
Mineral workings	1.25
Nature reserves	1.00
Open water	0.50
Other	5.00

(data from Countryside Commission 1978, 20)
*Excludes multiple land use

Fig 4   Ruined post-medieval building and enclosure at Hafod-y-garreg, Afon Dulyn, Tal-y-Bont (Gwynedd) (photo Mick Sharp)

1 *Constants* of the environment, such as geology and topography, will have had an influence on human activity over the last 10,000 years much as they do today; some slopes are too steep to cultivate and only certain places are suitable for settlement.

2 *Variables* of the environment such as climate are continually changing the potential land-use of given areas. Even slight changes in mean air temperature or precipitation can drastically alter the altitude at which crops can be grown and land cultivated.

3 *Interference* with the environment by man through forest clearance, intensive agriculture, and excessive exploitation upsets the ecological balance and causes changes to vegetation and soil fertility. These in turn act as constraints for successive generations.

Social and economic factors also have a role to play in constraining or determining land-use. Population pressure, technical ability, and organizational capacity promote or retard upland land-use at different times. These factors are considered more fully in chapter 4 below.

It will be clear by now that the upland landscapes visible today are the result of many processes of change, involving both human and natural agencies, and are not the unchanged products of nature alone (Fig 4). When we turn to look for solutions to the problems that currently beset archaeological sites these long-term dynamics of landscape change must always be remembered. First, however, some consideration is given to the way in which perceptions of the uplands have changed over the last few centuries (ch 2) and to the sources, and nature, of the archaeological information available today (ch 3).

I Upland archaeology in the past

"In the highlands we found the people everywhere
civil enough. We met with several inscriptions,
but none of them Roman, nor indeed ancient:
however, we copied all we met of two hundred
years standing etc."

(Edward Lhwyd 1699)

2 Upland archaeology: approaches in the past

Richard Morris

This chapter examines the ways in which upland
archaeology has been perceived and interpreted over
the last 200 years.

2.1 To 1850: Travellers, clerics, and romantics

British archaeology as we know it today had its
beginnings in the 19th century. Its birth was preceded
by a conception in the work of 16th century topog-
raphers like John Leland and William Camden, and
two centuries of gestation, witnessed first in field
studies carried out by such men as Edward Lhwyd,
Robert Plot, and John Aubrey in the 17th century, and
then by an expansion of antiquarian research and
systematic collecting prompted in part by a reawaken-
ing of interest in antiquities abroad, and also by the
development of natural history at home. The story has
been told by Professor Daniel (1975, 14–33); it does not
often take us far into the uplands.

Several factors placed upland studies at a disadvantage during the late 17th and earlier 18th century.
Inaccessibility was one. The intellectual climate of the
period, which until the 1740s tended to view disorderly
extremes, like mountains, with displeasure, did not
assist. Another suppressive influence may be traced,
perhaps unexpectedly, to the essentially 12th century
system of parochial organization which has been inher-
ited by the Anglican Church. Rectors of the 18th
century are more often remembered for their achievements in such spheres as literature (Crabbe, Sterne),
botany (Gilbert White), and antiquarianism (Doug-
las, Faussett) than theology. Pluralism, and its con-
comitant, absenteeism, are also recalled as a feature of
the age. Both had consequences for the uplands, where
medieval parishes could be vast, benefices were sometimes impoverished, and resident clergy correspon-
dingly few. This meant that the population of leisured,
educated clerics, with time to devote to antiquarian
pursuits, was smaller than elsewhere.

In any case, until the overthrow of the biblically-
derived chronology that placed the origin of the world
in 4004 BC, antiquaries and early archaeologists "could
not get far because there was no chronological *depth* to
their ideas of prehistory" (Daniel 1975, 39). This
blocked progress in archaeology everywhere, but the
impediment loomed large in the uplands, where those
who took the trouble to visit them often found that
prehistoric remains were both prominent and copious.
Until revised estimates of geological time, put forward
for instance by Charles Lyell in his *Principles of Geology*
(1830–3), and mightily extended by Darwin's *Origin of
Species* (1859), began to win acceptance, prehistoric
archaeology was characterized by a helplessness man-
ifested in the telescoping of chronology, and a sweeping
together of all monuments and remains as works of
"ancient Britons" or as "Druidical".

The tendency – which still exists in popular belief – to
hold the Druids accountable for stone circles and other
field monuments is traceable in part to the influence of
William Stukeley (1687–1765) (Piggott 1950) and to a
section of opinion which idealized primitive peoples
(Piggott 1968; 1976, 69–75). Druids and Britons were
also recruited by 18th century writers on liberty and
nationalism as "upholders of British resistance against
Imperial Rome" (Piggott 1976, 121). Remote history,
ruins, and the melancholy pleasures of decay were
given yet wider projection by the Gothick tastes of men
like Horace Walpole, who during the second half of the
18th century encouraged a revolt against gentility and
complacent rationalism.

The Romantics took matters further. Their themes
encompassed man's relationship with nature. Poets
and painters explored the possibilities of landscape as
"inscape", to reflect, dramatize, or act in sympathy
with the emotional states of people. Whereas artists
before *c* 1750 preferred restraint to enthusiasm,
avoided extremes, and shunned the barbaric, the
Romantics reversed these values. In result, mountains,
moors, and hills assumed a new importance within the
arts. Not only did they lend themselves to exaggerated
visions, like John Martin's painting *The Bard*, were
visited by extremes of weather, as caught by the eye of
Turner who was prowling Wharfedale early in the 19th
century, and provided habitat for schools of poets, but
the archaeology of barbarism was especially well represented (Fig 5).

"Scarce images of life, one here, one there,
Lay vast and edgeways; like a dismal cirque
Of Druid stones, upon a forlorn moor,
When the chill rain begins at shut of eve,
In dull November..."

Keats, *Hyperion* II, 33–37 (1820)

Fig 5   Uplands in the Romantic imagination: The Bard *by John Martin (from the collection at the Laing Art Gallery, Newcastle upon Tyne; reproduced by permission of Tyne and Wear Museums Service)*

8

Such agreeably horrifying images cast their shadows down the decades that followed.

2.2 Early fieldwork and interpretation

The composition of *Hyperion* coincided with the publication of Colt Hoare's *Ancient Wiltshire* (1812–20), which dealt "specifically with the archaeological history of a county" and attempted "to be comprehensive and complete" (Daniel 1975, 31). "We speak from facts, not theory" was the famous superscription to this work. But in remoter parts, until railways were introduced (cf Rollinson 1967, 139–40), and regional and county societies grew up, records of systematic field observations were few and excavations rare. Where facts were lacking, historians applied their imaginations. Early in the 19th century Wales entered upon a period of Celtic Revivalism, shortly to be embroidered by speculations upon linguistic and racial history. In the Lake District the habitations of ancient Britons were pronounced to have been "rude and incommodious" by Hutchinson in his *History of the County of Cumberland* (1794–7): "they knew not even the common conveniences of the household, they entered the hovel, laid down to rest, waked and departed to their several avocations in the field." Hutchinson added (1794–7, 7): "It is certain, they knew nothing of tillage in these northern districts; they had a few herds and flocks, and in summer subsisted chiefly by the chase."

A century later – the century of Worsaae, who put forward the scheme involving ages of Stone, Bronze, and Iron and which saw much field research in lowland Britain – another historian of Cumberland is found writing in staggeringly similar terms. In 1890 R S Ferguson quoted approvingly from Elton's *Origins of English history*, asserting that Britain had been "a land of uncleared forests, with a climate as yet not mitigated by the organized labours of mankind.... It is certain that the island, when it fell under the Roman power, was little better in most parts than a cold and watery desert." According to Ferguson (1890, 9), late prehistoric Britain in general, and Cumberland in particular, was subject to "continual" rain, and such meagre crops as were raised "grew rankly". Fanciful as this description is, the glimmerings of two fundamental concepts can be perceived through the curtain of Cumbrian drizzle: the importance of environmental variables, such as climate and the fertility of soils; and man's power to act upon his surroundings.

Eighteen years on, Hadrian Allcroft's *Earthwork of England* (1908) marked an epoch in the development of field research. But even Allcroft was unable to shrug off the conditioning: "A map of Britain at any date antecedent to the Romans' coming would present only isolated areas of cultivable land of greater or lesser extent scattered amongst stretches of unbroken forest and fen" (Allcroft 1908, 29). Just two pages later, however, Allcroft is discovered musing in a footnote on the apparent fact that Exmoor and Dartmoor had sustained large populations in "primitive times".

In fact, antiquaries working in their own neighbourhoods had been making similar observations for some time. The southern Pennines were perhaps particularly well served, for here there were conurbations inter-spersed between blocks of upland, and access to the moors was comparatively straightforward. Leafing through county journals of the later 19th and early 20th centuries one is left in no doubt that the extensiveness of remains of human activity in the uplands was coming to be well grasped by those who had seen the evidence on the ground for themselves. This knowledge was augmented between the wars, for example by F Elgee in his book *Early man in north-east Yorkshire*, and R Hansford Worth (1868–1950), a civil engineer from Plymouth who produced some 200 papers on aspects of the history of Dartmoor. The Royal Commission's inventory for Westmorland, published in 1936, gave clear acknowledgement to the evidence for widespread Bronze Age colonization above the 305 m (1000 ft) contour.

But there were still gaps. Westmorland apart, the Royal Commission in England ventured into no upland county. In Wales "The hills teem with the vestiges of early man" wrote Mortimer Wheeler in the preface to his book *Prehistoric and Roman Wales* (1925). He continued: "Much of the evidence is still unmapped." Six Welsh counties had by then been surveyed by the Royal Commission on Ancient and Historical Monuments in Wales. Four had been published before the Great War, and were to some extent lacking in the detail and accuracy that were now being called for. During the next 30 years only two more counties were to be covered: Pembroke (1925), and low-lying Anglesey (1937). When in 1946 W F Grimes ended his review of the prehistoric period in *A hundred years of Welsh archaeology* he did so by observing how *many* pre-Roman field monuments existed, and how these constituted still "a largely untapped reservoir of information" (Grimes 1946, 79).

Where data had been gathered they called for interpretation. In the higher, supposedly wild, areas this posed a problem. How could copious indications that such districts once supported large populations be reconciled with broader theories about the condition of prehistoric Britain as a whole?

2.3 The effect of the landscape upon man

As we have seen, historians who wrote before the First World War (and, as we shall see, some who have written since the Second), looked upon pre-Roman Britain as a country cloaked by forest and fen. Alongside this belief was erected a theory which stated that valley floors would have been too thickly wooded to permit much habitation or easy travel, and that the heavier lowland soils could not have been cultivated under prehistoric technology. Prehistoric man was therefore associated with light soils. Indeed, until very recently it was the Anglo-Saxons who were credited with bringing the lowlands into general agricultural use, especially the heavy midland clays. The first edition of the Collins *Field guide to archaeology* (Wood 1963) asserted that in Roman Britain "still only about 2 to 3 per cent of the possible land was used, and most of that in the southern half of the country", and went on to state, with qualifications, that the Anglo-Saxons had a virtually free choice of sites for their settlements and farms (Wood 1963, 26–7).

Of course, the commentators who invoked soils and forests as inexorable determinants of the whereabouts of prehistoric settlement did so with relatively congenial neighbourhoods foremost in mind. In areas such as the South Downs of Sussex, the wolds of Lincolnshire and eastern Yorkshire, and the rolling chalklands of Wessex, the region recently reinvented by Thomas Hardy, the evidence for abundant settlement on the one hand, and suppositions about a primeval, generally intractable Britain on the other, could be brought into a balance. Wessex, in particular, was looked upon as a prehistoric cultural nexus. Sir Cyril Fox declared (1947, 89):
"The most complete and full manifestations of any *primitive* culture entering eastern or southern Britain from the continent will come to be in the Lowland Zone. The centre and focus in the Lowland Zone of such culture will tend to be the Salisbury Plain region ("Wessex"), because it has the largest area of habitable country, is close to south-coast seaports conveniently reached by Atlantic and Armorican trade, and is the meeting point of the (natural) traffic routes of the Lowland Zone."

Looking back, we might add that Wessex had also been unusually favoured by the attentions of antiquaries and archaeologists, both before and after the days of Cunnington and Colt Hoare, and more recently had been subjected to intensive fieldwork on the ground, and scrutiny from the air, not least by O G S Crawford (Crawford & Keiller 1928), who from 1920 had been stationed as Archaeological Officer with the Ordnance Survey at nearby Southampton.

In the 1930s and 1940s the interpretation of prehistoric Britain as a kind of archipelago of areas of "habitable country" seemed to work well enough at low and intermediate altitudes. But it was not so easily applied to the evidence which was being recorded on much higher terrain. Here indeed was a paradox, for if technical limitations and natural obstacles conspired to inhibit settlement throughout much of lowland Britain, why should man exchange one set of hardships for another by electing to reside upon windswept mountainsides or to cultivate moorland fields?

The theory which attributed to "Early Man" a preference for open or lightly forested country with pervious soil was formally enunciated by Sir Cyril Fox in his book *The personality of Britain*, first published in 1932. Here Fox independently developed an analysis which resembled another that had been advanced 30 years before by the geographer Sir Halford Mackinder. In *Britain and the British seas* (1902) Mackinder explored contrasts between Highland and Lowland Britain. The fundamental contrast was one of geology, reinforced by climatic differences, which together were held to have exerted decisive influence upon the course of agrarian, racial, and cultural history. Fox, likewise, explored the structural and environmental contrasts as between a Highland and a Lowland Zone, considering these in conjunction with what he defined as "areas of Easy and Difficult settlement" (1947, 78). Out of both came a theory of cultural differentiation. In the Lowland "cultures of continental origin...tend to be imposed. In the Highland...these tend to be absorbed.... There is greater *unity* of culture in the Lowland Zone, but greater *continuity* of culture in the Highland Zone" (Fox 1947, 88).

2.4 The effect of man upon the landscape

The phrases Highland Zone and Lowland Zone are still current, and have indeed featured in the titles of a pair of CBA research reports, deriving from conferences, within the last ten years (Evans *et al* 1975; Limbrey & Evans 1978). The full titles of these books are, however, enormously significant: both of them deal with the effect of man upon the two "Zones". The opening essay of the Lowland volume (Fowler 1978) was in part a critique of some of Fox's propositions. The *personality* of Fox's Britain was observed to have been essentially natural: an amalgam of position, relief, structure, and climate, which determined soil, dependent vegetation, and animal life. "The whole represents man's environment" (Fox 1947, 86). In the Britain of Dr Fowler's perception, by contrast, man has been neither a prisoner of, nor external to, his environment; rather, he is part of it (Fowler 1978, 1).

The changes which have been wrought upon our understanding of the history of settlement in southern Britain during the last quarter century have been extensive and dramatic. One effect of the rapidity with which new knowledge has accrued is that archaeologists, as if dazed by the implications of their own discoveries, have done little to make their findings available in forms accessible to the public. The "Zones" live on because they have not yet been superseded by a model that is clear-cut. But landscape analysis of the type found in the writings of C C Taylor, perhaps especially in his recent book *Village and farmstead* (1983), provides the basis for a more coherent understanding, not based on a model but on observable evidence.

It emerges that our antiquarian predecessors were blinkered by three misapprehensions. First, the abundant evidence for early settlement that they saw on open areas of pervious soils *and in the uplands* was visible because the land in these districts was of marginal quality and much of it had reverted to pasture or moor, with the result that archaeological remains of earlier periods were well preserved (Fig 6). Second, evidence for early occupation in heavy-soiled lowland regions was not lacking, but it had been rendered obscure to earlier generations of workers by medieval and modern cultivation, by the absence of technical aids and methods that we now take for granted, and perhaps also by their own preconceptions. Third, too little was known about the nature and chronology of past changes in the environment. The scope and scale of man's responses to, and in some respects responsibilities for, such changes were not well apprehended, and in general underestimated.

Today, following the application of a range of methods (see ch 3) to which our predecessors either did not have full access or which they did not attempt to use, and the emergence of new approaches to the manipulation and interpretation of data, it is suggested that "far from there being dense inpenetrable forests throughout prehistoric times, the great attack on woodland in England started as early as 5500 BC, and this continued fairly steadily so that by about 1000 BC there was probably less woodland in England than there is now" (Taylor 1983, 20). As we shall see in chapter 4, the upland evidence has been placed in an entirely new light.

Fig 6   The Druid's Circle, Penmaenmawr, Gwynedd. This embanked stone circle of Bronze Age date set high on the open moorland near the Craig Lwyd stone axe factory was probably first called the Druid's Circle in the late 18th century under the influence of the romantic movement prevalent at that time. Earlier records, which date back to 1625, show that it was formerly known as Meini Hirion - *"the tall stones" (photo Tim Darvill, copyright reserved)*

The revolution in settlement studies has not been limited to prehistory. Population estimates for Roman Britain have been variously revised, always upwards; some now entertain a figure up to three times larger than the 1.5 million put forward by Wheeler in 1930. This in turn has repercussions for the study of Anglo-Saxon settlement, for although it seems that the population total fell after the 4th century, the notion that Anglo-Saxon settlers were at liberty to pick and choose their settlement sites and farms is no longer plausible. The idea that post-Roman Cumbria, Wales, and the south-western peninsula were occupied by large numbers of British refugees dies hard, but is equally fallacious. Beyond this, recent fieldwork, and reassessments of information contained in Anglo-Saxon written records, have led to the claim that rural resources were often as fully exploited in the 7th and 8th centuries as they were just before the Norman Conquest (Sawyer 1978, 144–5, 148).

So it is that archaeologists today visualize an early Britain which was thoroughly settled, at some periods and in some areas even crowded, long before the arrival of the Romans. The archaeology of the uplands is thus open to radical reinterpretation, not as the product of an uncomfortable (and, in terms of argument, unconvincing) compromise between the peak and the deep green forest, but rather as a series of cultural tide-lines deposited by washes of expansion from below. What the evidence actually consists of, and the ways in which we recognize it, are topics which form the theme of the chapter that follows.

II Upland archaeology in the present

"But there are not many places where one can feel with such complete assurance that this is exactly as the first inhabitants saw it in the freshness of the early world. Not much of England, even in its more withdrawn, inhuman places, has escaped being altered by man in some subtle way or other, however untouched we may fancy it is at first sight"

(W G Hoskins 1955, 19)

3 The upland resource

As attitudes have changed so it has become increasingly clear that the uplands preserve a rich archaeological heritage. In this chapter the nature and scale of this resource is described, and the ways in which we can find out more about it are explained.

3.1 The nature of the evidence

The archaeological remains in the uplands mostly represent focal points in the lives of long vanished societies: their settlements, enclosures, fields, paddocks, quarries, industrial sites, burial grounds, and ritual centres. Some of these functions are represented by massive earthworks and upstanding features, others by only the faintest traces. All types of evidence are important. Of course, knowledge of an individual site depends upon its preservation and the amount of investigation that has taken place (Stevenson 1975). Thus small collections of surface finds or the occasional "stray find" of a stone axe or other artefact are as significant as the features revealed on an aerial photograph, at least until the site has been carefully checked on the ground and its true nature established. However, common to all evidence of man's activities in the uplands are three characteristics which may be summarized as follows:

Physical structure

More than anything else, the physical structure of upland remains differentiates them from lowland sites. The extensive use of stone by upland societies makes the surviving evidence materially robust, if structurally fragile. Walls can be easily toppled and cairns dispersed even when light vegetation protects the structures. But stone was not the only material used. Wood and turf were integral parts of many structures with stone foundations, and entirely wooden buildings were constructed in the uplands from early prehistoric times onwards. Such structures might be thought to leave no surface traces once they have decayed, but visible traces of prehistoric timber houses and palisades are a notable feature of the upland archaeological record. At Moel-y-Gerddi near Harlech (Gwynedd), for example, postholes of a circular wooden house of c 450 BC were found beneath a later stone structure. In north Tynedale (Northumberland), three Iron Age/Romano-British settlements – at Tower Knowe, Belling Law, and Kennel Hall Knowe – all display sequences where

timber houses within wooden fenced enclosures were superseded by stone houses surrounded by stone walls or a bank and ditch (Jobey 1973; 1977; 1978). Localized soil conditions can sometimes cause the preservation of wooden structures themselves. There is no indication at present as to the distribution of timber buildings in the uplands, except where they have been revealed during the investigation of stone-built structures.

Generally speaking, upland sites are not deeply buried, and tend to have shallow, but often complex, stratigraphy. Episodes of living and working have created a palimpsest of remains. Relationships between successive periods of activity can sometimes be seen on the surface because the evidence is upstanding.

Upland sites tend to be poor in artefacts. This is partly a problem of preservation, since soil chemistry usually militates against the survival of calcareous matter such as bone, and partly because the kinds of context best suited to long-term preservation – pits and ditches – are rare. Furthermore, the activities connected with the use of upland sites (eg transhumance) create rather specialized deposition patterns and for this reason we should not expect upland evidence to resemble lowland evidence except on those types of site where similar activities took place. The inhabitants of some upland areas probably lacked pottery during certain phases of prehistoric and early historic times; presumably they made use of wooden and leather utensils instead.

Environmental indicators are fairly well preserved on most upland sites, and are given separate consideration below (3.3).

Archaeological form

The variety of site types in the uplands is impressive. Many can be broadly paralleled by lowland equivalents, the differences simply representing regional traditions and constraints imposed by available building materials: round barrows, later prehistoric houses, Roman forts, field systems, and long barrows represent just a few examples. In addition, there are types of site common in the uplands which certainly existed outside the uplands in the past, but which are now very rare in lowland areas. These include stone circles, vermin traps, warrens or pillow mounds, and early prehistoric field systems. Lastly there are classes of site which are almost exclusive to the uplands and result from the demands of specific activities. Clearance cairns, tin-

PALÆOLITHIC
MESOLITHIC
NEOLITHIC
BRONZE AGE
IRON AGE
ROMAN
DARK AGE
MEDIEVAL
PREHISTORIC?
UNKNOWN

%
100
80
60
40
20
0
20
40
60
80
100

DATUM

%
100
80
60
40
20
0
20
40
60
80
100

DYFED. Actual landscape - 21% above 244 m (800 ft), 79% below

CLWYD. Actual landscape - 35% above 244 m (800 ft), 65% below

Concentrations of recorded sites greater than expected

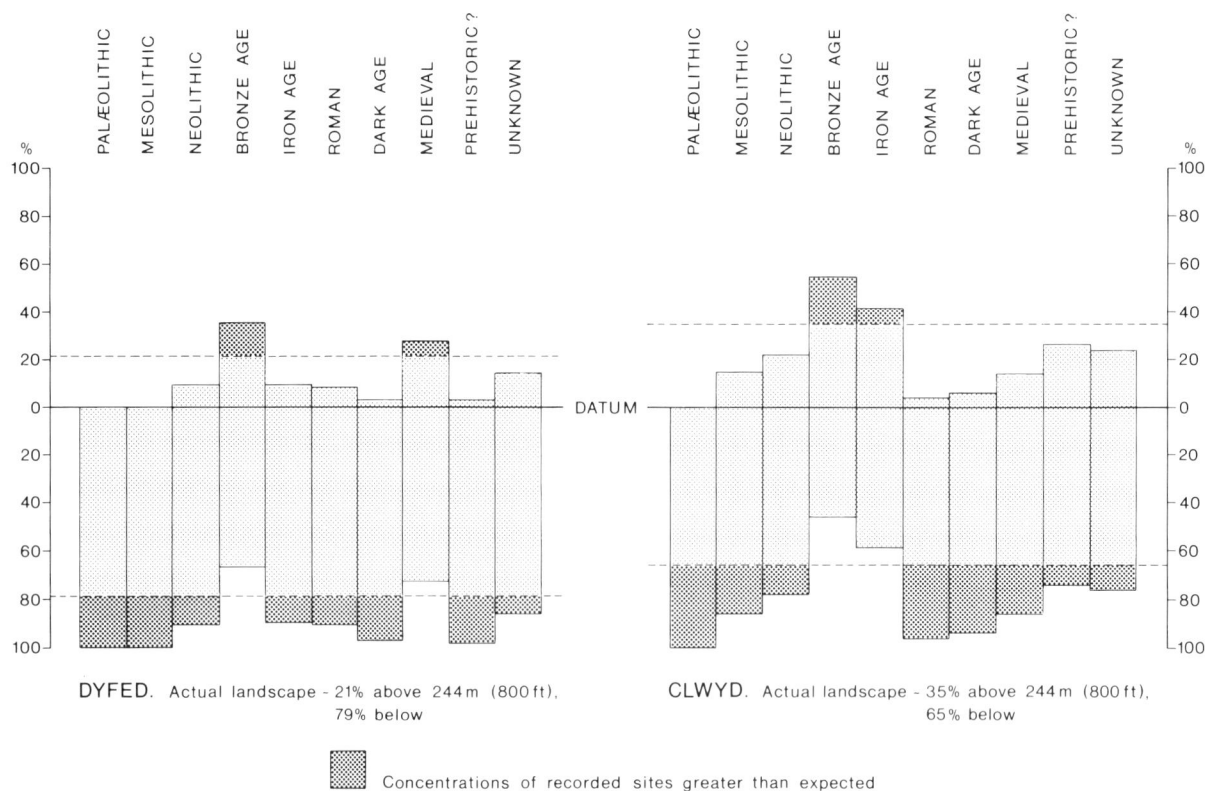

Fig 7   Summary of the recorded evidence from Clwyd and Dyfed by period and altitude. The percentage of recorded evidence is shown as a bar relative to the 244m (800 ft) contour which forms a datum for the graph. The dotted horizontal lines represent the actual division of land, as a percentage, above and below the 244m contour

Fig 8   Bronze Age land boundaries (reaves) on Holne Moor, Dartmoor, during excavation. The modern wall in the distance is on the site of the reave. To the left is open moorland, to the right, two smaller reaves representing field divisions join the main reave at right angles (photo Andrew Fleming)

streaming channels, blowing houses, stone rows, and shielings are examples.

Not all periods are equally well represented by field evidence (see Fig 7). In Dyfed it is clear that more Bronze Age and medieval sites are recorded from the uplands than would be expected if the distribution of sites was in rough accord with the distribution of land. In Clywd the Bronze Age and Iron Age are better represented by sites on high ground. For all other periods the lower ground offers a slightly higher stock of evidence (and see ch 4.1 below). How far these distributions are the product of geographically uneven investigation in the past is open to debate. Within the uplands, however, the relative quantities of evidence observed for different periods are probably acceptable as a guide to the actuality.

Preservation

Although there is variation in the distribution of evidence and the factors which determine the preservation and recognition of evidence, as a general rule sites situated above 244 m (800 ft) OD are more likely to be better preserved than sites on lower ground. This is well illustrated by data from Clwyd which have been supplied by Mr J Manley. In all, 1306 upstanding monuments have been recorded in the county. Of this total 36% lie above 244 m – a percentage which broadly corresponds to the actual land area above 244 m. Only 19% (254) of the 1306 are described on the Clwyd Sites and Monuments Register as "intact", but of these 44% lie above 244 m.

The quality of preservation in the uplands is intimately connected with the fact that upland sites tend to be more complete (Fig 8). Rather than being collections of isolated, discrete sites, many areas of upland, especially open moorlands, preserve neighbourhoods where foci of localized activities (settlements, burial sites, ritual complexes) are linked by evidence relating to activities of a more general kind (eg fields, paddocks, land boundaries). With so many coexistent features preserved, and relationships between them clear, such survivals can only be described as relict landscapes.

3.2 How the evidence is recognized

Throughout the history of upland studies the techniques for locating and examining sites on the ground have changed very little. What has changed is the organization of the work, and the thoroughness with which it is undertaken. The small, low-budget operations that for long characterized upland reconnaissance are now giving way to more highly organized projects where cost-effective recovery of maximum information, and the safety of the personnel involved, have come to the fore.

Naturally, the range of techniques available for a particular project must be adapted to suit its aims. Although most techniques are familiar to field archaeologists, many present special difficulties in upland settings. Universal among such difficulties is the problem of accessibility. Transporting personnel to where they are needed means having reliable cross-country vehicles (preferably with four-wheel drive). Safety procedures must be well understood by all

involved and the criteria for implementing emergency procedures strictly adhered to. Equipment needs to be light since it will have to be carried considerable distances. Thorough preparation for outdoor work is essential as a return to base for forgotten equipment is extremely time-consuming, if not impossible. These factors make work in the uplands more expensive than is often imagined.

The following techniques are used:

Field survey

This involves the careful scrutiny of selected areas and the detailed plotting of visible archaeological features. The technique was largely pioneered by the investigators of the Royal Commissions on Historical Monuments (England and Wales), and in the uplands it is the most widely used of all reconnaissance methods. It can be applied to an area of any size. Plotting features in a landscape with few landmarks can be difficult and requires competent surveyors (Fig 9). In the case of the Bodmin Moor survey, transcription of aerial photographs by the National Monuments Record Air Photographic Unit using a Thomson-Watts Mk II stereo plotting machine provided a base map for field checking, annotation, amendment, and elaboration (Johnson 1983). The south Cheviots are currently the subject of a similar survey by the Northern Local Office of RCHME. The success of any survey depends on covering the study area systematically, and on recording as much detail as is possible within the limitations set by the terrain. Because of constraints imposed by vegetation cover and bad weather, effective survey is really only practical in March and April in most areas, although in the far north it remains feasible until June. Mercer (1980) provides a clear outline of the practicalities and methodology of field survey in upland areas.

Fieldwalking

This involves the systematic recovery of artefacts from disturbed ground. Areas of archaeological debris may relate to sites not marked by standing features. Fieldwalking has a wide application on upland fringes where ploughed fields are present, but there are many opportunities for its use during forestry operations and ground improvement schemes. As with field survey, an area of almost any size can be tackled, although the need to be systematic is paramount if the distributions of artefacts are to be understood. Ground conditions suitable for fieldwalking are usually confined to a few months of the year. Fieldwalking has a long history in upland areas (Robinson 1948; Fell & Hildyard 1953; Grinsell 1964) but the methodological refinements necessary for objective application have only recently been developed (see Hayfield 1980). The results of studies on the Cotswolds (Darvill 1984) and the southern Pennines (Garton & Beswick 1983) illustrate what can be achieved.

Aerial photography

This has long been recognized as a vital part of reconnaissance in upland areas (Wilson 1975). Rapid access to remote areas, and cost effectiveness as a high resolution recording technique, make it particularly suited to upland work. Low-angle sunlight, light snow cover, and the use of infra-red film allow a great variety

14

Fig 9   Plane-table survey in progress at Hallshill (Northumberland) (photo Tim Gates)

of archaeological features to be identified and recorded. Cropmark evidence is less important in the uplands than elsewhere, although such marks have been recognized on peripheral areas where arable cultivation takes place, and growth marks have been recorded on reseeded pasture. Differential vegetation cover on moorland can be significant, but the masking effects of bracken and blanket bog diminish the effectiveness of aerial photography in some areas. Computer-assisted plotting of both vertical and oblique pictures is an important methodological advance which facilitates rapid interpretation and provides high quality maps for checking on the ground (Palmer 1977). Aerial survey in conjunction with field survey and/or fieldwalking gives high returns (Fig 10). Aerial photography also provides a rapid method of monitoring landscape change, threats or damage to archaeological sites, and the effects of management agreements.

Excavation
In the past much emphasis has been placed on excavation as a means of providing information of high quality but, by comparison with the techniques already discussed, excavation can only be undertaken on a small scale, focusing on the individual site or a tiny segment of a landscape (Fig 11). Excavation in the upland context is valuable in three respects: firstly as a last resort when sites of high importance are threatened by obliteration, secondly as a way of elucidating observations made during field survey, and thirdly as a research tool. No textbooks adequately cover the special problems of excavating upland sites, although

the general principles are well presented by Barker (1977).

Geophysical survey
Geophysical techniques find little application on the higher uplands, although they are widely used on the upland fringes, on enclosed land with deeper soils, and in conjunction with fieldwalking. Proton magnetometer surveys may be used alongside field survey. Further research is needed to harness the potential of geophysical survey to upland contexts.

Phosphate survey
Differences in soil phosphate levels can reflect variations in the type and intensity of activity over an area. Studies at Shaugh Moor, Dartmoor (Balaam & Porter 1982), illustrate the potential of phosphate surveys on upland sites, especially when linked to excavation or field survey (Fig 12). General comments on the application of phosphate analysis in archaeology are given by Bakhevig (1980).

Written records
Written records, including old maps, provide information for the post-Roman periods. Upland areas are, in general, less well covered by documentary sources than other parts of Britain, but some records are available. Aston (1983), for example, examined deserted farmsteads on Exmoor as revealed through the lay subsidy of 1327 and Harbottle and Newman (1973) have explored the change from transhumance to permanent

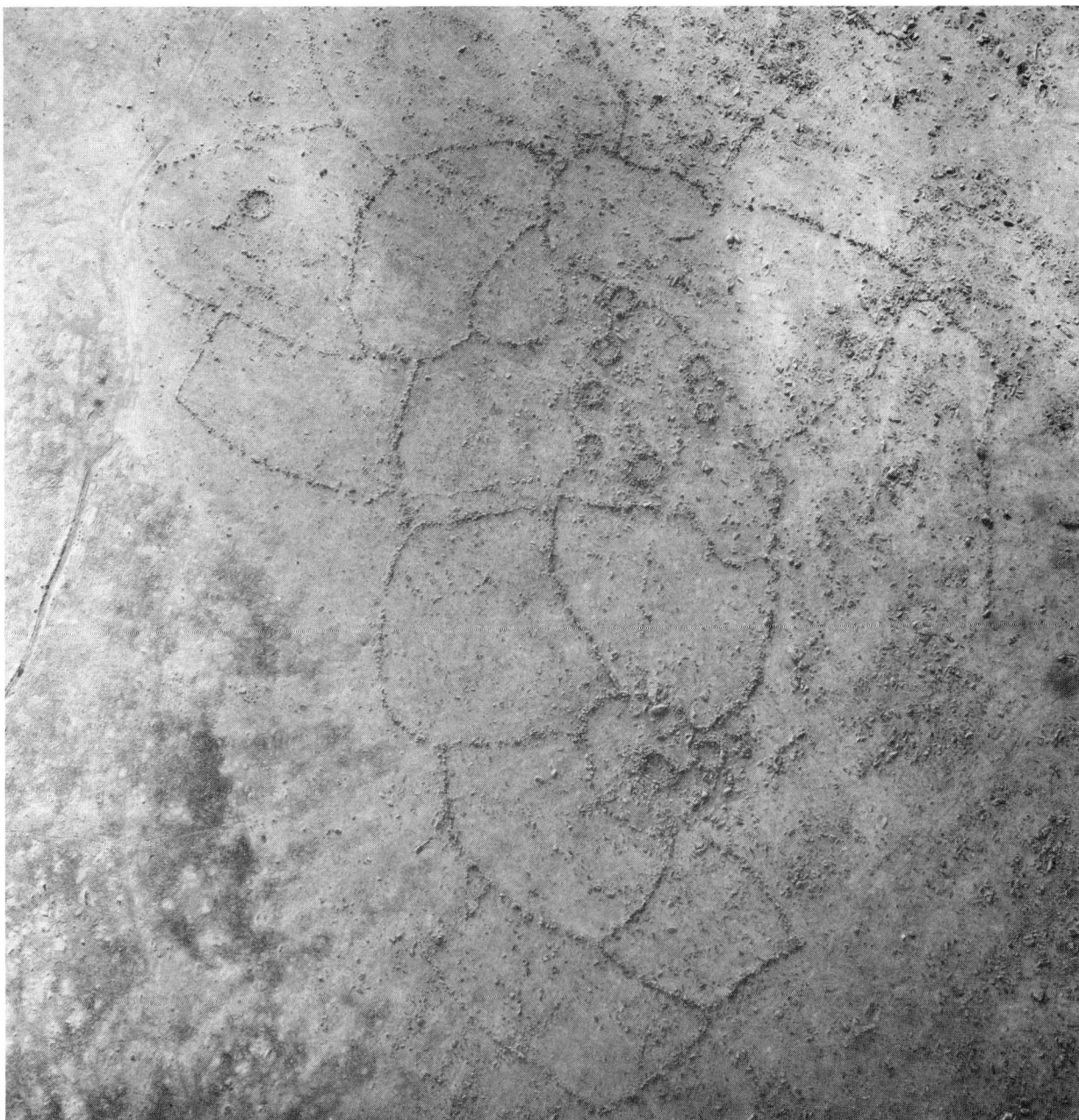

Fig 10 (A) Aerial view of Bronze Age settlements and fields at Leskernick Hill, Bodmin Moor (Cornwall). Clusters of huts amid irregular shaped fields defined by low stone walls can be clearly seen. Some of the fields appear to have been partly cleared of stones (photo National Monuments Record, Crown copyright reserved)

settlement in North Tynedale (Northumberland) between the 12th and 17th centuries.

Chance finds

The cumulative evidence from chance finds made during ground disturbances of all types is considerable. Museums play a major part in recording such finds, but probably only a fraction of the actual number of discoveries made are ever reported. Checks on the circumstances of recovery, to shed light on the context of the find, are becoming a regular part of archaeological work where resources permit.

There is a real need for more research aimed at the development of new techniques and the refinement and extension of those that already exist. In the past funding has gravitated towards excavation, to the detriment of other methods of reconnaissance (Jones

1985) which have been viewed as preliminaries or ancillary to excavation (Fowler 1980, 13). In fact, all the techniques mentioned above can be used in their own right as the basis for projects. Their power increases when they are used in combination, within structured programmes of research (Mercer 1982).

The lack of people qualified for upland work is a matter for concern. University departments represent the most important training ground for qualified staff, but only four out of the 22 departments which responded to the questionnaire run practical sessions on survey techniques appropriate for upland work. Several others run upland projects outside, but related to, the curriculum, and these will provide experience for some students.

Some reconnaissance projects are conceived in relation to specific problems, such as the appraisal of

Boulders

Rock outcrop

Hut Group

Hut Group

Hut
Group

Hut Group

Approximate area of photograph

100   0   100   200 m
100   0   600 ft

Fig 10   (B) Plot of Bronze Age settlements and field systems on Leskernick Hill, Bodmin Moor (Cornwall). The area covered by the photograph (Fig 10 (A)) is marked on the plan. (Reproduced by permission of Royal Commission on the Historical Monuments of England)

Fig 11   Excavation of a pair of Bronze Age burial cairns at Trelystan (Powys). The furthermost cairn has been almost totally excavated except for the central grave pit (to right of people). The cairn in the foreground has a stone curb and a rubble core. It is surrounded by a ditch. Two concentric rings of stake-holes representing some kind of wooded fence can also be seen. (photo W Britnell; copyright Clwyd Powys Archaeological Trust)

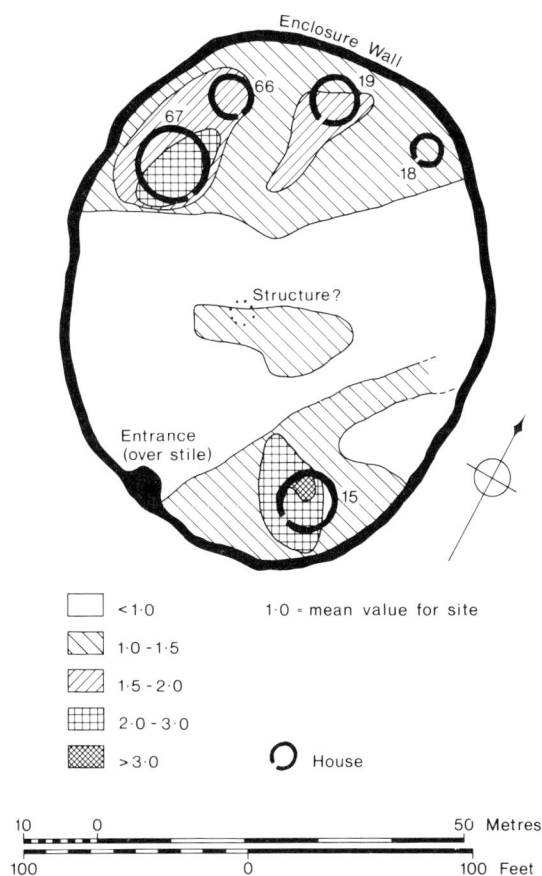

Fig 12 Plot of phosphate survey in Bronze Age enclosure on Shaugh Moor, Dartmoor. The areas of phosphate enrichment around the houses suggests human occupation rather than animal penning which would produce more widespread concentrations. There is no entrance gap in the enclosure wall; entry was probably over the stile on the south side (after Balaam et al 1982)

damage to monuments (Crawford 1980; Saville 1980). These tend to be low intensity surveys. High intensity systematic surveys of land blocks are increasingly being devoted to total archaeology, the recording of every-thing which is visible, of whatever period. The argu-ment that field survey is a repeatable exercise must be set alongside the fact that in some cases the surveyor may well be the last person to see the site intact. This calls for the widespread use, and further development, of comprehensive recording systems. Here there may be lessons to be learned from experience gained in the recording of complex urban excavations.

3.3 Expansion of the database

Interrogation of the principal Sites and Monuments Records (SMRs) covering upland areas revealed that c 31,881 sites have so far been recorded. This gives an overall average density of about 0.6 sites per sq km.

These records derive largely from the long tradition of fieldwork in the uplands, including the inventories by the RCHME for England and the RCAHM for Wales, the work of the former Ordnance Survey Archaeologic-al Division, and of course numerous individuals and local societies. The quality of information varies from single stray finds to dense concentrations of individual features forming relict landscapes. Also, the thorough-ness of work and the completeness of the record varies

from one area to the next. Table 2 presents a break-down of the recorded evidence by county. It should, however, be emphasized that with incomplete records the proportion of work remaining may not yield a commensurate increase in the number of sites re-corded.

By themselves, however, these figures mean very little. The information on which they are based has often been collected and catalogued using procedures suitable for work in lowland Britain, but which rarely do justice to the complexity of the evidence from upland areas. In particular, such figures fail to convey any idea of the area of archaeologically significant land. Some moorlands, for example, must be considered as total archaeological landscapes, and quantification of the archaeological resource should be in hectares or acres rather than numbers of sites. Nationally, this cannot be done; the data simply are not available at present.

In recent years the number of intensive archaeologic-al surveys undertaken, including field surveys, fieldwalking, and aerial surveys, has increased (see RCHME 1978 and below, ch 6.3). The result is that knowledge of the nature and density of recorded evidence has also increased (Fig 13). Using traditional methods of quantification, most counties have average densities lower than three sites per sq km. In these, any survey work has tended to be small in scale, records are often incomplete, and little or no record enhancement

Table 2 Summary of recorded sites by area and period

County	Area of upland Km²	%	Prehistoric density*	Prehistoric no.	Roman density	Roman no.	Medieval density	Medieval no.	Post-medieval density	Post-medieval no.	Unknown Date density	Unknown Date no.	Total density	Total no.	SMR complete† for uplands?
1 Northumberland	1408	28%	0.15	212	0.08	212	0.03	53	0.04	67	0.13	187	0.45	751	no (25%)
2 Cumbria	2451	36%	0.18	416	0.04	113	0.04	108	0.09	235	0.12	305	0.49	1177	no (50%)
3 Durham	950	39%	0.18	172	0.02	20	0.16	160	0.32	311	0.06	61	0.76	724	no (75%)
4 Cleveland	29	5%	2.75	80	0.17	5	0.44	13	1.79	34	1.20	35	5.75	167	yes
5 North Yorkshire (Moors)†	2079	25%	–	1084	–	8	–	150	–	38	–	238	1.30	1518	no (75%)
North Yorkshire (Dales)†			–	–	–	–	–	–	–	–	–	–	–	1200	no (25%)
6 Lancashire	574	21%	0.16	96	0.02	13	0.03	22	0.06	35	0.18	108	0.47	274	yes
7 West Yorkshire	427	21%	1.39	594	0.55	236	1.33	569	0.24	103	0.08	36	3.64	1538	no (75%)
8 Greater Manchester	205	16%	0.37	76	0.03	8	0.05	12	0.25	52	0.02	5	0.74	153	no (50%)
9 South Yorkshire	93	6%	1.79	167	0.36	34	2.82	263	1.75	163	0.03	3	6.77	630	yes
10 Derbyshire§	920	35%	1.98	1828	0.45	418	0.54	501	0.53	496	0.33	307	3.85	3550	no (75%)
11 Cheshire	116	5%	0.37	43	0.05	6	0.18	21	0.18	22	0.11	13	0.90	105	no (75%)
12 Clwyd	866	35%	0.56	489	0.01	8	0.09	84	0.08	76	0.04	42	0.80	699	yes
13 Gwynedd	1745	43%	0.17	299	0.01	4	0.04	85	0.01	15	0.10	186	0.33	589	no (75%)
14 Staffordshire	163	6%	1.15	188	0.03	6	0.14	24	0.50	91	0.20	33	2.09	342	no (50%)
15 Shropshire§	314	9%	1.87	589	0.34	108	0.82	259	0.24	76	0.87	275	4.16	1307	yes
16 Powys	3553	70%	0.43	1543	0.01	41	0.12	455	0.10	381	0.81	487	0.81	2907	no (75%)
17 Hereford & Worcester	157	4%	0.37	59	0.01	2	0.29	47	0.04	7	0.06	10	0.79	125	no (75%)
18 Dyfed	1211	21%	0.70	848	0.02	29	0.66	805	1.68	2041	0.15	187	3.22	3910	no (75%)
19 West Glamorgan															
20 Mid Glamorgan	563	30%	0.89	505	0.01	10	0.31	175	0.15	86	0.11	67	1.49	843	no (50%)
21 Gwent	123	9%	0.39	48	0.04	5	0.39	49	2.56	316	0.28	35	3.68	453	no (75%)
22 Gloucestershire	132	5%	1.03	136	0.18	24	0.15	20	0.06	8	0.31	42	1.74	230	no (25%)
23 Somerset§	449	13%	1.61	726	0.12	54	0.54	243	1.02	461	0.21	97	3.52	1581	no (50%)
24 Devon†	738	11%	3.39	2502	0.04	31	1.14	848	2.15	1592	1.21	898	7.95	5871	yes
25 Cornwall†	175	5%	8.5	1500	0.03	6	1.71	300	4.00	700	–	0	14.32	2506	yes
	19444			14200		1401		5266		7406		3657		33130	

* all density values recorded as sites per Km²
† complete = all available sources catalogued (uplands only)
‡ figures estimated from upland grid squares
§ figures estimated from upland parishes

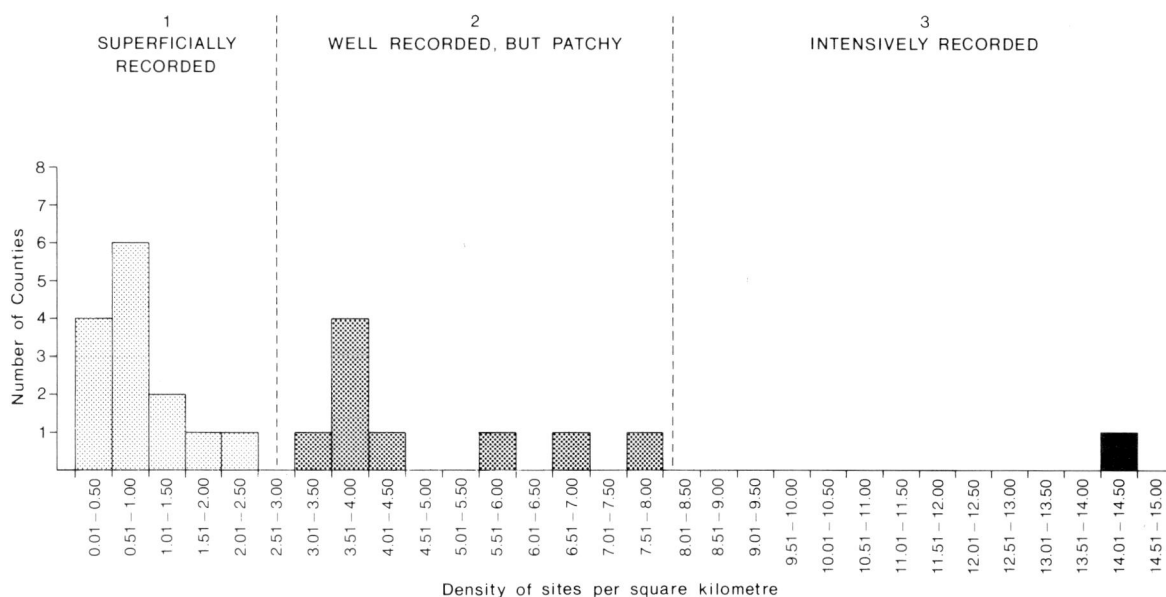

Fig 13   Histogram showing the number of areas (counties) with specified densities of recorded sites. Three components can be seen

through fieldwork has taken place. In the second group are those counties in which survey work has taken place, sometimes on a considerable scale, or where there has been diligent fieldwork by local groups or individuals. One or two counties with very small areas of upland fall into this group by virtue of having a local abundance of monuments. The final category contains counties in which survey work has been intensive over wide areas. Several counties in group 2 will move into group 3 in the near future as the results of survey work are processed. At present Cornwall stands alone in group 3 as a result of the recent survey of Bodmin Moor (Johnson 1983) where an average density of about fourteen sites per sq km has been recorded.

Average densities above ten sites per sq km are often to be expected after detailed survey in the uplands. Locally, much higher concentrations are possible. In the Lake District, Leech (1983) recorded over 520 sites in an area of 5 sq km, and on Danby Rigg (Durham) over 680 sites were recorded in an area of less than 1 sq km by a six-man team over two and a half weeks (Harding 1984). A study of the Otterburn Ranges (Northumberland) by members of the Society of Antiquaries of Newcastle-upon-Tyne revealed over 650 monuments in an area where only sixteen had previously been recorded (Selkirk 1978, 152; Charlton & Day 1978). Wherever survey work takes place the increase in sites recorded is dramatic (Fig 14). Given that under 5% of the uplands has so far been surveyed in detail, a total upland archaeological resource of over half a million sites might be expected, but records quantified by simple site-counts can be ambiguous. In some cases dramatic increases are due to how a "site" is defined, and as a result comparisons are very misleading. For example, Leech (1983) assigned a separate primary record number to every individual clearance cairn within a cairnfield.

Concealed beneath these general increases in the number of recorded sites, recent field surveys have highlighted, and for the first time allowed quantification of, three important features of the upland

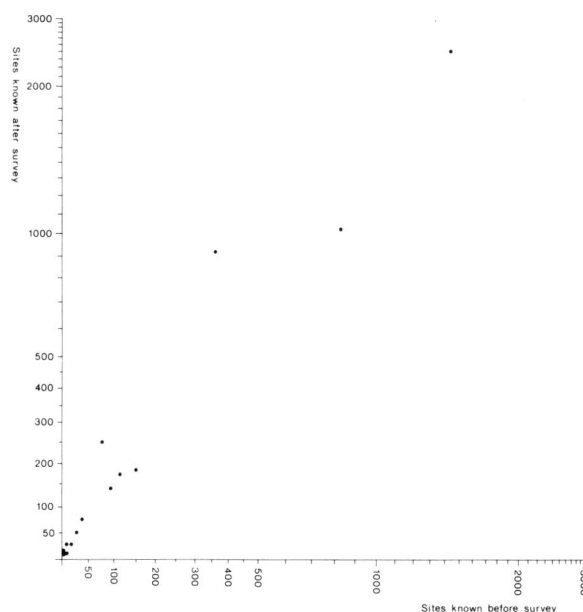

Fig 14   Graph showing the numerical increase in sites recorded by a sample of fourteen surveys

archaeological resource. Perhaps most important is the quality of the evidence, and here results from the south-west are particularly illuminating. On Bodmin Moor, although the number of medieval fields known increased by a factor of four (from 30 to 120), the area of fields recorded represents an increase of 700% (information from N Johnson, CCRA). On Dartmoor, surveys of Bronze Age fields have revealed that over 1000 ha (2471 acres) of field systems and perhaps 200–300 km (125–185 miles) of field boundary earthwork of the same antiquity survive largely intact (Fleming 1975; 1983a). Some individual Bronze Age boundaries (reaves, as they are called locally) extend for over 5 km (3 miles). Among the best preserved systems are those around Holne Moor, Rippon Tor, and Corndon Tor (Fleming 1983b). Equally complete

20

evidence survives from medieval times (Fleming & Ralph 1982).

It is not only the south-western uplands where extensive tracts of continuous archaeological remains lie preserved. In north Yorkshire plotting of aerial photographs allows similar patterns to be recognized. Around Wharfedale in the Yorkshire Dales almost uninterrupted ancient field systems cover areas as large as 5 km (3 miles) by 1 km (0.6 miles) (Fig 15). Work currently being undertaken by the RCHME in Cheviot, Peak District, and Welsh Marches confirms that such high quality preservation is widespread.

A second important finding is that although the uplands are indeed very rich in archaeological remains, the distribution of evidence is not uniform. In particular the density of sites tends to diminish as altitude increases, especially above 430 m (1400 ft). Thus, the interior of the Cheviot massif is almost devoid of settlements or early fields (Gates 1983) and it has long been recognized that in Northumberland the fells north of Hadrian's Wall and west of the North Tyne contain very little evidence for settlement (Jobey 1974). Any suspected voids must, however, be fully substantiated through field survey before being declared archaeologically sterile.

The third important result of extensive survey is that variations in the form of evidence between regions is easier to document. For example, aerial survey in the Welsh borders and in Cumbria revealed the presence of dyke systems and earthwork enclosures comparable with well-known examples in Wessex (Guilbert 1975; Higham 1978). Only through the detailed recording of the evidence can morphological studies of specific classes of site really begin (Mercer 1982).

3.4 The importance of the environmental evidence

In the uplands, the preservation of pollen and the abundance of slowly accumulating peat bogs and lake sediments provide ample scope for the study of past patterns of vegetation and climatic fluctuations. Even within archaeological sites pollen can be trapped in ground surfaces and under walls or cairns, thus providing data to illuminate the conditions which preceded occupation or perhaps the immediate surroundings of the site during occupation.

Many studies of upland pollen sequences have been undertaken, particularly on Dartmoor, in Wales, and in the Lake District. The changing patterns represented have been well summarized by Godwin (1975) and Birks et al (1975). The archaeological implications of environmental work have recently been reviewed in a volume of regional essays (Keeley 1984). Preserved seeds and the remains of plants, insects, animals, and birds provide vivid insights into once thriving economies.

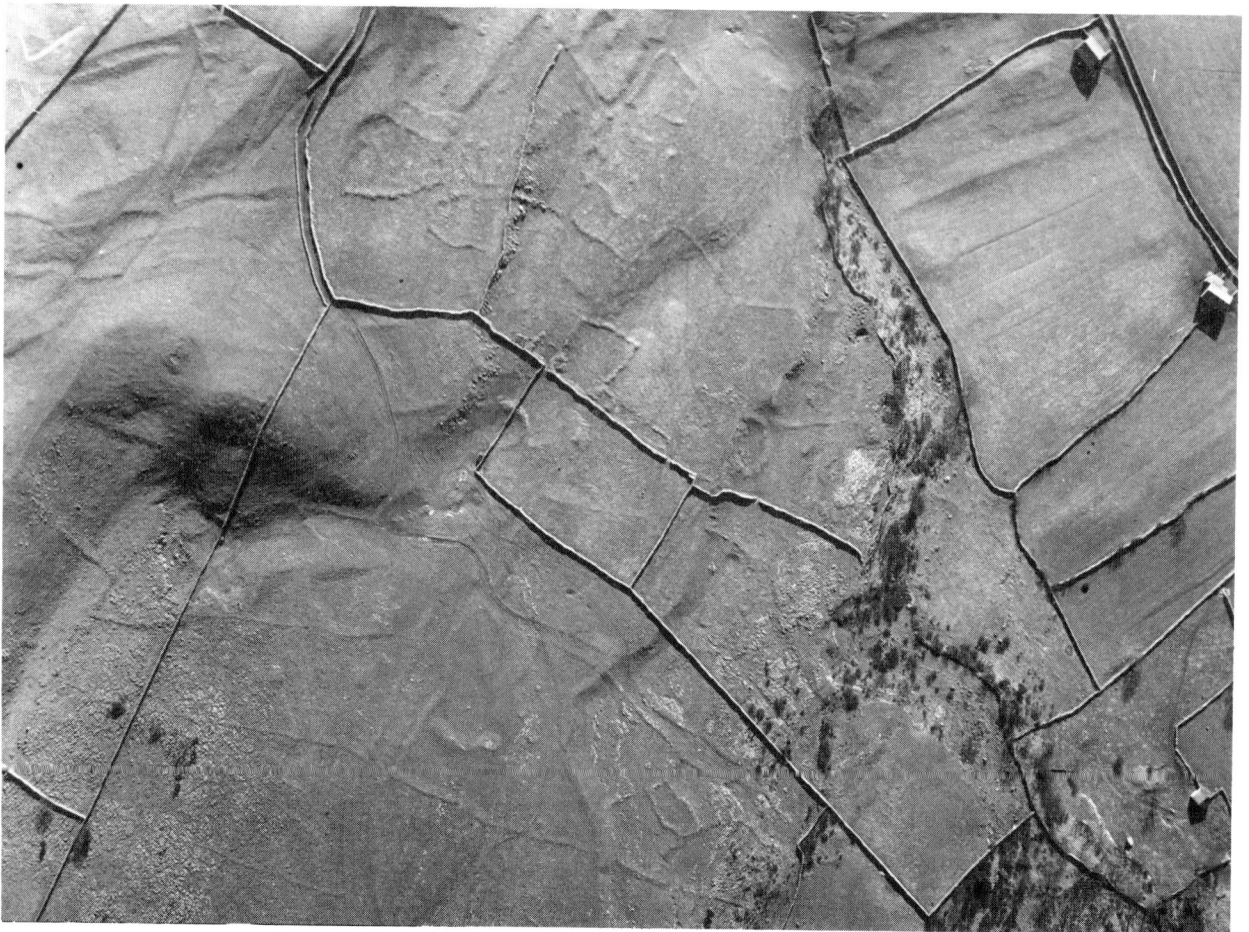

Fig 15 (A) Landscape at Grassington (North Yorkshire) where traces of Iron Age and Romano-British settlement and field system underlie more recent (? post-medieval) fields still in use today. The coincidence of some recent boundaries on ancient alignments is clearly visible. (photo National Monuments Record, Crown copyright reserved)

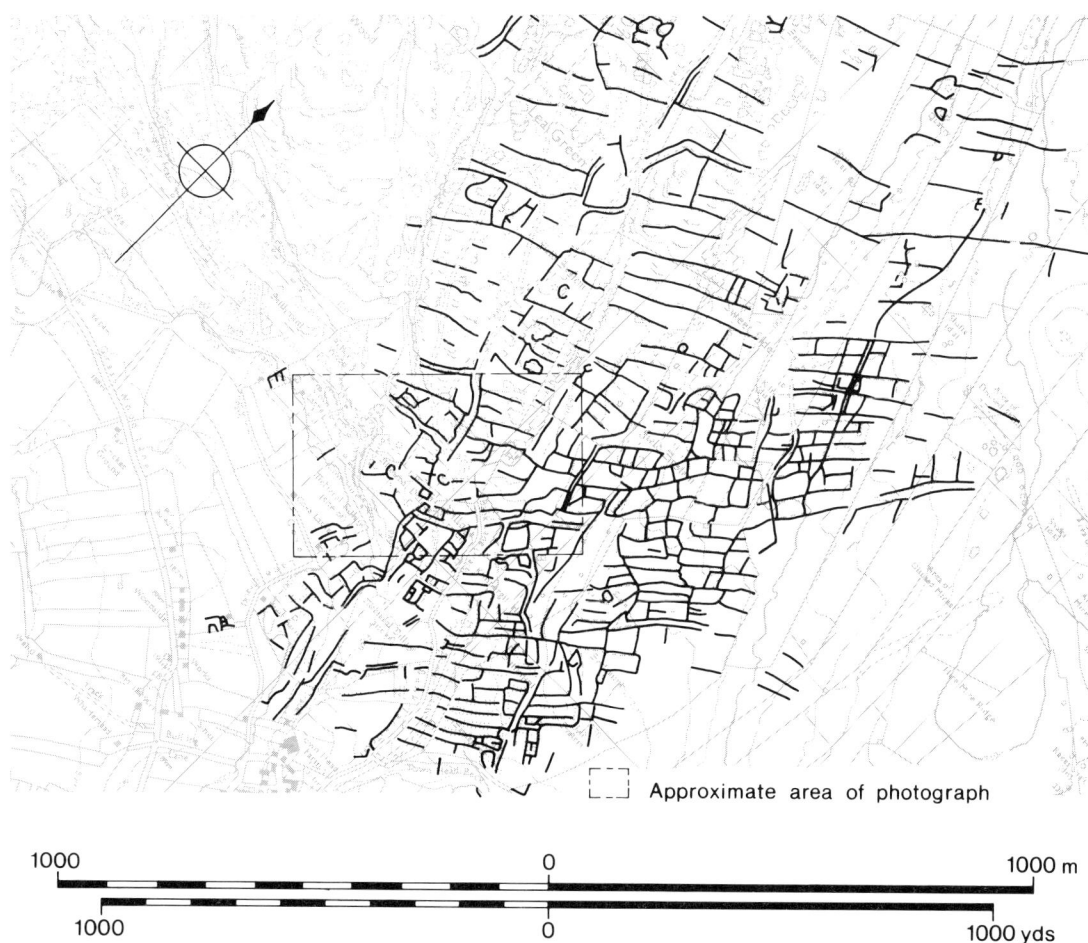

Fig 15 (B) Grassington, (North Yorkshire). Plot of prehistoric, Roman and medieval features recorded from aerial photographs. The area of Fig 15 (A) is indicated. (Copyright North Yorkshire County Council)

In many areas earlier prehistoric sites are sealed beneath blanket bog. This of course has the advantage of protecting them, but also prevents their identification so that conservation, preservation, and management needs can be assessed.

3.5 Methods of analysis and interpretation

We have seen that the reconstruction of the past requires evidence from a wide variety of sources and the use of a broad range of analytical techniques. The quantitative and qualitative increase in the number and disposition of known sites is of course important, but the results of reconnaissance work are only the first stage in the process of elucidating the past. The detailed analysis of information collected from surveys and excavations, the careful examination of artefacts, and the methodical searching for patterns in the data provide the framework for reconstruction onto which detail from individual projects can be added. These all-important aspects of archaeological work are easily overlooked because they take place indoors and do not fall within the role of the archaeologist as it is popularly perceived.

While the value of nuclear physics in the development of radiocarbon dating has become widely understood, the use of other techniques borrowed from the physical sciences – for example petrology, scanning electron microscopy, computer enhanced graphics, dendrochronology, optical emission spectroscopy, and neutron activation analysis – hardly registers with the general public. Contributions from the biological sciences are vital for understanding past environments and subsistence economies. The social sciences, too, have an important role to play, in helping archaeologists to distance themselves from the context of the 20th century, and in providing the theoretical apparatus with which to examine societies at different levels of complexity.

With particular reference to the uplands, the detailed morphological study of late prehistoric settlements (Smith 1977), the petrological studies of Neolithic stone axes (Cummins 1979), the spatial analysis of distribution maps (Bradley & Hart 1983), the examination of environmental records (Keeley 1984), and the analysis of social boundaries and land boundaries on Dartmoor (Fleming 1982) may be cited as examples of the many technical studies pertinent to reconstructing the past. For more recent times, written records provide a framework within which archaeological evidence may be interpreted, or with which it can be compared.

The expansion of knowledge about the number of sites, and about the environment of upland areas, provides much scope for the reinterpretation of traditional views. Such reinterpretation is offered in the chapter that follows.

4 Interpretations for today

This chapter brings together summaries of recent work
and interpretations to provide a general introduction to
the prehistoric and historic archaeology of the uplands.

4.1 The Palaeolithic and Mesolithic (to
c 3500 BC)

Paul Mellars

Evidence for exploitation of the uplands of England
and Wales during the Palaeolithic period (prior to *c*
8000 BC) remains sparse. Shortly before the end of the
last glacial period there is some evidence for exploitation around the margins of the uplands, apparently
concentrated during the period known as the "Windermere Interstadial", between 10500 and 9000 BC. The
clearest evidence at present comes from a number of
sites in the southern Peak District, best represented
perhaps at Ossom's Cave, Elder Bush Cave, and Thor's
Fissure in the Manifold Valley (Campbell 1977; Jacobi
1980a). Two radiocarbon dates for this horizon of
occupation in the Ossom's Cave are of 9980 ± 310 and
8640 ± 70 BC. A recent analysis of the animal bones
from Ossom's Cave suggests a very brief occupation,
apparently occasioned by the hunting of reindeer,
during the early spring months (Scott 1984). Most
probably this and other sites in the same area represent
brief visits by groups of Late-Glacial hunters who were
based for other seasons at adjacent sites in the lowlands
– for example at Creswell only 25 miles north-east of the
Manifold valley, or perhaps in lowland areas to the west
of the Pennines. Sporadic evidence for similar occupation may be represented at sites further north in the
Pennines, for example at the Victoria and Kinsey Caves
(North Yorkshire) (Campbell 1977). All the present

evidence is scanty, but it should make us aware of the
possibility that similar sporadic exploitation of other
upland areas of Britain occurred during the same time
range. Occupation at this time need not have been
confined to cave sites, and the possibility of occasional
summer-season occupation at open air locations in the
uplands should be kept in mind.

Evidence for relatively extensive, systematic exploitation of upland areas first comes into focus shortly after
the end of the last glacial period, around the middle of
the 8th millennium BC. Throughout the Mesolithic
period there is comparatively abundant evidence for
occupation in most if not all upland areas of England
and Wales. At present the richest and best documented
evidence comes from the southern and central Pennines – mainly to the south of the Aire valley – and from
the North York Moors (Fig 16). Material in other areas
is more scattered, but has now been well documented
in certain areas of the northern Pennines, the Welsh
uplands, and the major upland areas of south-west
England (Wainwright 1963; Jacobi 1979; 1980b). The
critical question is how far this concentration of finds in
the southern Pennines and North York Moors truly
represents a concentration of Mesolithic occupation,
and how far it is the product of extensive peat erosion
on these moorlands, coupled with the long history of

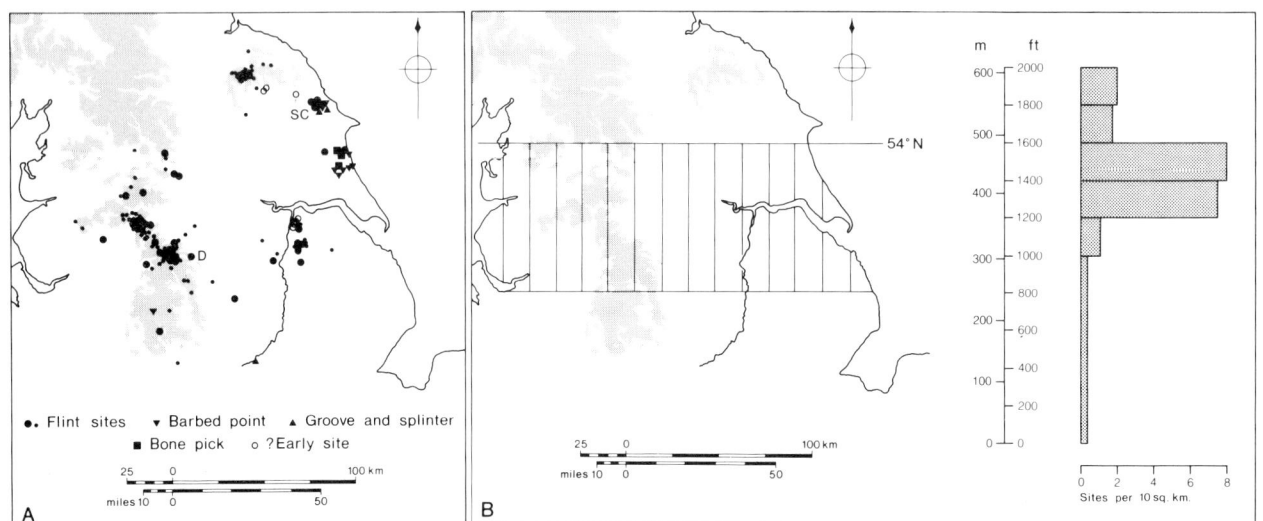

Fig 16 (A) Distribution of sites and finds of Early Mesolithic age (8000–7000 BC) in northern England, showing major
concentrations in the southern Pennines and North York Moors. SC= Star Carr; D= Deepcar (after Jacobi 1978)
(B) General distribution of Mesolithic sites at varying altitudes in northern England (i) shows transect surveyed for sites –
uplands shaded. (ii) densities of sites recorded at different altitudes (after Jacobi, Tallis and Mellars 1976)

archaeological exploration centred on the northern industrial towns. Heavy peat cover elsewhere, for example in the northern Pennines, the Lake District and parts of the Welsh uplands, presents an obvious obstacle to the discovery of Mesolithic sites, and must be seen as a factor which distorts current distribution patterns.

It is now clear that extensive exploitation of the southern Pennines, the North York Moors and the south-western uplands must have extended over a period of at least 4000 years, spanning virtually the whole of the earlier and later Mesolithic periods (Mellars 1974). Well documented assemblages of early Mesolithic flint work have been recovered from at least a dozen sites in the southern Pennines, four or five sites on the North York Moors, and at least one site in the south-western uplands (Jacobi 1978, 1979). Four of these sites are dated to around the middle of the 8th millennium BC (Jacobi 1978). As such, the sites are broadly contemporaneous with such well known lowland Mesolithic locations as Star Carr (Yorkshire) and Thatcham (Berkshire). Distinctive assemblages of later Mesolithic flintwork first make their appearance in the middle of the 7th millennium. Typical industries in the Pennines, such as Warcock Hill, site III (Lancashire), date to 6656 ± 110 BC. From this point on there is a scatter of later radiocarbon dates extending down to the middle of the 4th millennium (Mellars 1976b; Switsur & Jacobi 1975; 1979). Whether or not the occupation of the uplands was strictly continuous over this time range must remain a matter for speculation.

The striking concentration of Mesolithic sites in the southern Pennines and North York Moors is perhaps one of the most impressive features of the British Mesolithic (Spratt 1982; Spratt & Simmons 1976; Jacobi et al 1976). Most are simply surface concentrations of artefacts, reflecting the energetic activities of several generations of amateur collectors extending back into the 1870s. Material recovered from controlled excavations is rather scarce, although during the past 25 years systematic excavations have been carried out in the Pennines and North Yorkshire and the evidence from these is beginning to shed more light on the character and chronology of the Mesolithic occupation.

The major limitation of the data lies in the almost total lack of organic material from these leached upland environments. Inevitably, any assessment of the specific economic activities undertaken from these sites, or the precise seasons of their occupation, must remain largely speculative. Most of the published interpretations assume that the occupation of the upland sites was essentially seasonal in character, that it was connected with seasonal migrations of animal populations, and that it took place largely if not entirely during the summer months (Clark 1972; Mellars 1976a; Jacobi 1978). Certainly, supplies of flint for tool manufacture are known to have been carried between the upland and lowland areas, though it would of course be possible to postulate other mechanisms for the movement of these raw materials without invoking systematic patterns of transhumance between the two areas. There is little doubt that the hunting of game was an important activity at these settlements. On the other hand, remains of burnt hazelnut shells have been recovered from many of these upland sites, and argue both for the

systematic collection of plant food resources at these sites and the extension of at least some of the occupation into the later summer or early autumn months (Mellars 1976a). The evidence for seasonal patterns of occupation in these upland sites is persuasive, but not conclusive.

Reconstruction of the detailed social and settlement patterns of these upland Mesolithic groups poses similar problems. Many of the individual flint scatters recorded on the moorlands occupy tightly concentrated areas, and appear to reflect the activities of very small human groups – perhaps individual family units, or conceivably all-male hunting parties (Mellars 1976a; Jacobi 1978). In other cases, however, these individual flint concentrations have been found to occur in groups of two to four associated clusters, which could reflect either the occupations of larger social groups, perhaps several families, or, alternatively, simply repeated visits to the same location by small groups in different years. One of the major problems here is that excavations have rarely been extended beyond the immediate limits of the individual flint scatters to assess the wider contexts and associations of the sites. Substantial traces of occupation structures have been recorded in excavations in at least three upland sites (Broomhead site V (North Yorkshire), Sheldon (Derbyshire) and Deepcar (South Yorkshire)) and more almost certainly await discovery by careful excavation at many other upland locations. Hearths seem to be frequent if not invariable features on the occupation sites, where these have been specifically looked for (Radley & Mellars 1964; Radley 1968; Radley et al 1974).

Work carried out over the past twenty years has begun to shed light on the environmental context of Mesolithic occupation in the uplands. In the southern Pennines, for example, it has been shown that the highest concentrations of Mesolithic sites seem to occur within a relatively narrow range of altitudes, mostly between 366 and 488 m (1200 and 1600 ft), which were probably located just above the main limits of full forest cover (Jacobi et al 1976). The situation is not so fully documented in other areas, but in all parts of Britain it is likely that the prime attraction of upland habitats to Mesolithic groups lay in the comparatively open character of the vegetation, which would have provided optimal grazing conditions for most of the species of larger herbivorous animals – particularly red deer, roe deer and aurochs (Simmons 1975). In Wales and the central Pennines, exploitation is known to have extended up to altitudes of at least 550–610 m (1800–2000 ft), with most of the higher elevations being extensively blanketed by thick deposits of late peat (Jacobi 1980b). More controversial, but potentially more interesting, is the suggestion that many of these upland habitats may have been deliberately managed by Mesolithic groups, through a policy of systematic burning of the local plant communities at regular intervals (Dimbleby 1961; Simmons 1969, 1975; Smith 1970; Mellars 1976c). Present evidence for this comes partly from the pollen record (which appears to indicate well defined episodes of clearance in demonstrably Mesolithic contexts) and partly from the occurrence of concentrated charcoal particles in the same horizons as the pollen sequences. Evidence of this kind has been recorded from three separate areas: the southern Pennines, North York Moors, and the south-western uplands. It appears to

24

extend over several periods of the Mesolithic occupation (Dimbleby 1961; Simmons 1969; Simmons & Innes 1981; Simmons et al 1983; Jacobi et al 1976). Deliberate manipulation of vegetation patterns in this way has of course been widely documented in many recent groups of hunters and gatherers, and might be seen as an intermediate stage towards the more intensive and systematic use of subsistence resources which culminated in the transition from Mesolithic to Neolithic economies in many parts of northern Europe (Mellars 1976c). Further work on this question should perhaps be seen as one of the central aims of future research into the character of man/land relationships in the Mesolithic occupation of upland habitats.

Bibliography

Campbell, J B, 1977 *The Upper Palaeolithic of Britain: a study of man and nature in the late ice age*, Oxford, Clarendon Press

Clark, J G D, 1972 *Star Carr: A case study in bioarchaeology*, Addison-Wesley Module No 10

Dimbleby, G W, 1961 "The ancient forest of Blackamore" *Antiquity* **35**, 123-8

Jacobi, R M, 1978 "The settlement of northern Britain in the eighth millennium BC" in P Mellars (ed) *The early post-glacial settlement of northern Europe: an ecological perspective*, London, Duckworth, 295-332

Jacobi, R M, 1979 "Early flandrian hunters in the south west" *Proc. Devon Archaeol Soc* **37**, 48-93

Jacobi, R M, 1980a "The Upper Palaeolithic of Britain with special reference to Wales" in J A Taylor (ed) *Culture and environment in prehistoric Wales* (British Archaeological Reports **76**), Oxford, BAR, 15-99

Jacobi, R M, 1980b "The early Holocene settlement of Wales" in J.A.Taylor (ed) *Culture and environment in prehistoric Wales* (British Archaeological Reports **76**), Oxford, BAR, 131-206

Jacobi, R M, Tallis, J H & Mellars, P A, 1976 "The southern Pennine Mesolithic and the ecological record" *J Archaeol Sci* **3**, 307-20

Mellars, P A, 1974 "The Palaeolithic and Mesolithic" in C Renfrew (ed) *British prehistory: a new outline*, London, Duckworth, 41-99

Mellars, P A, 1976a "Settlement patterns and industrial variability in the British Mesolithic" in G de G Sieveking, I H Longworth & K E Wilson (eds) *Problems in economic and social archaeology*, London, Duckworth, 375-99

Mellars, P A, 1976b "The appearance of "narrow blade" microlithic industries in Britain: the radiocarbon evidence" in S K Kozlowski (ed) *Les civilisations du 8e au 5e millennaire avant Nortre Ere en Europe*, Nice, International Union of Prehistoric and Protohistoric Sciences, 166-74

Mellars, P A, 1976c "Fire ecology, animal populations and man: a study of some ecological relationships in prehistory" *Proc Prehist Soc*, **42**, 15-45

Radley, J, 1968 "A Mesolithic structure at Sheldon, with a note on chert as a raw material on Mesolithic sites in the southern Pennines" *Derbyshire Archaeol J*, **88**, 26-36

Radley, J & Marshall, G, 1965 "Maglemosian sites in the Pennines" *Yorkshire Archaeol J*, **41**, 394-402

Radley, J & Mellars, P, 1964 "A Mesolithic structure at Deepcar, Yorkshire, England, and the affinities of its associated flint industries" *Proc Prehist Soc* **30**, 1-24

Radley, J, Tallis, J H & Switsur, V R, 1974 "The excavation of three narrow blade" Mesolithic sites in the southern Pennines, England", *Proc Prehist Soc*, **40**, 1-19

Scott, K, 1984 "Hunter-gatherers and large mammals in glacial Britain" in R Foley (ed) *Hominid evolution and community ecology*, London, Academic Press, 219-35

Simmons, I G, 1969 "Evidence for vegetation changes associated with Mesolithic man in Britain" in P J Ucko and G W Dimbleby (eds) *The domestication and exploitation of plants and animals*, London, Duckworth, 111-19

Simmons, I G, 1975 "Towards an ecology of Mesolithic man in the uplands of Great Britain" *J Archaeol Sci*, **2**, 1-15

Simmons, I G, 1979 "Late Mesolithic societies and the environment of the uplands of England and Wales", *Bull Inst Archaeol*, **16**, 111-29

Simmons, I G & Innes, J B, 1981 "Tree remains in a North York Moors peat profile", *Nature*, **294**, 76-8

Simmons, I G, Rand, J I & Crabtree, K, 1983 "A further pollen analytical study of the Blacklane peat section on Dartmoor, England", *New Phytologist*, **94**, 655-67

Smith, A G, 1970 "The influence of Mesolithic and Neolithic man on British vegetation: a discussion" in D Walker and R G West (eds) *Studies in the vegetational history of the British Isles*, Cambridge, At the University Press, 81-96

Spratt, D A, (ed) 1982 *Prehistoric and Roman archaeology of north east Yorkshire* (British Archaeological Reports **104**), Oxford, BAR

Spratt, D A & Simmons, I G, 1976 "Prehistoric archaeology and environment on the North York Moors" *J Archaeol Sci*, **3**, 193-210

Switsur, V R & Jacobi, R M, 1975 "Radiocarbon dates for the Pennine Mesolithic", *Nature*, **256**, 32-4

Switsur, V R & Jacobi, R M, 1979 "A radiocarbon chronology for the early post-glacial stone industries of England and Wales" in R Berger and H E Suess (eds) *Radiocarbon dating*, Berkeley, University of California Press, 41-68

Wainwright, G J, 1963 "A reinterpretation of the microlithic industries of Wales", *Proc Prehist Soc*, **29**, 99-132

4.2 The Neolithic (3500–2000 BC)

Tim Darvill

With the exception of a few peripheral areas, such as the Cotswolds and the southern Peak District, the uplands of England and Wales were not intensively settled during Neolithic times. The range of field monuments known from upland areas is small, but there is a considerable body of excavated evidence, together with stray finds and environmental data, to provide the basis from which to reconstruct events during the period.

At the beginning of the Neolithic, when agriculture and animal husbandry were becoming commonplace in most lowland areas, much of the uplands was covered by woodland. Oak, pine, hazel and birch were the dominant species. Only the highest ground was open moorland, but in some parts, for example the Lake District, the high Pennines and mid Wales, blanket bog had begun to form by about 3500 BC (A G Smith 1981). The climate was more continental than today, with long summers and hard winters (Taylor 1975).

During the early and middle Neolithic (3500–2500 BC) farming groups established themselves for the first time around the periphery of most upland areas, exploiting fertile soils in river valleys and along the coastal plains for cultivation of cereals – wheat and barley – and animal husbandry – cattle, pigs and sheep. The stability offered by the farming economy meant that groups occupied rather smaller territories than in Mesolithic times. Chambered tombs, comprising stone-built chambers set within a long or round stone cairn, provided ritual centres and burial places for these early farming groups. Architecturally the chambered tombs vary from region to region. Usually they are located around the fringes of the uplands, and their occurrence on the periphery of occupied land may indicate a wish to minimize disruption of agriculture. Capel Garmon (Gwynedd) is typical of the siting of many examples (Fig 17). Recent surveys of Dartmoor, Bodmin Moor, the north Pennines and the Cheviots have all brought to light previously unknown possible Neolithic tombs further into the uplands than expected. These hint that perhaps more traces of upland

Fig 17 Capel Garmon (Gwynedd): Neolithic chambered tomb. The long trapezoidal shape, forecourt and horns, and stone chamber can be clearly seen (photo Mick Sharp)

settlement belonging to this early farming period await discovery.

Axes of flint and stone are common as stray finds in upland areas. In a study of Neolithic land-use in the Lake District, Richard Bradley (1972) tentatively linked the spread of such finds with fodder collecting, something which was probably more widespread in the uplands than a cursory glance at the evidence would allow. Arrowheads and low-density flint scatters betray hunting or perhaps warfare in the uplands. At Moel-y-Gaer (Clwyd) a small upland hunting camp represented by a wooden windbreak, the remains of broken weapons and the debris from making and repairing arrowheads and knives dates to about 2900 BC (Bradley 1978, 80).

Environmental records relating to the early and middle Neolithic suggest occasional small scale clearances, not of the sort associated with cultivation but more likely relating to the use of the uplands for seasonal pasture. Caves were sometimes used as temporary refuge during such expeditions, or while hunting. Where caves were not available temporary encampments can be recognized by flint scatters and, sometimes, small quantities of broken pottery.

Fine-grained igneous and metamorphic rocks such as are available in some upland areas were used for making axes and edged tools (I F Smith 1974, 105). At Graig Lwyd in north Wales and Great Langdale in the Lake District very large quantities of rock were quarried from wide areas. The piles of waste debris from primary working can still be seen as scree flows. Axes manufactured in the uplands were exchanged widely with communities in other parts of Britain.

The light calcareous soils covering the limestones of the Cotswolds and the White Peak supported higher populations than other upland areas. The density of chambered tombs was greater, and settlements much more common. On the Cotswolds, enclosed settlements similar to those well represented in southern and eastern England are known (Darvill 1984,88).

In much of southern England there seems to have been a hiatus in the expansion of farming groups in the middle of the third millennium BC (c 2500 BC) but evidence of this is hard to find in upland areas. Only in the Lake District do environmental records suggest forest regeneration, and only on the Cotswolds and in a few other peripheral areas is there a sharp break in the use of earlier sites. Elsewhere the pattern of peripheral settlement, coupled with low intensity use of upland resources, continued.

From about 2300 BC, however, use of the uplands became more intensive. Population pressure, technical advances in farming technology and slight climatic changes may all have played a part in promoting greater activity. Environmental records indicate an increase in small-scale woodland clearances. Flint scatters and small occupation sites yielding typical late Neolithic (grooved ware and beaker) pottery are common. At Trelystan (Powys) two small square huts, each with wooden walls and a central hearth, were revealed during recent excavations, and are best interpreted as upland summer dwellings connected with transhumance (Britnell 1982). Caves continued to be used as settlements or for temporary refuge.

Fine stone remained an important resource. Several new areas, for example around Mynydd Preseli (Dyfed) and Corndon Hill (Powys) supplemented earlier sources in supplying traditional axes and also perforated tools of various kinds. These products were widely exchanged. Carn Meini in the Preseli Mountains of Dyfed provided the "blue stones" used in the remodelling of Stonehenge in Wiltshire about 2000 BC.

By the later Neolithic the traditional burial monuments of earlier times had been superseded by new types of structures, including cist graves and round cairns/barrows covering one or more burial. Stone circles, standing stones and stone alignments began to be constructed at this time, and, like the new types of burials, continued to be built and used into the Bronze Age. In a few areas, including Dartmoor, the Mendips, the Cotswolds and the Peak District, henge monuments – large circular ditched ritual enclosures – were constructed around 2000 BC or a little earlier. The example at Arbor Low (Derbyshire) contains the remains of a stone circle and a central stone setting (Fig 18), which, when upstanding, must have resembled early phases at Stonehenge (Wiltshire).

The metal ores of Wales and the uplands of the south-west peninsula gave these areas an added importance at the end of the Neolithic when the technology to

Fig 18   Late Neolithic (c 2200 BC) henge monument at Arbor Low (Derbyshire). The bank (about 76.5m (250 ft) in diameter) with internal quarry ditch defines a roughly circular area in which are the remains of a stone circle and central stone cove (photo National Monuments Record, Crown copyright reserved)

work copper and gold, and later to produce bronze by mixing copper and tin, became available.

In summary, it was during the Neolithic period that the natural wealth of the uplands was first really tapped. Subsistence resources of leaf fodder for animals, lightly wooded hunting grounds and open grazing areas were integral to the economies of early farming groups settled around the upland fringes. Stone was important for the manufacture of edged tools. By the end of the Neolithic circumstances favoured more intensive use of the uplands. Close relationships between upland communities and those further south and east on the lower ground are attested by similarities in burial monuments, ritual structures and through the acquisition and exchange of raw materials. The uplands remained largely wooded at the end of the Neolithic. A dramatic transformation was to follow.

Bibliography

Bradley, R, 1972, "Prehistorians and pastoralists in Neolithic and Bronze Age England", *World Archaeology*, **4**, 192-203

Bradley, R, 1978, *The prehistoric settlement of Britain*, London, Routledge and Kegan Paul

Britnell, W J, 1982 "The excavation of two round barrows at Trelystan,Powys", *Proc Prehist Soc*, **48**, 133-202

Darvill, T C, 1984 "Neolithic Gloucestershire", in A Saville (ed) *Archaeology in Gloucestershire: From the earliest hunters to the Industrial Age*, Cheltenham, Bristol and Gloucestershire Archaeological Society & Cheltenham Museum, 80-112

Piggott, S, 1954 *The Neolithic cultures of the British Isles*, Cambridge, At the University Press

Savory, H N, 1980 "The Neolithic in Wales" in J A Taylor (ed) *Culture and environment in prehistoric Wales* (British Archaeological Reports 76), Oxford, BAR, 207-31

Smith, A G, 1981 "The Neolithic" in I Simmons & M Tooley (eds) *The environment in British Prehistory*, London, Duckworth, 100-28

Smith, I F, 1974 "The Neolithic" in C Renfrew (ed) *British Prehistory – A new outline*, London, Duckworth, 125-209

Taylor, J A, 1975 "The role of climatic factors in environmental and cultural changes in prehistoric time", in J G Evans, S Limbrey & H Cleere (eds) *The effect of man on the landscape: The highland Zone*, (CBA Res Rep 11), London, CBA, 6-19

4.3 The Bronze Age (2000–800 BC)

Frances Lynch

In much of Britain it was during the Bronze Age that the uplands began to assume the aspect that we know today - open landscape, virtually treeless with vulnerable soils whose fertility may be short-lived and where the agricultural returns for much hard work may be meagre. But if this is the picture at the end of the Bronze Age, it was almost certainly not so at the beginning; it is a sobering thought that the deterioration with which we are still living today may be as much the result of man's mismanagement of a marginal environment as of the worsening of climate for which we have evidence towards the end of the period.

Throughout Britain the broad pattern of activity is the same. Wide expanses of upland, seemingly under-used by the first farming communities, are colonized from the Late Neolithic onwards, and used during the earlier Bronze Age not only for burial and religious observances, but for living and farming on what is now emerging as a surprisingly large and permanent scale.

Precisely when and why the retreat from this high point of exploitation begins are still matters for research; the answer is likely to be found in a complex mixture of social and environmental pressures. However, the fact that these areas have seldom been so extensively reoccupied has meant that the Bronze Age remains offer a uniquely complete fossil landscape from which the content of human history is only beginning to be distilled.

The Bronze Age evidence covers two areas of human activity: the spiritual domain of ritual and ceremony, still concentrated around the burial of the dead, and the everyday life of farmers and herdsmen. The ceremonial and burial sites have long been recognized, but it is only relatively recently that it has been realized that the homes of the living could also be found on the same hills (Fig 19).

In most areas the Bronze Age round barrows must be the commonest and best known of prehistoric antiquities, set on hill and ridge tops to be seen for miles around. In the uplands they are built of stone or of turves and, except where they have been robbed for boundary walls, they survive as imposing monuments and markers because they have not interfered with subsequent land use (Fig 20). These solid mounds are normally found to cover burials, most often cremated bones in an urn or bag. Superficially they appear very simple but closer study, especially of the stone examples, can often reveal quite complex structures and a good deal of architectural sophistication, especially in their placing within the landscape (Lynch 1979). Such considerations may have been even more important in the siting of contemporary ceremonial sites. Some have claimed that these stone circles were designed primarily in relation to the stars and the sky for the purpose of recording the ritual calendar; others have stressed a link with more earthly concerns of death and fertility, and pointed to the variety of circular monuments built for subtly different ceremonies at this time (see Burl 1976). Such arguments within the realm of religious thought will never be satisfactorily resolved, but it is only in the uplands that fieldwork can amass the quantity of data necessary even to reveal the fascinating complexity of the problems.

Just as uniformity of social attitudes should not be expected, so a complete identity of religious practice should not be assumed. In this aspect, as in others, the south-west shows greater individuality, though often less architectural finesse. In the Lake District a preference for certain distinctive monuments may be observed; and even in regions such as Wales and the south Pennines, where structures are very similar, excavation has suggested that ceremonies may have had a different emphasis.

Whereas the cairns and stone circles have been known for a long time and have always been assigned to the Bronze Age, the full extent of evidence for houses, farmyards and fields is only now being recognized. Dating may still be uncertain. In some regions, such as Dartmoor, the physical evidence – regular fields and formal boundaries – has been known for some time, but an early date was not always credited; in others, such as the Pennines, the North York Moors and the Cheviots, the agricultural significance of commonly observed features such as clearance cairns was not previously understood. In Wales problems of dating, which

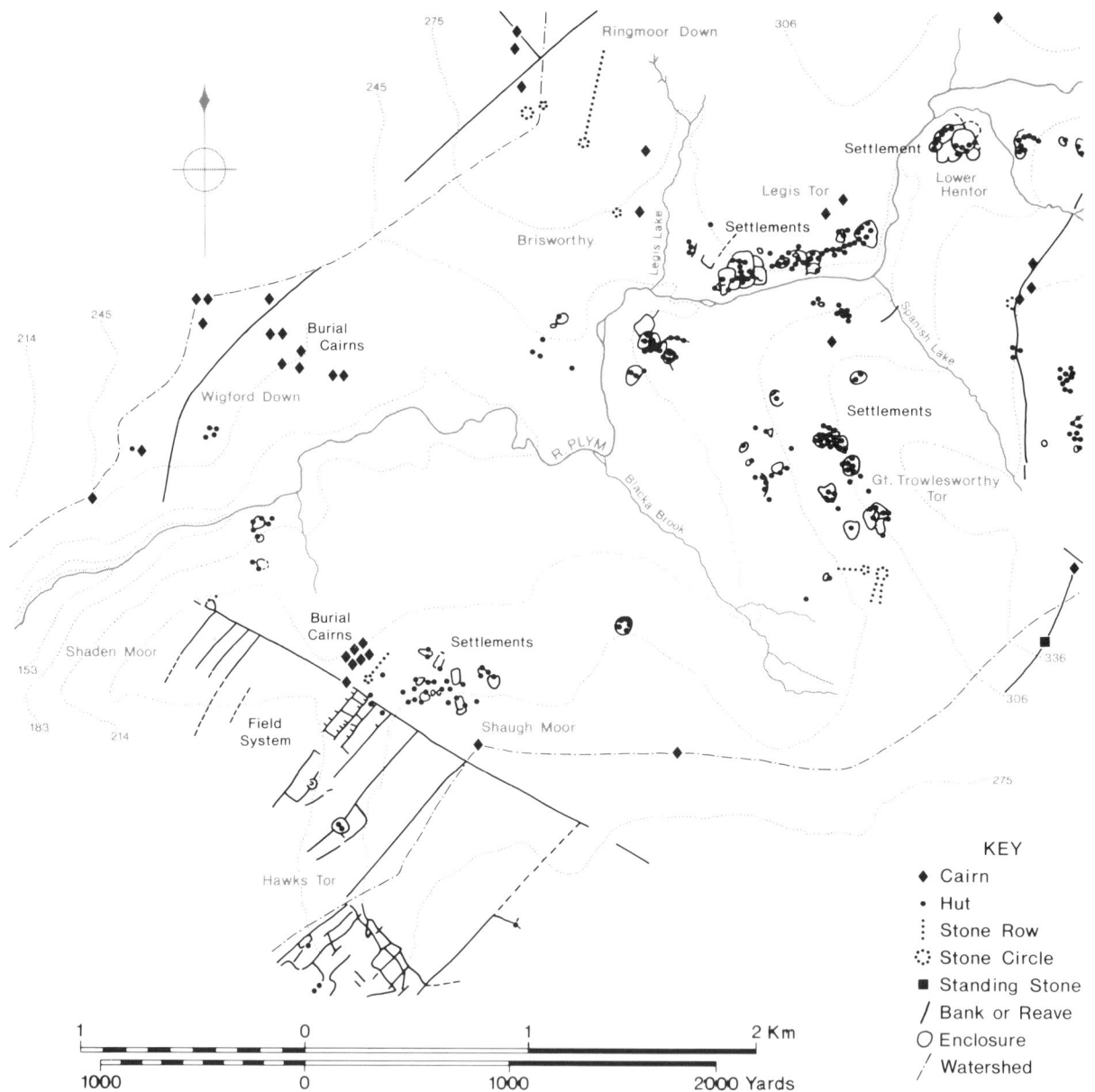

Fig 19 *Bronze Age fields, settlements, ritual sites and burial areas recorded in the upper Plym Valley, Dartmoor (after Balaam et al 1982)*

persist, have precluded the confident separation of different periods of occupation. Elsewhere, as in upland Lancashire and the Lake District, much primary fieldwork still remains to be done.

The fact that the uplands were occupied in the Bronze Age for living and working should not, perhaps, have occasioned so much surprise. Climatic history suggests that at the beginning of the period a more continental climate would have prevailed, giving a growing season five weeks longer than today's, and an environment favourable to agriculture at higher altitudes. The extent of forest cover and the date of its clearance will have varied from region to region - even valley to valley - but the broad picture is much the same in all upland districts. Although sedge and heather began to invade the tree-succeeding grasslands from an early date and incipient podsolization has been noticed beneath barrows, there could have been good grazing for several centuries, while regular enclosed fields denote a successful arable regime. It is this aspect of the

economy which must first have fallen victim to its own success, and to the increasing damp and cold of the later second millennium. In some favoured lowland areas ranch boundaries succeed the arable fields; in bleaker parts the farms seem to have been abandoned altogether. What happened to the displaced population is hard to say. Had the upland farms always been linked to lowland centres which could reabsorb them peacefully ? Did their redistribution to growing nucleated settlements cause stress? Did starvation and plague solve the problem more brutally?

Archaeologically, the homes of the living have always been more ephemeral than the monuments to the dead, being but the collapsed stone residues of structures which originally may have incorporated a good deal of wood and turf. Houses which are known to be of Bronze Age date are generally round, between 4 m (13 ft) and 10 m (33 ft) in diameter. Normally the houses are associated with low walls and the farmed area may be distinguished by a peripheral scatter of

Fig 20 Bronze Age round barrow, partly excavated, Llyn Brenig (Clwyd). The barrow was built in several stages. First, a marker circle of stakes, and a central small mortuary house were built. Funeral rites took place and bodies were placed in the centre before the mortuary house was burnt down. Then a ditch was dug out and the spoil piled up to form a low bank on its inner lip. Finally the barrow mound was built from turves and soil (photo Frances Lynch)

small cairns, laboriously formed by picking stones from the fields. Although clearance suggests grass improvement and even tillage, the heaps themselves are an encumbrance and must indicate that the plough was not always used on these farms. The walled fields are often irregular and some enclosures now appear incomplete and may have served as shelters rather than as pens. More regular fields on gently sloping terraces may have developed lynchets, but this is not always the case.

Mounds of burnt stone are another upland phenomenon in Wales, not found as yet in the south-west or the north of England. They are traditionally interpreted as "cooking places" where large joints might be boiled in water heated with hot stones, but because they have seldom been found very close to habitation it is difficult to understand their social role. However, they are not restricted to upland areas and it may be that their function varied; it has been suggested that some in Anglesey were connected with metal working. Upland areas in general were the source of metal ores and their exploitation would have been another reason for occupation in remote parts of the region.

Thanks to intensive study over recent years the best known Bronze Age landscapes are those of Dartmoor (Fleming 1983), especially around Shaugh Moor (Balaam *et al* 1982). An astonishing picture has been revealed of land management on an enormous scale with a rigid pattern of territorial blocks containing

fields laid out according to some "master plan" which must have been imposed by powerful authority, whether generated internally among the communities of farmers, or dictated from outside. The system is thought to succeed a less tangible division of the territory hinted at by the clustering of slightly earlier religious monuments on the higher slopes. Although there are other parts of the country, not necessarily upland, where surprisingly large blocks of fields seem to have been laid out in ordered schemes, implying the existence of a planned society which few would have credited in prehistory, such a pattern is clearly not universal. For instance, it may be repeated in parts of the Pennines (eg Swaledale: see Fleming 1976), but not in the Cheviots.

The circular houses of Bronze Age date may be grouped in various ways, clustered as small hamlets or scattered amongst their fields. It is these fields which, within a broad similarity of morphology, materials and environment, may show greater regional diversity in the way in which they are organized. Such variation may be a sensitive indicator of social structures. Bronze Age fields in the north of England, for instance, are sometimes regular, sometimes irregular, but their pattern suggests a more organic growth than is implied in the south west. In north Wales there is little regularity among the enclosures around the small huts of postulated Bronze Age date, although they are surprisingly extensive. The same is true of the haphazard layout of walled fields around the Swine Sty enclosure near Sheffield. On the North York Moors it has been suggested that estate boundaries run with the streams and ridges and are not imposed across the topography as in some other areas (Spratt 1982).

Bibliography

Balaam, N D, Smith, K, & Wainwright, G J, 1982 "The Shaugh Moor Project: Fourth report: environment, context and conclusion", *Proc Prehist Soc*, **48**, 203-78

Burgess, C, 1980 *The age of Stonehenge*, London, Dent

Burgess, C, 1984 "Prehistoric settlement in Northumberland: a speculative survey", in R Miket and C Burgess (eds) *Between and beyond the walls: essays in the prehistory and history of north Britain in honour of George Jobey*, Edinburgh, John Donald, 126-75

Burl, H A W, 1976 *Stone circles of the British Isles*, New Haven and London, Yale University Press

Fleming, A, 1976 "Early settlement and the landscape of west Yorkshire", in G de G Sieveking *et al* (eds) *Problems in economic and social archaeology*, London, Duckworth, 395-73

Fleming, A, 1983 "The prehistoric landscape of Dartmoor. Part 2: north and east Dartmoor", *Proc Prehist Soc*, **49**, 195-241

Gates, T, 1983 "Unenclosed settlements in Northumberland", in J C Chapman & H C Mytum (eds) *Settlement in northern Britain, 1000 BC – 1000 AD: Papers presented to George Jobey*, Brit Archaeol Rep, **118**, Oxford, BAR, 103-48

Griffiths, W E, 1950 "Early settlements in Caernarvonshire", *Archaeol Camb*, **101**, 38-70

Hart, C, 1981 *The North Derbyshire archaeological survey*, Chesterfield, *Derbyshire Archaeol Soc*

Lynch, F M, 1979 "Ring cairns in Britain and Ireland: their designs and purpose", *Ulster J Archaeol*, **42**, 1-19

Spratt, D, 1982 *Prehistoric and Roman archaeology of north east Yorkshire*, Brit Archaeol Rep, **104**, Oxford, BAR, (see ch 5)

4.4 The Iron Age (800 BC — 43 AD)

Barry Cunliffe

The retreat from the uplands, which began in the Late Bronze Age, continued. The cause is best sought in the general climatic change affecting the British Isles in the first half of the first millennium. Although the evidence is, in detail, open to debate, the general view is that there was a comparatively rapid change to cooler and wetter conditions during the three or four centuries following 1000 BC (Barber 1982, 100; Simmons & Tooley 1981, 256–61). The wetter conditions would have been even more accentuated in the upland areas of Britain, which fringe the western side of the island, and are thus directly exposed to the Atlantic weather. The slight lowering of temperature suggested for this period would have had a dramatic effect on upland farming. Lamb (1981, 55) has estimated a fall of nearly 2°C between 1000 and 750 BC, which would have shortened the growing season by more than five weeks. Clearly, if these estimates are correct, the altitude at which arable farming was possible would have been significantly lowered. The archaeological evidence is consistent with this view.

On Dartmoor, where intensive fieldwork has been carried out, relict landscapes extending up to about 400m (*c* 1400 ft) have been recorded, but there is little evidence of occupation after the middle of the first millennium BC. Instead the moor-top blanket bog had begun to extend. Only in sheltered areas of good soil do farming settlements, like Kestor, persist. Much the same process of upland abandonment is suggested by

recent field surveys on Bodmin Moor (Johnson & Rose 1982) and Northumberland (Gates 1983). Lack of precise chronological control, however, makes detailed assessment difficult.

However, while arable farming and the associated settlement systems retreat from the uplands, mixed farming, adopting a variety of regimes, continues and even intensifies in the valleys. Recent work on the North York Moors has shown a very considerable density of Iron Age quernstones coincident with areas of good arable land around the moorland fringes, even though settlement traces are difficult to find (Spratt 1982). Elsewhere, for example in North Derbyshire (Hart 1981) and Northumberland (Jobey 1974), settlements defended by palisades and banks and ditches abound, often up to quite considerable heights. The impression gained from a wide variety of surveys is that while the uplands were abandoned in many parts of the country, the lower slopes were occupied and farmed on a far more intensive basis (Fig 21). It is quite possible that the readjustment, consequent upon the climatic decline, created stress conditions which are reflected in the increasing trend towards defensive works.

The nature of the agricultural regimes adopted by the hill farms is not easy to ascertain and only in Northumberland have a sufficient number of sites been excavated to provide a comprehensive data-set. This, together with systematic pollen analysis of cores taken from bogs, has indicated mixed farming. The previously held view that the northern counties depended upon a pastoral system can now be shown to be largely incorrect. However, there can be little doubt that animal husbandry must have played a significant role in the economy. Areas of upland, previously farmed, may now have become sheep runs. In more exposed areas, where the ripening season was too short for successful cereal growing, oats and barley cut green could have provided adequate cattle feed. The study of these upland economies with their regional variations is a particularly fruitful field for further research.

While it is a fair generalization to say that the settlement pattern of much of the uplands of northern and western Britain was dominated by scattered enclosed farmsteads of single-family or extended-family size, there do occur occasional examples of larger, defended enclosures which can be categorized as hillforts. Some of them are on exposed hill crests well above 244 m (800 ft): sites like Foel Trigarn (Dyfed), the Breiddin (Powys), Mam Tor (Derbyshire) and Ingleborough (North Yorkshire). Excavation at the Breiddin has demonstrated a long sequence of use beginning in the Late Bronze Age and a range of structures which suggest a storage capacity and occupation though there is no way to show whether this was sporadic, periodic or continuous. Rather more limited work at Mam Tor exposed circular huts of late second or early first millennium date but there was no easy way to show whether they predated the rampart or were contemporary with it. At Foel Trigarn superficial observation strongly suggests that some of the many hut circles predate the defences. Overall the evidence is a little ambiguous but it could be that prominent hilltop locations of this kind were places where the larger community assembled for social, political or economic purposes over many generations beginning in the second millennium BC when climatic conditions were

Fig 21   Circular Iron Age enclosure and hut under excavation at Cyfannyd, Arthog (Gwynedd). The first phase of this site was built in timber, but later rebuilt in stone. The early phase dates to about 450 BC. The site was excavated in advance of upland pasture improvement (photo Richard Kelly for Gwynedd Archaeological Trust)

more favourable, the communal function continuing into the first millennium, eventually being monumentalized with defensive architecture. Whatever the explanation, as places redolent of coercive of power these upland fortified enclosures deserve careful attention. Other hillforts exist in upland areas but usually fringing the main massifs on rather lower summits (Fig 22). Few have been adequately examined but where evidence is available – eg Moel y Gaer (Clwyd) and Midsummer Hill (Hereford and Worcester) – internal occupation appears to be intense, ordered and long-lived. Both sites, however, are part of a central southern British socio-economic zone which is not typical of the truly upland areas of the north and west where structures of this kind are rare.

Another settlement phenomenon, restricted to the upland area, is the occupied cave, best known from the limestone areas of the Mendips and Wharfedale in the Pennines. Most have been inadequately explored and recorded, but the quantity of debris recovered is suggestive of intensive use. While ritual activity cannot be ruled out, the simplest explanation is that the caves were used by a segment of the population pursuing seasonal activities such as flock-minding or resource-gathering. As a potentially significant element in the social system cave sites have hitherto been sadly neglected.

The mineral wealth of the upland region must have continued to have been exploited. Little is known of the actual winning of copper from the Pennines and Wales, of the gold from South Wales or, indeed, of the tin from the river gravels deriving from Dartmoor or Bodmin Moor, but production must have been on a considerable scale. Lead from the Mendips was also exploited, and there is some evidence from Hengistbury Head (Dorset) that argentiferous lead was treated to extract silver. The Late Iron Age leadworkings probably underlie the Roman mining settlement at Charterhouse (Somerset). It is possible that the occupants of the Mendip caves may have been engaged in metal collecting, perhaps as a seasonal activity.

Evidence for burial in the Iron Age is notoriously sparse except from the north-east (the Arras Culture) and the extreme south west. For much of the rest of the country, including the upland areas we can only suppose that the normal rite involved exposure of bodies (excarnation) with the possible retention of part of the skeleton after the liminal period had ended. Such a procedure, attested in may parts of the country, may well have been prevalent in the uplands, accounting for the almost total lack of burial monuments.

Finally, some mention should be made of ritual behaviour. The first millennium BC sees a dramatic

32

Fig 22   Aerial view of double ditched (?Iron Age) hillfort at Shoulsbury, Exmoor (Somerset). Disturbance of the ramparts by a trackway can be seen (photo National Monuments Record, Crown copyright reserved)

increase in the deposition of prestige goods, especially weapons, in watery contexts. Chance finds of Iron Age metalwork are therefore only to be expected from the bogs and lakes of the uplands. They range from the large assemblage of material, including two cauldrons, thrown into the lake of Llyn Fawr (Glamorgan) to the pair of bronze spoons from Crosby Ravensworth (Cumbria). There can be little doubt that many more votive deposits of this kind lurk beneath the waters of the peat of the upland regions adding to the very considerable potential of this distinctive sector of the British landscape.

Bibliography

Barber, K E, 1982 "Peat-bog stratigraphy as a proxy climate record", in A Harding (ed) *Climatic change in later prehistory*, Edinburgh, At the University Press, 103-13

Gates, T, 1983 "Unenclosed settlement in Northumberland", in J C Chapman & H C Mytum (eds) *Settlement in northern Britain, 1000 BC – 1000 AD: Papers presented to George Jobey* (British Archaeological Reports 118), Oxford, BAR, 103-48

Hart, C, 1981 *The North Derbyshire archaeological survey*, Chesterfield, The Derbyshire Archaeological Society

Jobey, G, 1974 *A field-guide to prehistoric Northumberland*, Gateshead, Frank Graham

Johnson, N, & Rose, P, 1982 "Defended settlements in Cornwall – an illustrated discussion", in D Miles (ed) *The Romano-British countryside* (British Archaeological Reports 103), Oxford, BAR, 151-207

Lamb, H H, 1981 "Climate from 1000 BC to 1000 AD", in M Jones & G Dimbleby (eds) *The environment of Man: The Iron Age to the Anglo-Saxon period* (British Archaeological Reports 87), Oxford, BAR, 53-65

Simmons, I, & Tooley, M, (eds) 1981 *The environment in British prehistory*, London, Duckworth

Spratt, D, 1982 *Prehistoric and Roman archaeology of north east Yorkshire* (British Archaeological Reports 104), Oxford, BAR, (esp ch 5)

4.5 The Roman and Romano-British Iron Age (43 − 400 AD)

Malcolm Todd

Under Roman administration the uplands of Britain were subjected to unusually close supervision by the occupying power. The northern frontier of the province, for most of the period of Roman rule, ran across the northern hills through the Tyne–Solway gap, marked by Hadrian's Wall, although a substantial area beyond this was also controlled. A substantial proportion of the Roman units in Britain were stationed in the Pennines and in Wales, and the legionary garrisons were sited in strategic positions where upland and lowland met, at York, Chester and Caerleon. Some of the most arduous campaigning in the conquest of Britain had been conducted against the inhabitants of the hilly country of Wales and northern Britain, and even when that conquest had been achieved a substantial reserve of troops was left in those regions. As a result, the remains of Roman military works in northern and western Britain are among the finest and most informative of any part of the Roman Empire and their study has long been recognized as one of the most important contributions of Roman Britain to the study of the Empire at large (Richmond 1955).

A large number of military works survive on the uplands as earthworks, some of which attracted atten-tion in the eighteenth and nineteenth century. Some of the best surviving examples of marching-camps and practice-camps lie on high ground in Wales and the north, for instance the practice-works on Llandrindod Common (Powys) the camps at Y Pigwn (Dyfed) and the complex of works at Chew Green near the Scottish border (Northumberland) (Fig 23). Sites like these have usually been well studied or at least thoroughly surveyed. Much less well recorded are sites at lower altitudes, for example in the Welsh Marches and the Pennine Dales. More of these sites exist than is commonly realized (a survey of Roman camps in northern England by RCHME is now nearing comple-tion).

Most of the mineral deposits in which the Roman state was particularly interested lay in upland areas. These include the gold deposits at Dolau Cothi (Dyfed) the silver–lead of Northumberland, Derbyshire, Flint-shire and the Mendips, and perhaps the copper of north Wales. Aside from the workings of these minerals, about which relatively little is known, various installa-tions are to be expected in these areas, whether forts or *stationes* like that at Dolau Cothi, or sizable settlements like that at Charterhouse-on-Mendip. Other forms of mineral extraction are still less well documented as yet, such as the tin-streaming presumably practised in Cornwall and Devon. Identification of such Roman workings will never be easy, but it should not be despaired of.

Fig 23   Five successive superimposed Roman forts at Chew Green (Northumberland). The different sizes reflect the various army units that erected and used the forts; their purpose was to guard Dere Street (not visible on this picture) as it crossed the Cheviots. (photo National Monuments Record, Crown copyright reserved)

A complex network of roads developed to serve the military establishments and the mines. Many can still be seen crossing upland areas, as at Pen-y-Crogbren (Powys) (Frere and St Joseph 1983,139)

It is too readily assumed that the wealth of Roman Britain was concentrated in the south and east of the province, in the areas where towns and villas flourished and where arable cultivation was widely practised. The few references we have to the products of Roman Britain make it clear that animal products, especially wool, were among the most prominent (and most profitable) exports from the province. These are likely to have come from most parts of Britain, but the uplands most probably provided the largest expanses of pasture for sheep (wool), goats (leather) and cattle (hides). Many parts of upland Britain were largely pastoral, notably Wales, the Pennines and the south-western hills, and may have supplied more of the raw material upon which the prosperity of later Roman Britain was based than is often recognized.

Remains of the settlements which were associated with upland farming are familiar features of the landscape, not only in the moorland areas of the Pennines and Wales, but also on the limestones of the Midlands. Field systems dating to the Roman period are also well known, as for example at Grassington (North Yorkshire) (Fig 24). In all these areas, we are confronted by essentially Iron Age culture and economy, little changed (if at all) by the demands of Rome. In some areas, for instance Northumberland, we are well informed about such settlements and their material remains. In others, knowledge is still patchy and unsatisfactory.

Among many aspects which are still uncertain, it is not clear what settlement forms existed in the uplands in the Romano-British period, and what changes in settlement types were wrought in those four centuries. The single farmstead appears to be a constant feature of all the upland areas, but small agglomerations occur in Cumbria, and in Wales (Higham & Jones 1975). It

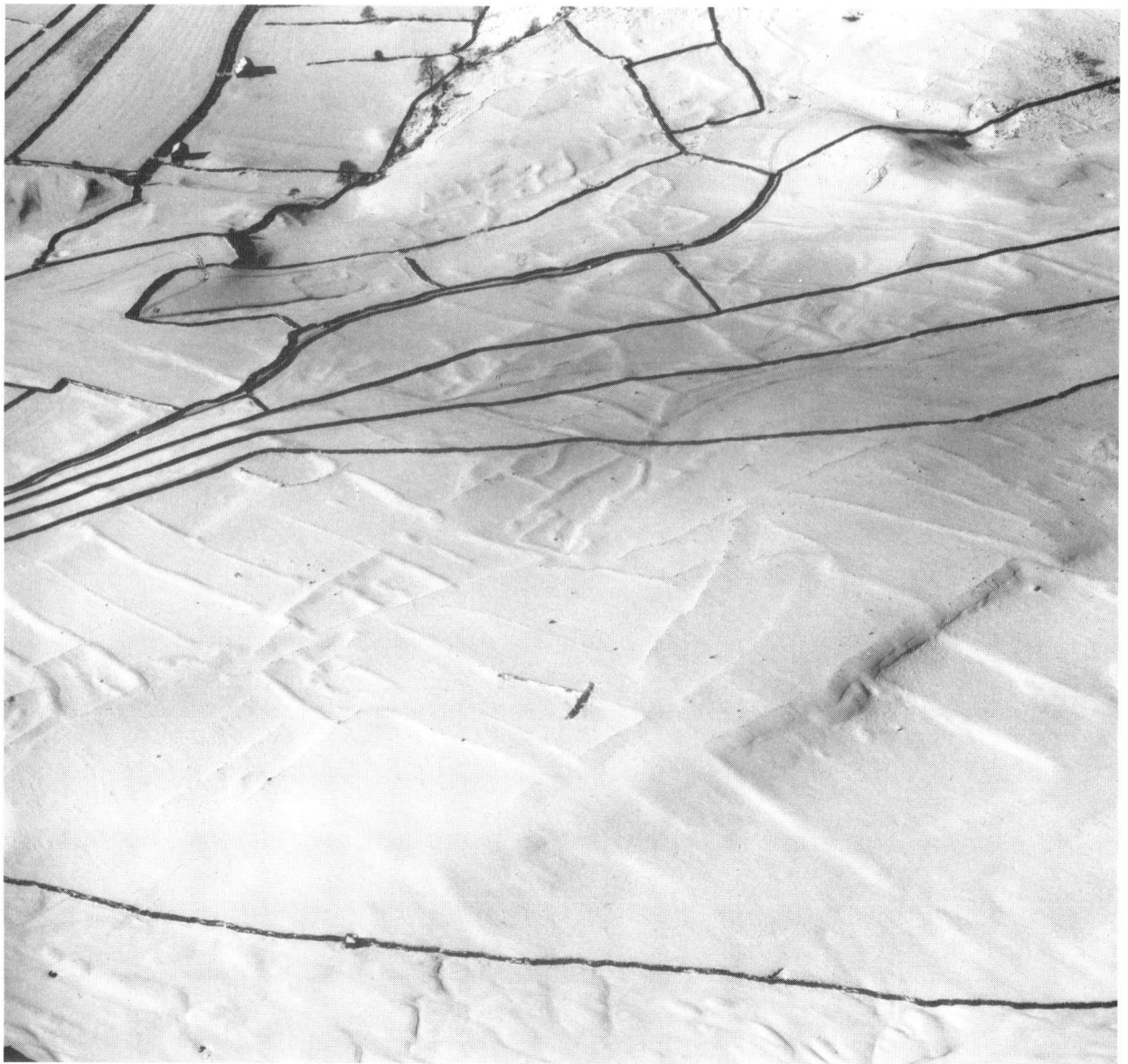

Fig 24   Romano-British fields and settlements near Grassington (North Yorkshire), seen when the ground was under a light covering of snow. Modern walls are superimposed on the earlier field pattern (photo Cambridge University Collection, copyright reserved)

appears increasingly likely that more nucleated settlements came into being, probably during the later Roman period. The possibility of synoecism or association between settlements which now appear to have been scattered in the landscape must also be entertained. Reoccupation of earlier enclosed sites, including hillforts, occurred in a number of areas, especially parts of Wales, Somerset, Devon and Cornwall, foreshadowing important developments in the early sub-Roman period and possibly hinting at social change in late Roman Britain. Few of these sites have yet been as carefully examined as they deserve. Some may well have been occupied from late Roman times into the early medieval period.

Above all else, settlement in the uplands is characterized by its essential continuity, from the pre-Roman Iron Age into Roman Britain, and probably beyond. Merely because the impress of Rome was slighter in these environments, it in no way detracts from their significance for an understanding of the province. In several parts of upland Roman Britain, population may have been denser than at any time until the early modern period. In no sense were these peripheral or impoverished areas. Rather, their contribution to the Romano-British economy may have been far greater than the evidence at our command can demonstrate.

Bibliography

Clack, P A G & Haselgrove, S, (eds) 1982 *Rural settlement in the Roman North*, Durham, CBA Regional Group 3

Frere, S S & St Joseph, J K S, 1983 *Roman Britain from the air*, Cambridge, At the University Press

Higham, N J & Jones, G D B, 1975 "Frontier, forts and farmers", *Archaeol J*, **132**, 16-53

Manning, W H, 1975 "Economic influences on land use in the military areas of the Highland Zone during the Roman period", in J G Evans, S Limbrey and H Cleere (eds) *The effect of man on the landscape: the Highland Zone* (CBA Res Rep 11), London, CBA, 112-6

Richmond, I A, 1955 "Roman Britain and Roman military antiquities", *Proc Brit Acad*, 41, **297-315**

4.6 The post-Roman period (400–1000 AD)

Harold Mytum

The archaeological evidence for post-Roman activity in the uplands is limited to a few excavated settlements, some burial monuments (both barrows and inscribed stones) and certain recognizable earthworks such as Offa's Dyke.

Place-names can sometimes give an indication of the extent of settlement at this period, but their interpretation is controversial. Documentary sources provide an outline of political and economic changes, and in some areas estates can be reconstructed from early charters. Documentary evidence also suggests that there was a climatic deterioration immediately after the Roman period, with some improvement by the 9th or 10th century. The colder winters would have made the marginal farmlands unsuitable, and this probably explains the apparent hiatus in settlement and exploitation around the 7th–8th century AD.

Pollen diagrams suggest that land use in both the north-east of England and in north Wales continued as before during the 5th and 6th centuries, while in the north-west there was substantial forest clearance for the first time in some areas. Unfortunately there is little pollen evidence for the later part of this period because the deposits have been removed in peat cutting.

In north-east England it is likely that the farmsteads in the Cheviots continued in use for a while after the withdrawl of the Romans. Similar evidence of continuity for a century or two is indicated in north Wales, though the best evidence comes from just off the uplands proper at Cefn Graeanog (Gwynedd). Some hillforts, such as the Breiddin (Powys) were briefly reoccupied.

A few inscribed memorial stones in Wales and south-west England occur on higher ground. Examples include that of Caratacus on Exmoor, the group written in the Irish Ogam script in south Powys, and the group

Fig 25 Christian inscribed stone from near Penmachno (Gwynedd). Translated it reads "Cantiori lies here. He was a citizen of vendos (and) cousin of Maglos the Magistrate". Dated to c 500 AD (photo Mick Sharp, copyright Gwynedd Archaeological Trust)

from Penmachno (Gwynedd) (Fig 25). All these monuments, traditionally dated to the 5th and 6th centuries, suggest that the uplands were still visited if not sporadically occupied. The greatest concentrations, however, were in the lowlands, suggesting that much of the higher marginal land was already being abandoned in favour of the more productive areas.

By the end of the 6th century there appears to be little evidence of upland management, and during the 7th century the only area with certain evidence of activity is the Peak District, where numerous barrow burials, both inhumation and cremations, took place (Ozanne 1964). Thanks almost exclusively to 19th century excavations, an important collection of 7th century Anglian material has been assembled from this region. The quality of this evidence is not high, and only Wigber Low (Derbyshire) has been excavated in recent times, but some conclusions can be drawn. Many burials were put in pre-existing Bronze Age barrows, as at Garratt Piece (Cumbria) but new barrows such as Benty Grange (Derbyshire) were also built. Some barrows are close to veins of lead and they may have reinforced claims over such resources. In general, however, Anglian barrow burials tend to be on unused marginal land, so the presence of these in the uplands probably only indicates settlement in the adjoining lowlands.

By the late 8th century there is evidence for the reoccupation of the uplands as at Simy Folds in Upper Teesdale (Coggins et al 1983). Three small farmsteads were in use at this time, set in a line among fields on a terrace in the limestone hills and practising a mixed farming strategy. The buildings were no longer in the earlier roundhouse tradition, but instead were rectangular and sometimes of two rooms. Heaps of ironworking slag suggest that perhaps from the beginning of the settlement, and certainly from the 9th century, iron production was a significant activity, and this seems to continue into the medieval period (Fig 26).

Few other settlements are known from pre-conquest northern England, but at Ribblehead (North Yorkshire) another farmstead has been identified and excavated, and it is likely that many still remain to be recognized (King 1978). A cluster of three rectangular buildings can be tentatively dated on coin evidence to the later 9th century, and represents a family group engaged in the rearing of cattle, sheep and horses, with some smithying.

By the 10th century and perhaps earlier there is evidence that many upland areas were being used. At Holne Moor on Dartmoor there was arable as well as pastoral farming, and this expansion continued in the medieval period (Fleming & Ralph 1982). Small fields

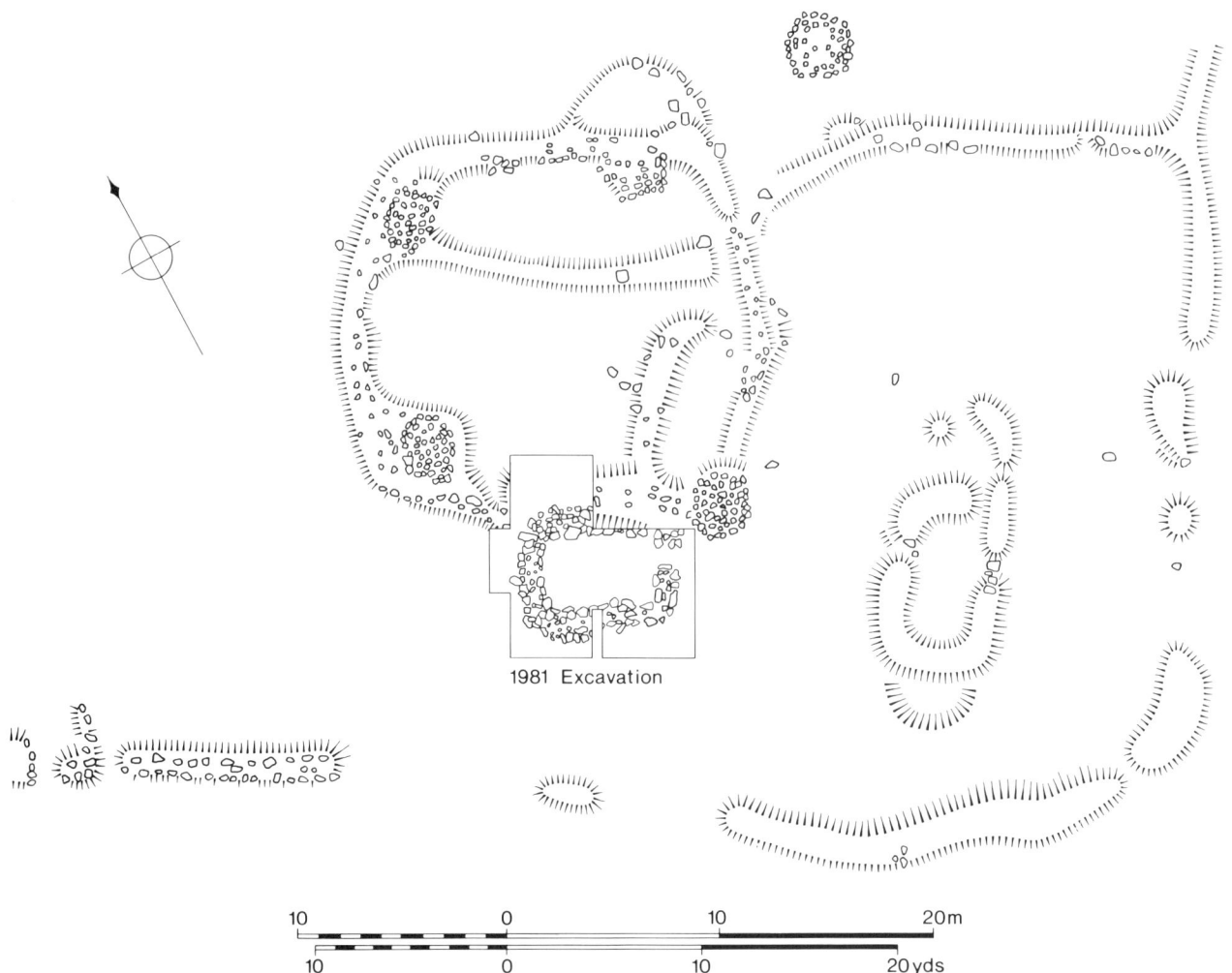

1981 Excavation

Fig 26 Simy Folds (North Yorkshire): plan of a small late 8th century farmstead comprising rectangular buildings and enclosures (after Coggins et al 1983)

were being marked off with hedges and characteristic block-walls, but unenclosed upland was also used for extensive grazing. Excavated evidence from Hound Tor, also on Dartmoor, reinforces the image of intensified upland exploitation by the end of the first millennium AD.

Elsewhere archaeological evidence for the incorporation of upland areas into estates has yet to be found, though documents clearly indicate this. Upland and lowland elements were combined in substantial single or multiple estates designed to be as self-sufficient as possible. A Welsh example is that of Trefwyddog (Dyfed) and others have been identified in the Pennines. Anglo-Scandinavian carved stones (and by implication settlements) in northern England have a lowland distribution, but some, such as Falstone (Northumberland) are in locations which suggest that upland pastures would have been used in the summer months at least. It is likely that the transhumant pattern of exploitation in north Wales began at this time (Davies 1982), with the permanent lowland *hendre* settlements and summer upland *hafoty* sites used as bases for seasonal grazing.

The material culture from most sites of the post-Roman period is limited, and those few that have been excavated in the uplands are no exception. No material apart from the western British memorial stones with their Latin or Ogam inscriptions and simple inscribed cross decorations can be dated to before the 7th century, when the Anglian grave goods from the Pennines were deposited. Some of these, such as the Benty Grange helmet and the gold and garnet pendant from White Low, are spectacular, but most were humble personal possessions. The late 8th century settlement of Simy Folds, and Ribblehead a century later, produced stone spindle-whorls and a range of simple iron tools. The finds from the earliest, probably pre-conquest phases at Hound Tor were similar in their range (Beresford 1979).

In conclusion, the period shows a continuation of the native Roman pattern of upland exploitation until the 6th century, with gradual abandonment of marginal land. This was then brought back into use from the late 8th century, by which time the deteriorating climate may have started to improve. Sometimes permanent settlements were placed in upland areas, but in many cases exploitation was either seasonal or carried out from a centre in the adjacent lowland.

The post-Roman period can be seen as a time when one phase of upland use comes to an end and, after a period of abandonment, a new and vigorous expansion begins in a different cultural and economic milieu. While relatively little is known so far, the combination of documentary and field evidence can suggest main trends which will be further elaborated as more work is carried out.

Bibliography

Beresford, G, 1979 "Three deserted medieval settlements on Dartmoor: A report on the late E Marie Winter's excavations", *Medieval Archaeol* 23, 98-158
Coggins, D, Fairless, K J & Batey, C E, 1983 "Simy Folds: an early medieval settlement in Upper Teesdale", *Medieval Archaeol*, 27, 1-26
Davies, W, 1982 *Wales in the early Middle Ages*, Leicester, At the University Press
Fleming, A, & Ralph, N, 1982 "Medieval settlement and land use on Holne Moor, Dartmoor: The landscape evidence", *Medieval Archaeol*, 26, 101-37
King, A, 1978 "Gauber high pasture, Ribblehead – an interim report", in R A Hall (ed) *Viking Age York and the north* (CBA Res Rep 27), London, CBA, 21-5
Ozanne, A, 1964 "The Peak dwellers", *Medieval Archaeol*, 6/7, 15-52

4.7 Medieval (1000–1700 AD)

Stephen Moorhouse

Use of the uplands throughout the Middle Ages was dictated by three factors: natural environment, geology and tenure. The first constrained the type of farming practised, the second attracted the extraction of a wide range of minerals, while the third dictated the way in which the uplands were exploited. Unlike earlier periods a wide range of written records was produced, many of which have survived. These allow us to see how the landscape was laid out, who moulded it for what purpose, and to chart its progress. The manor as an economic unit played a major role in forming the landscape and changing it. Large estates held by politically and financially powerful landlords included vast tracts of upland, which provided essential resources for a balanced manorial economy. Mineral resources, large open grazing areas and unrestricted hunting grounds were rarely available in the lowlands, either because such resources did not exist there or because space was at a premium. Often, large areas of upland were in the hands of one landlord. In the central Pennines the vast adjoining honours of Pontefract and Clitheroe straddled the uplands, and belonged to the Lacy family. The exploitation of the uplands during the Middle Ages produced its own very specialized economy and a landscape totally different from that which developed at lower altitudes. Deteriorating climate and a retraction of population has left a relic landscape which is as varied in its content as it is rich in its surviving heritage (Parry 1978; Fleming & Ralph 1982).

The changing patterns of settlement during the Middle Ages were governed by many factors, most of which were purely regional in their influence. Two, however, were paramount: changes in population and climatic deterioration. The rising population of the 13th century saw an expansion of settlement and clearance of moorland for both pastoral and subsistence arable use. The decline in population from the late 13th century was accelerated, but not precipitated, by the plagues of the 14th century, and it only began to rise again during the 15th century. Many upland regions saw a second wave of land reclamation following the rise in population during the later Middle Ages, with the creation of new isolated farmsteads with their surrounding fields (see Roberts 1977, 173–86; Taylor 1984, 175).

The influence of climate on settlement in the uplands is at present uncertain. Climatic historians suggest that the series of very wet summers towards the middle of the 14th century heralded the agricultural and economic decline in north-west Europe during the later Middle Ages. Archaeological investigation of settlements on the fringes of the uplands suggests a preponderance of desertion and abandonment during the

38

14th century (Fig 27). However, reasons for desertion were complex and often purely regional (Beresford 1964; Aston 1983; Moorhouse 1981). While historians are agreed about general climatic trends during the Middle Ages they also point out that the weather, like today, was extremely regional and followed different patterns in different parts of the country (Hallam 1984).

This development is seen rather clearly at Houndtor 1 on Dartmoor. Here a group of post-Roman shielings were superseded by a series of permanent houses forming a village in the 13th century, only to be finally abandoned during the 14th century (Beresford 1979). Houndtor illustrates another not unusual trend in the medieval uplands: the builders of the 13th century farmstead at Houndtor 2 used the ruins of a stone-built Bronze Age farmstead. The hard-won clearances in the uplands tended to be reused in successive periods, settlements and fields alike, with expansion to old and the creation of new settlements. This is certainly true during the Middle Ages.

The natural elements of geology, geography, soil cover and climate dictated a predominantly pastoral economy in the uplands. Arable farming was practised at a purely subsistence level to provide cereals for those in permanent occupation. Wide variations in the way in which people organized themselves into communities in the uplands, and also in the patterns through which they held property, created an equally wide range of composite field systems (Baker & Butlin 1973). Individual field enclosures were usually small, up to 1 ha (2.4 acres), and were added piecemeal to the settlement. Often the fields outlived the settlements around which they had originally developed. The methods of constructing field boundaries varied throughout the uplands, not through the availability of material but, like building materials, through fashion. In many areas stone was used. Elsewhere banks with quickset hedges upon them are found, even though stone was easily available in the area. In the central and northern Pennines these were replaced by stone walls during the post-medieval period (Moorhouse 1981, 614). Here, medieval enclosures within later field systems or as abandoned isolated groups can be detected not only by their small, irregular shapes, but also by the stone walls which have been set into the earlier banks, using them as bases.

The uplands provided large areas of often lush grazing during the summer months, but were inhospitable during winter. This gave rise to seasonal occupation where shepherds and herdsmen, their families, or even whole communities, would migrate from the lowlands to take up summer residence in temporary accommodation (Fig 28). Abandoned hut sites from such occupation are to be found over most of the uplands (Ramm, McDowall & Mercer 1976; Davies 1980). In many areas these temporary sites later became permanently settled. This was well advanced in

Fig 27 Deserted medieval settlement at Trewortha Marsh, Smallacombe, Bodmin Moor (Cornwall). The rectangular houses can be seen amid a field system which contains and partly overlies prehistoric fields and settlements. A prehistoric enclosure is visible top left. A medieval track approaches the settlement from the bottom right (photo National Monuments Record, Crown copyright reserved)

Cumbria by the 11th century, but in neighbouring Northumberland, for different reasons, transhumance sites did not become settled until the 13th century. In many areas these temporary medieval settlements survive as thriving farms, their origins betrayed by regionally distinctive place-name elements, such as "shield" or "erg" in the northern Dales, "booth" in the central Pennines or "hafod" in Wales.

The settlement of the uplands created a need for communication. Many upland areas preserve little-used or more often abandoned routes which were important in the Middle Ages. Some provided access to abandoned farming or industrial settlements or to the temporary shielings. Others were more important, acting as manorial thoroughfares, connecting distant parts of dispersed estates. Such a route crossed the northern Pennines linking Clitheroe and Pontefract, the centres of two very large estates owned by the powerful Lacy family. Much of this route is now minor roads, other parts are footpaths, while some portions have fallen out of use altogether, although its entire length survives. One of the major changes in the use of medieval upland routes occurred during the turnpike era in the late 18th and 19th centuries when new routes, particularly in the industrial valleys of the central and southern Pennines, led to the downgrading of many long-trodden important moorland routes to the status of footpath, which thereafter were used only infrequently. It is likely that many upland routeways have a medieval if not earlier origin. The very large areas of upland township or vill territories meant that manorial and farming features essential to everyday life, such as the manorial corn mill or the parish church, could be widely separate. The effects of such dispersal upon the development of communities are perhaps underestimated.

Many of the larger estates deliberately included upland areas as well as fertile lowland. Apart from parks, the uplands provided rich and expansive grazing areas and were ideal for large sheep or cattle farms, the lay equivalent of the monastic grange. Many such farms, formerly more extensive, persist as much smaller complexes, with the earthworks of their medieval predecessors surrounding the surviving buildings. Typical of such sites, particularly in the northern Pennines, is a series of successive well-worn hollow ways fanning out over the moors – long since abandoned routes which frequently point in the direction of summer grazing areas (Moorhouse 1981, 614). As with parks, the boundary of their adjacent grazing area, and distant summer pastures, would be defined physically with a bank surmounted by a fence, hedge or stone wall and an external ditch. Feed storage barns are documented on the larger and more isolated grazing areas.

Cattle farms and sheep ranches exerted influences of their own upon the pattern of routes in the uplands, through droveways and other paths which connected distant parts of the farms and linked them with the outside world.

Fig 28 Brenig (Clwyd): excavated foundations of a 16th century hafod with two small rooms. Scale totals 2m (photo Frances Lynch)

The geology of the uplands dictated that the most abundant building material was stone, whether it be the Millstone Grits of the Pennines, the granites of Dartmoor or the limestones of the Cotswolds. In most areas this was the material used, sometimes in combination with timbering in the upper part of the structure. In other areas fashion was more important or more adaptable to the kind of buildings. Wood was the dominant material for building at all social levels and for field boundaries during the Middle Ages in the central Pennines. These were superseded only in the 17th century by the most abundant and easily available stone, which in the Middle Ages was used almost exclusively for stone slates to roof the buildings.

A variety of minerals was exploited, and scattered communities of miners and craftsmen added to the upland population. Coal was mined extensively wherever it outcropped. Sophisticated gallery techniques were in use at least from the 14th century in the north, while drift mining was commonplace by the 15th century - two techniques which leave very different surface remains. Iron mining and smelting were mainly restricted to the northern uplands (Crossley 1981; Moorhouse 1981, 1984; Jewell, Michelmore & Moorhouse 1981). Iron had been exploited from the Roman period at least, and was a major industry by the 13th century in the Yorkshire Pennines and the North York Moors, rivalling the better-known lowland centres of the Weald. Sites are often isolated, self-contained, and as such usually extensive. Where water power was harnessed the remains of one or more dams may survive. The central Pennines have produced the earliest documented examples in the country of a water-powered iron smelting site, dating to the late 13th century, and the earliest recorded oliver (1349/50). Small and scattered deposits of silver were mined in Northumberland, Derbyshire, the Mendips, Wales and on Exmoor and Dartmoor, while tin mining was restricted to the south-western uplands (Greeves 1981). Lead was the most widely exploited of all upland minerals and was mined in most regions (Blanchard 1981).

Quarrying was common in many regions on the upland fringes (Moorhouse f.c.). Building stone and roofing slates were thriving industries in some areas. Stone slates became very important during the later Middle Ages in the central Pennines, and these products achieved a wide distribution. Millstones were quarried wherever the appropriate type of stone existed, mainly over the Millstone Grit areas. The absence of wheat for bread meant that oat cakes or their local versions were staple foods in the uplands. Bread ovens gave way to open baking shelves or bakestones. These were quarried mainly from local sites, but were scattered over large areas of northern England. The wide, mainly southern English distribution of a series of Millstone Grit mortars suggest that one or more mortar and quern centres lie on the gritstones of central northern England. Personal knives and whetstones to keep them sharp were commonly carried on the belt by men among the lower ranks of society. The common use of such knives is reflected by the number and distribution of documented whetstone quarries. Movement of population has meant that many of the upland medieval quarries have been preserved because of their isolation and inaccessibility. Those nearer to the later centres of population have been used continually, destroying the earlier workings.

The natural resources of the uplands provided raw materials for an essentially lowland market. The exploitation of some minerals was as intensive as at any time during the Industrial Revolution of some centuries later. At the moment documentary evidence is the main source of information for the existence, extent and changing patterns of their exploitation. Fieldwork is beginning to make an impact, particularly for iron production in the north, and is suggesting that primary mining and secondary working sites survive in abundance in the uplands (Everson & Welfare 1984). Their isolation means that the larger permanent sites were self-contained with bakers and brewers to service them, with the primary extractive and secondary processes taking place on the same site. It is probably through the well-preserved upland industrial sites that knowledge of medieval technology will be advanced, for comparable sites in the lowlands are rare, having been destroyed either in antiquity or through modern development.

The open moors of the uplands made them ideal for use as hunting reserves. A number of royal forests existed within the English and Welsh uplands, as did many forests and parks belonging to wealthy landlords (Cantor 1982). Forests in either lay or royal ownership were administered separately and their landscapes tend to be geared more to hunting requirements than farming or industrial use. Parks were generally smaller, and excluded settlements and their attendant field systems, being almost exclusively the private hunting reserve of the landlord. Their boundaries were well defined, usually surviving as a substantial bank with internal ditch, designed to keep animals in and humans out. Their contents varied, but commonly included at least one lodge where the keeper would live and the visiting landlord and his guests would stay. A number of scattered barns for storage and winter feed would be essential. Rabbits were often reared in parks in a conygarth, commonly extensive with a minimum of artificial earths and surrounded by a stout fence to exclude predators. A variety of hunting features existed. Net positions for animals and birds were common, as were pit traps. In large parks hunting positions, or "stands", were fashionable during the Middle Ages. These were tall wooden towers with surrounding paddocks, into which the game was driven for easy shooting by the hunters in the tower.

Economic circumstances dictated that most parks over rich mineral deposits were not excluded from industrial activity. The mining of coal and iron, the smelting of the latter, and the quarrying of various stones were common practice in some medieval upland parks. Boundaries of former areas of woodland should also exist, as woodland was coppiced and managed as intensively within the parks as elsewhere. The existence of woodland assumes the existence of a range of woodland craftsmen. The two most likely to leave physical evidence for their activities are charcoal burners and carpenters. Carpenters' workshops, and especially saw-pits, should be expected in regions where timber buildings were fashionable, as in the central Pennines.

Monastic exploitation of the uplands was both extensive and intensive. Few monastic houses were themselves sited above the 800 foot contour. The estates of those on the fringes of the uplands covered vast tracts of open moorland, providing grazing for extensive cattle or sheep farms. The mineral wealth of the uplands was also exploited, particularly by the Cistercians (Donkin 1979) who deliberately acquired mineral rights and established major granges many miles from the mother house. Influential North Yorkshire houses set up a series of large granges with their attached estates in modern West Yorkshire, 50 miles to the south, specifically to exploit the rich iron ore deposits. Garendon Abbey (Leicestershire) established a grange at Roystone Grange in northern Derbyshire to mine the rich lead seams there.

In summary, the uplands of England and Wales supported a specialized economy which was not found in the lowlands. Many large estates included upland areas for their natural resources. The nature and development of this exploitation can only be fully understood and appreciated through the documentary evidence, which should pave the way for intensive fieldwork and selective excavation in the future. In contrast to their stark and abandoned appearance today, the uplands in the Middle Ages constituted a properly organized and well managed landscape, but changing times and circumstances saw fluctuations in their use and culminated in their abandonment. Climatic alterations, tenurial and economic influences all played their part, but perhaps it was the purely local factors which dominated. Tenurial evidence shows that in our wider understanding the uplands cannot be detached from lowland economies; the two were very much linked, each providing a different range of resources and facilities, but both essential to the commerce and pleasure which combined to support a large manorial estate.

Bibliography

Adams, I, 1976 *Agrarian landscape terms: a glossary for historical geography*, (Inst Hist Geogr Special Publication no 9), London, Institute of Historical Geography

Aston, M, 1983 "Deserted farmsteads on Exmoor and the Lay Subsidy of 1327 in west Somerset", *Proc Somerset Archaeol & Nat Hist Soc*, **127**, 71-104

Baker, A R H & Butlin, R A, 1973 *Studies in field systems in the British Isles*, Cambridge, At the University Press

Beresford, M W, 1964 "Dispersed and nucleated settlement in Medieval Cornwall", *Agr Hist Rev*, **12**, 13-27

Beresford, G, 1979 "Three deserted medieval settlements on Dartmoor: a report on the late E Marie Minter's excavation", *Medieval Archaeol*, **23**, 98-158

Blanchard, I S W, 1981 "Lead mining and smelting in Medieval England and Wales", in D W Crossley (ed) *Medieval industry* (CBA Res Rep no 40), London, CBA, 72-84

Cantor, L, 1982 "Forests, chases, parks and warrens", in L Cantor (ed) *The English Medieval landscape*, London, Croom Helm, 56-85

Crossley, D W, 1981 "Medieval iron and smelting", in D W Crossley (ed) *Medieval Industry*, (CBA Res Rep 40), London, CBA, 29-41

Davies, E, 1980 "Hafod, hafoty and lluest: their distribution, features and purpose", *Ceredigion* **9**, 1-41

Donkin, R A, 1979 *The Cistercians: studies in the geography of medieval England and Wales*, (Studies and Texts 38) Toronto

Everson, P E, & Welfare, H G, 1984 "Surveys of industrial landscapes: Clee Hill, Shropshire and Cockfield Fell, County Durham", in *Royal Commission on Historical Monuments (England) Annual Review 1983-84*, 18-21

Fleming, A & Ralph, N, 1982 "Medieval settlement and land use on Holne Moor, Dartmoor: the landscape evidence", *Medieval Archaeol*, **26**, 101-37

Greeves, T A P, 1981 "The archaeological potential of the Devon tin industry", in D W Crossley (ed) *Medieval industry*, (CBA Res Rep 40), London, CBA, 85-95

Hallam, H E, 1984 "The climate of eastern England 1250-1350", *Agr Hist Rev*, **32**, 124-32

Jewell, H, Michelmore, D J H & Moorhouse, S, 1981 "An oliver at Warley, West Yorkshire, AD 1349-50", *Hist Metall*, **18**, 39-40

Moorhouse, S, 1981 "The rural medieval landscape", in M L Faull & S Moorhouse (eds) *West Yorkshire: An archaeological survey to AD 1500*, Wakefield, West Yorkshire County Council, 581-850

Moorhouse, S, 1984 "Permanent ironworking sites in medieval West Yorkshire", *CBA Forum: Newsletter of CBA Group 4* (1984), 25-9

Moorhouse, S, forthcoming, "Mining and quarrying in medieval West Yorkshire", in [Old West Riding], forthcoming

Parry, M L, 1978 *Climatic change: agriculture and settlement*, London

Ramm, H G, McDowall, R W & Mercer, E, 1970 *Shielings and bastles*, London, RCHME

Roberts, B K, 1977 *Rural settlement in Britain*, Folkestone, Dawson

Taylor, C, 1984 *Village and farmstead*, London, George Philip

4.8 The Industrial Age (1700–1980)

Keith Falconer and Stafford Linsley

Until the advent of the motor car at the beginning of the 20th century three themes dominated the evolution of the upland landscape in the modern period – the enclosure of common grazing lands, the extraction of minerals and the exploitation of natural resources for use in the lowlands. These themes were well established before the beginning of the period, but it was to be the change in scale of these operations that differentiated the period from all others.

Previous chapters have identified a trend of increasing interdependence between the uplands and the adjacent lowlands, and this developed in the modern period to a point where subsistence and self-sufficient economies in the uplands were all but extinguished. They were replaced by an economy based on supplying an industrialized and urbanized society dependent for its basic needs on a much wider network of sources than hitherto. Transhumance, as a way of life, was to disappear by the end of the 18th century, while infield–outfield farming was to survive only to a limited extent in the 19th century.

The appearance of much of the present-day landscape is a result of relatively recent enclosure of common grazing lands by lowland landowners. In the Pennines, for example, enclosure was taking place in upper Wharfedale in the 1780s and 1790s, and in Swaledale a few years later. Many of the walled fields in Wensleydale, each with its barn tucked in the corner, date from around the time of the Napoleonic Wars. These were not the first enclosures; smaller enclosures, often of irregular configuration, had been taking place in the vicinity of settlements since the 16th century. But it was the period *c* 1750-1840 which saw the greatest change, when concern for the improvement of land and farming methods was accompanied by the systematic blocking-out of fields, and drystone walls were ruled up the sides of the Yorkshire Dales, or across the undulating limestone plateau of the Peak, as around Wardlow in Derbyshire. These new fields of the Georgian era have become the "traditional" landscapes with which residents and visitors are now familiar.

42

The steady rise in the level of extraction of mineral resources chronicled in previous essays continued at a much accelerated pace in the early part of the period. The extraction of non-ferrous ores had already achieved some measure of industrial organization with the incorporation of the Society of Mines Royal in 1568, and a few copper mines had been opened in the Lake District and Cornwall by 1600. The scale of mining remained small, however, until the beginning of the 18th century when there was a great increase in demand for brass, an alloy of copper. Brass was not only required for many types of household goods in an increasingly affluent society but for the expanding engineering industry and for military accoutrements for the large standing armies of that century.

Improved mining techniques included first the introduction of adit draining and then of steam pumping. These new technologies allowed the exploitation of much deeper ores and the established mining areas experienced dramatic growth. Thus, in the early 19th century, comparatively remote areas such as Coniston in the Lake District had mines employing up to 600 people. With the aid of some thirteen waterwheels, for both mine drainage and ore dressing, one site was capable of producing some 250 tons of ore a month. This activity has left a legacy of numerous mine adits and shafts, dressing floors and waste heaps (Figs 29 & 30).

In Cornwall and Devon the remains are even more impressive though not by any means restricted to the uplands. The copper mines of Cornwall as a whole achieved a peak output of 140,000 tons of ore by the middle of the 19th century, and although this ore was mostly shipped to south Wales for smelting, the profusion of empty engine houses, intermingled with those of the tin and lead industries, are a poignant reminder of the scale of operations.

The winning of lead ores and its smelting was more widespread in the uplands with notable concentrations in the Mendips, the south Shropshire hills, mid Wales, the Peak District and the northern Pennines, in addition to the Lake District and the south-west. In these areas mining had not only a significant physical impact on the landscape but also on the upland economy with ramifications far beyond the immediate mining site.

The Alston area in the northern Pennines provides a good example of the pervasive influence of the industry. Standing at more than 900 ft, Alston is the highest market town in England and a centre of lead mining since at least the 12th century. From that time onwards lead mining and processing, within the surrounding fells up to 914 m (3000 ft) above sea level, were the primary economic activities of the area, making it one of the richest mining areas of Britain. Most of the lead was exported from Newcastle, being carried over a complex and frequently high-level network of carriers' ways and later on roads that are among the highest in Britain. The present road from Alston to Weardale reaches a summit of 627 m (2056 ft) above sea level, having done so at least from the 18th century: an alternative route, occasionally used, went underground through a series of mine workings.

Fig 29   Park Level Mill, Killhope (Durham). Lead-crushing mill with large over-shot water wheel adjacent to the crushing house. The wheel is 10.2m (33.75 ft) in diameter (photo Stafford Linsley)

Fig 30   Smelt Mill flue at Nenthead (Durham) (photo Stafford Linsley)

Lead miners rarely had secure or regularly remunerative employment and a miner-farmer lifestyle became common through the development of smallholdings. Thus, with the help of locally produced lime to improve the poor soils, the moorland fringe in the Alston area was pushed to higher and higher altitudes, frequently to above 549 m (1800 ft), steadings, cottages and sometimes small settlements accompanying these extensions of farming land. Moreover, as the main commercial centre of this activity, and as a market town, Alston generated supporting industries such as small woollen mills, a brewery and baking enterprises. In the 19th century, just before the lead industry went into a fairly sharp, irreversible decline, Alston became the terminus of a branch line from the Newcastle to Carlisle railway. So even today it is possible to attribute almost any field evidence, structure or transport route in the area, directly or indirectly to its former lead industry.

Such interdependent economies developed to varying degrees in most other mining areas, including the slate-quarrying areas of north Wales and the Lake District. In these areas and especially around Blaenau Ffestiniog the ravages of extraction are particularly dramatic, with huge slate-waste tips dominating a landscape of vast, flooded quarries. Although the 20th century has seen the virtual cessation of metalliferous mining in the uplands, extraction of mineral resources such as phosphates, fluospar and barytes has continued apace, while there has been a dramatic expansion in the scale of stone-quarrying. With the increasing use of

crushed limestone as an aggregate for concrete, quarries which hitherto served local needs for building stone and fertilizer have developed into huge concerns meeting a national demand for hard core and concrete. Since the Second World War more stone has been removed from the Mendips and the Peak District than was extracted in all previous working.

In the modern period the uplands have become increasingly valued as gathering grounds for water to supply lowland centres of population. Not only have the waters of small valleys in the Pennines and Brecon Beacons been impounded to provide for local towns but huge reservoirs have been created in remoter areas such as mid Wales and the Lake District to supply far distant cities. The lake Vyrnwy scheme (1881–92) supplying Liverpool was the pioneer, to be followed closely by the Elan Valley and the Thirlmere schemes supplying Birmingham and Manchester respectively. The process still continues with the post-war drowning of the Meldon valley on the fringe of Dartmoor and the creation of the vast Keilder reservoir, close to the Scottish border, to supply the needs of Tyneside, Wearside and Teesside into the 21st century. Although these schemes drown existing landscapes, they have created their own landscapes of dams, valvehouses, aqueducts and pipelines, and have caused the growth of associated settlements not only to service the installations but increasingly to cater for the recreational use of these facilities.

The last two centuries have witnessed sporadic attempts to tame the uplands by the injection of outside capital. The reclamation of Exmoor by John Knight from 1815 involved the deep ploughing and sowing of 2,500 acres and an enclosure wall 29 miles long, while Thomas Johnes' experiments in the upper Ystwyth Valley involved planting some four million trees between 1796 and 1813. The creation of the Forestry Commission in 1921 has continued this process with dramatic effect on the appearance of the landscape.

Extensive areas have been deep-ploughed, destroying much archaeological material, and planted with comparatively few species of trees. The visual impact of these regimented conifers caused a popular reaction against the creation of such unfamiliar landscapes, and the Forestrey Commission has responded by planting a wider variety of trees and developing forest parks to promote greater leisure use of their properties.

Remote areas, suitable for water-gathering or forestry, have also been sought after by the military for firing ranges and for exercise purposes. Extensive tracts of uplands in south Wales, Dartmoor and the northern Pennines have had their landscapes virtually fossilized for these purposes. Surprisingly, they do less archaeological damage than might be imagined.

Throughout the period increased exploitation of the uplands demanded improved transport facilities. Many of the upland tracks of earlier periods were valued for their accessible grazing and used to provide networks of drove roads channelling cattle driven from western Wales and Scotland through the uplands of central Wales and northern England respectively to regional fairs and ultimately to Smithfield. In the 18th century this use of the uplands peaked, with as many as 20,000 head of cattle assembling at Malham Moor Fair each October. The alignments of many of the packhorse trails of medieval times were perpetuated by the boundary walls of the new enclosures and the paths continued to be used for local transport of commodities such as coal and woollen goods until displaced either by the turnpike roads radiating out from industrial towns or, somewhat later, by railways. In some cases the turnpike roads improved existing packhorse routes, and many packhorse ways continued in use after the coming of the turnpikes, but often their rationales were different and many paths gradually fell into disuse, leaving impressive remains in areas such as the moors above Todmorden (West Yorkshire).

Railway penetration of the uplands was comparatively early and lines such as the Cromford and High Peak Railway in Derbyshire, operational in 1831, and the 1834 Stanhope and Tyne Railway with its Rookhope branch in Weardale, reached altitudes between 244 and 509 m (800 and 1670 ft), while some mainline railways such as the South Durham and Lancashire Union and the Settle and Carlisle railways have summits in excess of 305 m (1000 ft). By the end of the 19th century railways had opened up all but the most remote areas with mineral lines and narrow-gauge railways, greatly facilitating the exploitation of slate and mineral ores in Wales and Cumbria. Railways and steam shipping also had the effect of extinguishing long-distance cattle droving with a subsequent abandonment of many upland paths. The retreat of railways from the uplands this century has left a rich legacy of engineering structures, the future of which is problematical. Latterly the motor car, or more strictly the internal combustion engine as lorries and buses have to be included, has opened up the uplands to an unprecedented extent. Now a journey from the lowland concentrations of population to formerly remote parts of the uplands has become a casual experience.

Bibliography

Buchanan, R A, 1972 *Industrial archaeology in Britain*, Harmondsworth, Penguin

Cossons, N, 1975 *The BP book of industrial archaeology*, Newton Abbot, David and Charles

Davies-Shiel, M & Marshall, J D, 1969 *The industrial archaeology of the Lake Counties*, Newton Abbot, David and Charles

Falconer, K, 1980 *Guide to England's industrial heritage*, London, Batsford

Millward, R & Robinson, A, 1980 *Upland Britain*, Newton Abbot, David and Charles

4.9 Patterns of exploitation and neglect

Taking the evidence summarized in this chapter as a whole, a number of patterns can be seen which encompass current changes in the uplands.

The uplands prospered as providers of critical resources – stone, metals, wood and of course agricultural produce. Changing environmental circumstances and the cumulative effects of earlier activities continually modify land-use potential. The density of settlement in the uplands is, on the whole, directly proportional to the labour needed to exploit the required resources. In the past additional demands on the uplands were relatively few; today they include water, recreation, forestry, military training, and intensive agriculture, thus increasing pressure on the availability of land.

We have seen that upland land-use was essentially episodic in the sense that periods of intensive use were interspersed with phases of neglect and abandonment. The Bronze Age, the Roman period and the early medieval period represent the high points of upland exploitation before the modern era. Each successful episode depended upon favourable environmental, technical and economic circumstances. The present intensification of land use in the uplands is thus only the latest in a series which stretches back into prehistory. But it is the technical achievements of this century in the form of machines able to modify the landscape on a scale previously unimagined, and the economic pressures to increase productivity, which underlie the current episode of exploitation.

There have always been many constraints on the use of the uplands. Physical environment largely dictates lines of communication, the availability of suitable land for settlement and the distribution of natural resources. For these reasons upland landscapes display a high degree of continuity from one stage of use to the next. Settlements tend to be sited in much the same places, and in some instances field boundaries and land divisions established in the Bronze Age still remain in use down to this day. This apparent conservatism, probably based largely on common sense, has undoubtedly played a major part in preserving the archaeological heritage of the uplands and may yet hold the key to their future.

As with other parts of Britain, the uplands display considerable regional variation, even over quite small areas. As Pryor (1983) has emphasized, regional development relates to the differing traditions of the people in each area since they make and perpetuate their own history. The search for regional traditions in the archaeological record is an area of research which is only just beginning, but one which will prove particularly rewarding in upland studies.

4.10 Problems of interpretation

In conclusion it is worth mentioning three groups of problems which affect our capacity or ability to interpret the archaeology of the uplands.

Conceptual difficulties
There is a widespread view, largely promoted by out-of-date textbooks, that regards the uplands of England and Wales as a cultural backwater throughout prehistory and much of the early historic period simply because, until recently, the evidence has not been recorded in the detail it deserves. This view is clearly quite wrong, since, as we have seen, the uplands sustained high populations during much of later pre-history and the Middle Ages. There is also the problem of educating the public to the fact that the uplands have not always looked as they now do.

Research difficulties
The pace of discovery through fieldwork has outstripped our understanding of some classes of site. Thus structures such as burnt mounds, stone rows and field systems are poorly understood despite the fact that thousands of them are now known. Excavations at hillforts such as Moel y Gaer (Powys) suggest that in some instances at least these enclosures were built much earlier than previously thought. Whether this is a widespread or a regionally variable phenomenon requires further research to determine.

Chronological difficulties
The research problems are directly related to questions of dating. Because many upland sites are artefactually poor it is difficult to reassess the date of features solely on the basis of finds. A programme of radiocarbon dating is badly needed, in conjunction with field survey and limited excavations, to revise the chronological framework for upland remains.

5 Upland archaeology in danger

Intensification of land-use and improved technology, both fuelled by government incentives, pose more threats to the upland archaeological heritage than ever before. This chapter examines the causes and effects of these threats.

5.1 Patterns of decay

In order to understand the long-term effects of threats to archaeological remains, and to provide a basis for discussion on how such threats may be averted (see below ch 9), it is useful to have a model of decay processes.

The archaeological record is a product of human activities. Inevitably, individual parts of the record – for example earthworks, timber buildings, bone needles or ironwork – begin to decay from the moment of deposition. The rate at which decay occurs depends upon two sets of factors: the durability of the components (eg wood, stone, bone, metal etc), and the processes of attrition (eg chemical action, physical erosion etc). It is helpful to visualize the operation of these processes graphically as curves (Fig 31). Characteristically a decay curve begins steeply, as the archaeological components become acclimatized to their surroundings, followed by a more shallow falloff as the components, now more stable, gradually change with those surroundings. Within any given site some remains of the activities undertaken will be more durable than others, and some sites themselves are more durable than others.

Decay processes relating to the survival of archaeolo-

gical features in Dorset have been discussed in this way by Groube (1978; Groube and Bowden 1982 and see Fig 31a). In the uplands the decay path is rather different, due partly to the nature of the evidence itself (see ch 3.1) and also to the history of the upland landscape (see ch 4). Unlike most lowland areas, where man's activities have been fairly continuous, settlement and exploitation of the uplands have been episodic to the extent that periods of high attrition and decay are sandwiched between periods which saw stabilization. Thus a *stepped*, and also less steep decay path may be proposed for upland areas (Fig 31b). This accords with the generally better condition of monuments in the uplands compared with those on lower ground (ch 3.1).

During the present century the increase in man's ability to modify the environment has led to a steepening of the natural decay curves (Groube & Bowden 1982,15; and see Fig 31c). In lowland areas this acceleration began in the 1940s. In the uplands it started somewhat later and gathered momentum slightly more slowly, but with technological developments and economic incentives it has, over the last decade, become equally steep (Fig 31d).

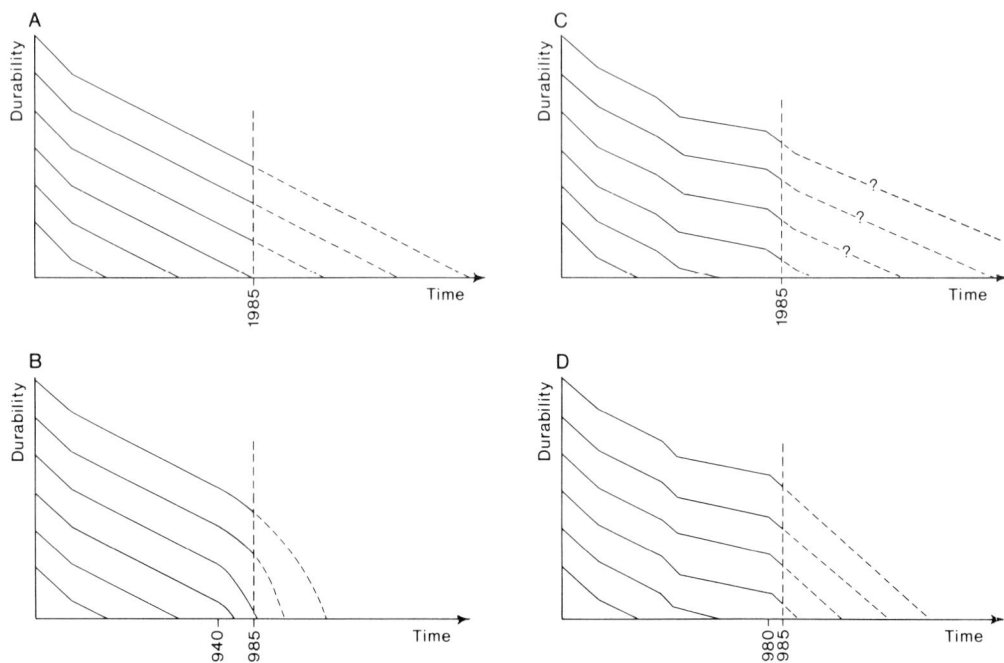

Fig 31   Specimen idealized decay paths for archaeological evidence of different durability plotted against a logarithmic time scale. (A) natural decay path assuming constant chemical and physical attrition (B) accelerated natural decay path (C) upland natural decay path with episodic intensification of physical attrition (D) accelerated upland decay path (A and B after Groube and Bowden 1982)

5.2 Present threats

Threats to the archaeological heritage may also endanger other features of the countryside such as wildlife, plants and landscape vistas. A precise quantification of the incidence of threats is impossible within the scope of this project. However, in order to obtain a general impression of the impact and extent of threats, all the county SMRs visited were asked to list, in rank order, the five most serious threats in their areas. Not all were able to give five. The results are summarized on Table 3. In this scoring system a lower value denotes the greatest threat.

The following 11 major threats may be considered:

Agricultural land improvement
This is the single most destructive and widespread threat to upland archaeological sites. It was reported as being serious in 23 out of the 25 "upland" counties; the score of 2.9 shows that it rated high on the list. Drainage schemes, stone clearance, reclamation of moorland, conversion of pasture to arable, the grubbing out of hedges and walls and reseeding cause the most damage. Such work is usually undertaken with central government improvement grants channelled through MAFF and WOAD. Except within National Parks (which do, however, cover nearly 60% of the uplands), grants are given retrospectively, and work is not covered by planning legislation.

The monitoring of agricultural improvements in the uplands is extremely difficult. Only a fraction of those cases which disturb archaeological features ever become known. However, the known density of archaeological sites in the uplands (Chapter 3.3) makes it certain that much is destroyed without trace. Since 1813 Bodmin Moor has shrunk by nearly 50%; within the last twenty years nearly 10 square kilometres (6.2 square miles) have been lost, mostly through agricultural improvement (Johnson 1983). As more land is improved so the total length of moorland edge that faces threat increases (Fig 32).

Some examples of damage caused by agricultural improvements in Wales illustrate the range of problems typically encountered elsewhere. At Tir Mostyn, Nantglyn (Clwyd), land improvement brought to light and disturbed two previously unrecorded small Bronze Age ring cairns (Lynch 1983). A similar cairn was found on Y Glonc near Carno (Powys) in 1980 but had to be excavated in 1983 by the Clwyd-Powys Archaeological Trust just after it had been heavily disturbed by upland pasture improvement (CPAT 1983, 9). At Moel Goedog near Harlech (Gwynedd) stone removal in 1978 damaged a well preserved stone circle. Excavations were able to trace the original stone holes and in this case the stones were re-erected. The excavations disclosed Bronze Age burials within the area of the circle (Lynch 1978). At Coelbren (Glamorgan) an agricultural drainage scheme cut through the flanking ditches of

Table 3 Spread and intensity of threats to upland archaeological heritage

Threat	Number of counties reporting threat	Rank value score*
1 Agricultural land improvements (incl drainage, reseeding, first ploughing, stone clearance, reclamation, pasture to arable conversions)	23	2.9
2 Agricultural facilities improvements (incl new roads, buildings etc)	3	4.0
3 Regular ploughing	2	4.0
4 Mineral extraction and quarrying (incl mines, quarries, waste dumps etc)	14	7.5
5 Industrial and domestic building	4	8.3
6 Forestry (incl new planting, replanting etc)	16	8.8
7 Natural erosion (incl acid rain, soil movement etc)	4	9.75
8 Visitor erosion (incl walkers, bike riders, horse riders, farm animals)	16	10.1
9 Public utilities (incl water schemes, pipelines, buildings etc)	7	17.8
10 Vandalism	2	20.5

*rank value score = Sum of assigned rank (1−5) squared, divided by reported incidence.

48

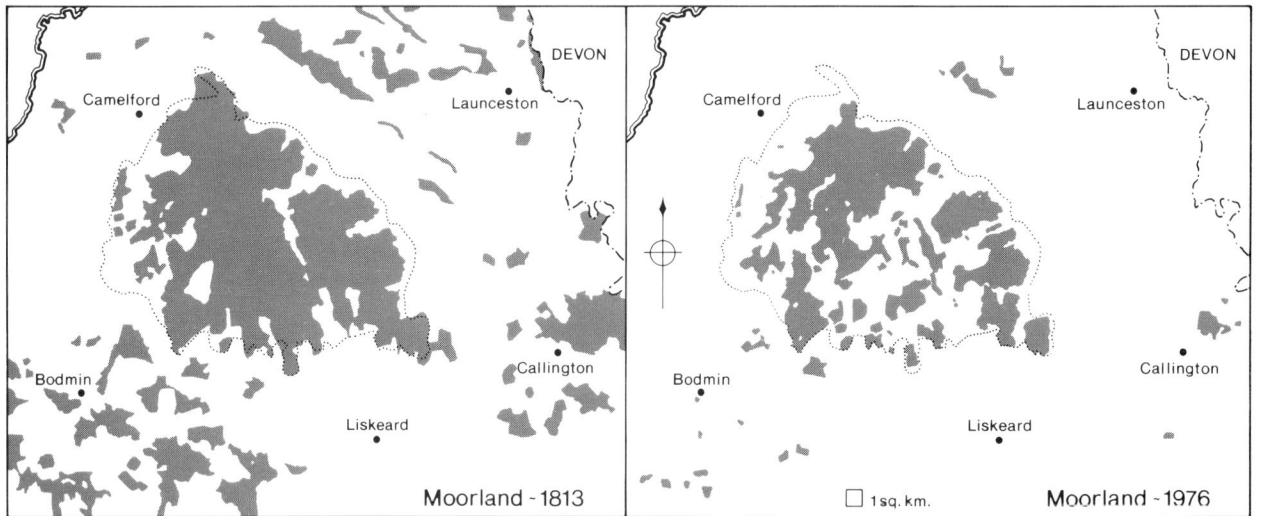

Fig 32   Bodmin Moor (Cornwall): extent of moorland loss 1813-1976 (after Johnson 1983)

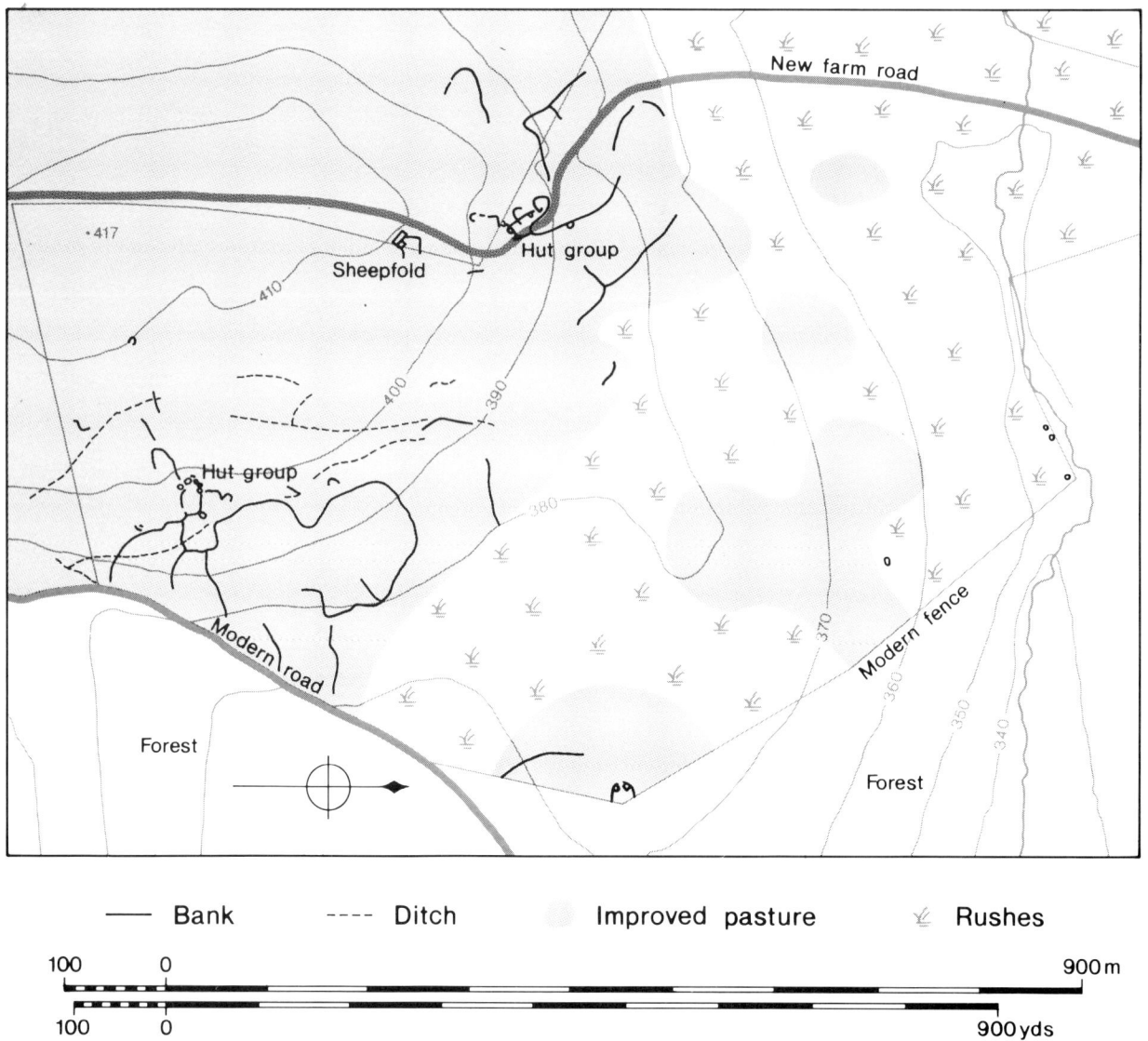

—— Bank   ---- Ditch   Improved pasture   ⚘ Rushes

100   0   900 m
100   0   900 yds

Fig 33   Plot of archaeological features recorded on Ffridd Brynhelen (Clwyd), and line of new agricultural road cutting through settlement features and field system (after Manley 1984, with additions)

Fig 34 Ploughing in progress over a scheduled Neolithic chambered tomb in the Gloucestershire Cotswolds. The tomb probably once stood over 3m (10 ft) high (photo Alan Saville)

a Roman fort and exposed the line of a road leading northwards from the fort (Sell 1983). In south-west Dyfed the practice of stone clearing became particularly prevalent in 1980 when contractors found that they could charge farmers for clearing the stone and then sell the stones for a coastal protection scheme. Several ancient monuments are known to have been affected, including a standing stone at Parc Maen where a beaker cremation burial dating to about 1800 BC was recovered from ground churned up by machines clearing stones (information from Mr D Benson, Dyfed Archaeological Trust).

Similar problems are also encountered on lower ground where land can be improved, for example in West Penwith (Cornwall) (Johnson & Rose 1983). In fairness to many landowners, however, it should be emphasised that much of the blame for the destruction of archaeological features rests with the contractors who seem blind to archaeological features which might hinder their work.

The improvement of agricultural facilities
Many improvements to agricultural land require corresponding improvements in facilities, for example the provision of new tracks and buildings. Government grants are available for this work although they were cut quite severely in December 1984. Most such work falls outside current planning legislation. Improvements to agricultural facilities occur throughout the

uplands; three counties (Shropshire, Glamorgan and Gwynedd) considered them to merit inclusion in their top five serious threats. Again, only a fraction of cases come to the attention of archaeologists. Typical of many, however, is the disaster at Ffridd Brynhelen (Clwyd) where a well preserved collection of prehistoric huts, burial cairns and field systems was bisected by a new farm road which was bulldozed through several upstanding features (cf Manley 1984 and Fig 33). A further point about farm roads is that they may enable heavy plant to be taken into areas previously inaccessible to such machines, thereby posing a new threat to remains that may be well preserved.

Regular ploughing
On many upland peripheries regular ploughing of arable land is a major destructive force, just as it is in lowland Britain (Hinchcliffe & Schadla Hall 1980). Two counties included it high on the list of serious threats, and a number of surveys underline the scale of the damage. On the Cotswolds, Saville (1980) found that of 906 recorded sites with above-ground traces, 38% were extensively affected by plough-damage and a further 8% partially affected. Within these overall figures some classes of monument, for example round barrows and long barrows, were clearly under even greater threat with 50–60% of both classes regularly ploughed (Fig 34). A similar pattern emerges from a survey of barrows on the North York Moors in

50

Cleveland (Crawford 1980). Here, about 15% of known sites have been totally ploughed out, and a further 10% have been ploughed within the last decade, or ploughed annually, as land which was previously pasture is converted to arable.

Mineral exploitation and quarrying

Over half the counties consulted cited mineral-working as a major threat. Coal, limestone, china clay, fluorspar, barytes, granite and slate are the most common workings that affect archaeology, not only in terms of the scale of the holes dug by modern machines but also by the dumping of waste and the construction of plant and ancillary buildings. At Shaugh Moor on southern Dartmoor, china clay workings threatened large areas of well preserved Bronze Age field systems and settlements (Fig 35). An extensive programme of excavation and field survey, occasioned largely by the extension of these quarries, was undertaken by the Central Excavation Unit of the Department of the Environment (now

HBMC) between 1976 and 1980 (see Balaam *et al* 1982 with earlier refs). Hillforts seem to be particularly at risk from quarrying, among them Moel Hiraddug on the northern end of the Clwydian range (Musson 1984a) and Meg Dyke camp in West Yorkshire (Fig 36).

Industrial and domestic development

Four counties (Greater Manchester, Powys, Derbyshire and Durham) reported this as a major threat, but it is mostly confined to the upland fringes and it tends to damage archaeological sites within small areas.

Forestry

Afforestation damages and destroys archaeological evidence through preplanting ploughing, forestry roads and root growth (see Jackson 1978) (Fig 37). Clear felling and replanting can also be extremely harmful. Forestry was reported by 16 out of 25 counties as a major threat, and presents a widespread problem.

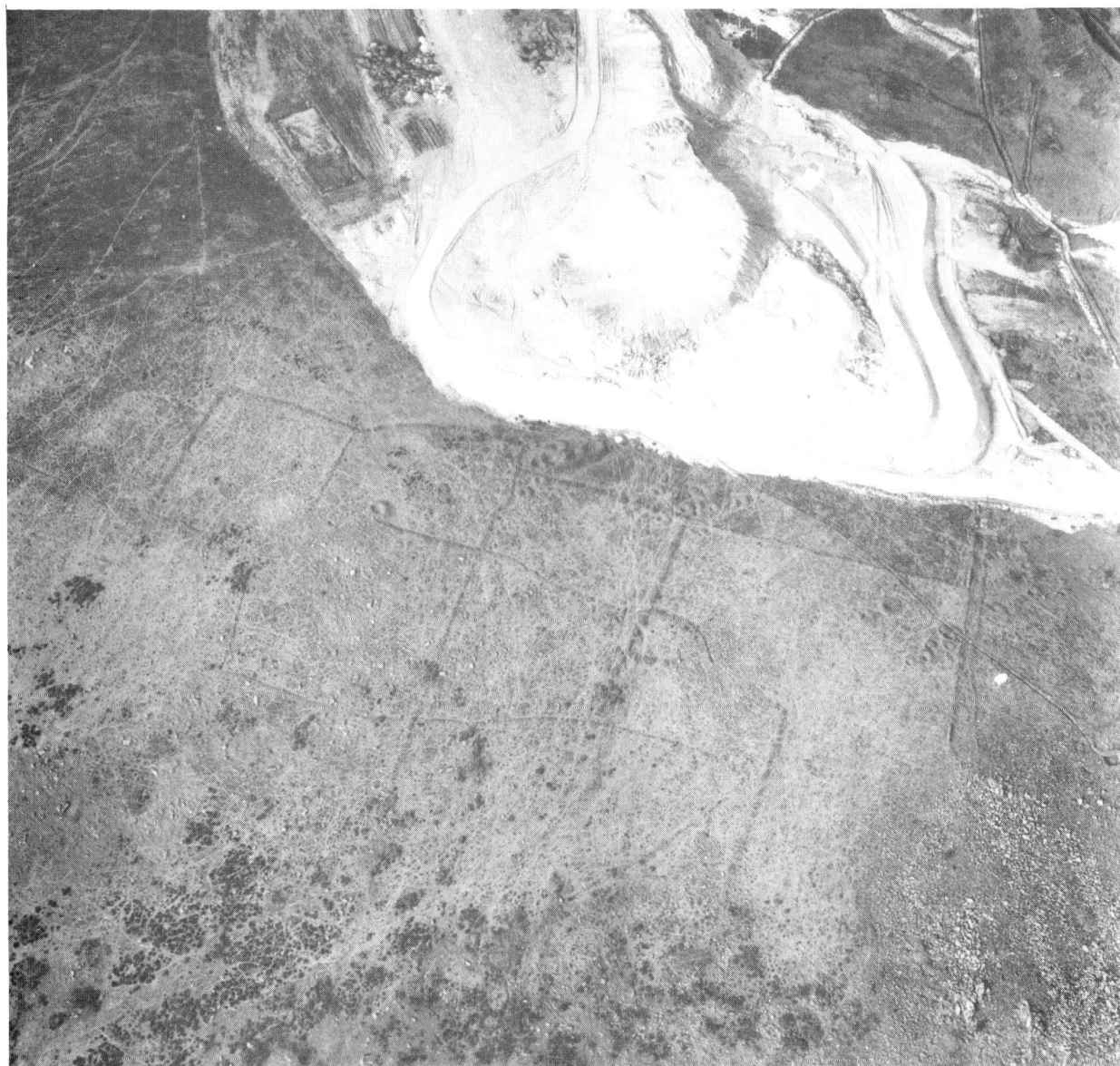

Fig 35   China clay waste at Shaugh Moor, Dartmoor. The remains of a prehistoric fieldsystem and prehistoric houses can be seen right up to the edge of the spoil heap. Some have disappeared under the heap (photo National Monuments Record, Crown copyright reserved)

Fig 36   *Quarrying within the Meg Dyke Iron Age hillfort (West Yorkshire). Little more than the enclosing ramparts now remain (photo John Hedges)*

Fig 37   *Pre-afforestation ploughing of cairnfield on Freddin Hill, Cheviots (Northumberland), in 1981. The rear wheels of the tractor are on a typical small cairn which is about to be ploughed away (photo Tim Gates)*

52

The problems posed by massive Forestry Commission conifer plantations have largely receded, although the legacy of damaged hillforts, tree-covered field systems and wrecked barrows remains. In Cleveland about 16% of known Bronze Age round barrows have been destroyed or seriously damaged by forestry operations (Crawford 1980,75). The Forestry Commission have in recent years adopted a more sympathetic approach to the preservation of archaeological remains. In north Wales a pre-afforestation survey at Cyfannedd by the Gwynedd Archaeological Trust (Kelly 1982a, 1983) led to a programme of action being successfully adopted whereby some sites were scheduled, planting boundaries were revised to avoid certain areas, and surveys, excavations and watching briefs were implemented for sites which could not be preserved (Fig 38). Similar arrangements have also been reported from Northumberland (Jobey 1981). However, while the presence of "islands" of unplanted land within forests can provide some protection for ancient monuments, they also produce undesirable consequences such as a lowering of the water table which can accelerate decay, and the growth of a thick blanket of tussocky grass and ungrazed scrub which can mask evidence. Add to this the severance of sites from their landscape context, and the loss of accessibility, and such preservation has decidedly less appeal. The recent increase in private forestry is also a matter for concern. In some areas, for example Northumberland, the activities of private forestry organisations such as EFG have actually *increased* at a faster rate than that at which those of the Forestry Commission have decreased.

Natural erosion

Localized but nonetheless serious threats come from natural erosion such as soil movement and peat decay. At Blackstone Edge in Greater Manchester, for example, water draining down the hillslope is washing away parts of the exposed ancient road surface causing pitting, deposition of silt and hillwash accumulation (Walker 1984). On the high Pennines peat decay, probably brought about by acid rain (Fry & Cooke

Fig 38   The results of pre-afforestation ploughing in Ardudwy (Gwynedd). The hut circle in the foreground was spared after an archaeological survey recorded visible sites and allowed their relative importance to be assessed (photo Richard Kelly for Gwynedd Archaeological Trust)

1984), is causing flint scatters and previously unexposed old land surfaces to come to light. At Waun Fignen Felin (Powys) peat erosion disclosed a number of Mesolithic sites, including one dated to the mid 6th millennium BC (Berridge 1979).

Over a longer period, the erosion which has caused limestone pavements in Cumbria has effectively sterilized a number of archaeological sites by leaving only the stone outlines of once impressive huts and field boundaries. Wind erosion was cited as contributing to the displacement of Mesolithic material from the surface of Stanage Barrows in the Pennines (Henderson 1979). Deep-rooted plants, including trees and bracken, cause serious disturbance to archaeological deposits.

Visitor erosion
Visitor erosion is widespread and was reported as a serious threat by 16 out of 25 counties. Tourists, farm animals, motor cross riders and horse riders are individually or collectively responsible for considerable erosion on archaeological sites near concentrations of population or in popular areas. The problems encountered along Hadrian's Wall are especially well known (Wingerson 1979; HWCC 1984).

Other examples serve to emphasize the point and illustrate the range of factors involved. In 1978, following erosion by visitors, it was discovered that the trigonometrical station erected by the Ordnance Survey on Pen-y-Fan in the Brecon Beacons surmounted a burial cist. By Easter 1983 a further cist had been revealed in the same way and, despite attempts to conceal the features, stone removal by visitors continues to threaten the site. Nearby the tramp of feet scoured a footpath and cut through a Bronze Age burial (Briggs 1984). On Dartmoor erosion by tourists and horse-riding is causing problems on the paths around the well known enclosure at Grimspound (Fig 39). Among the worst-hit sites in Clwyd is the Moel Fenlli hillfort. Visitors climbing up from the car park below have eroded several deep gullies to a depth of over 1 m (3.3 ft) through the multiple defensive banks and

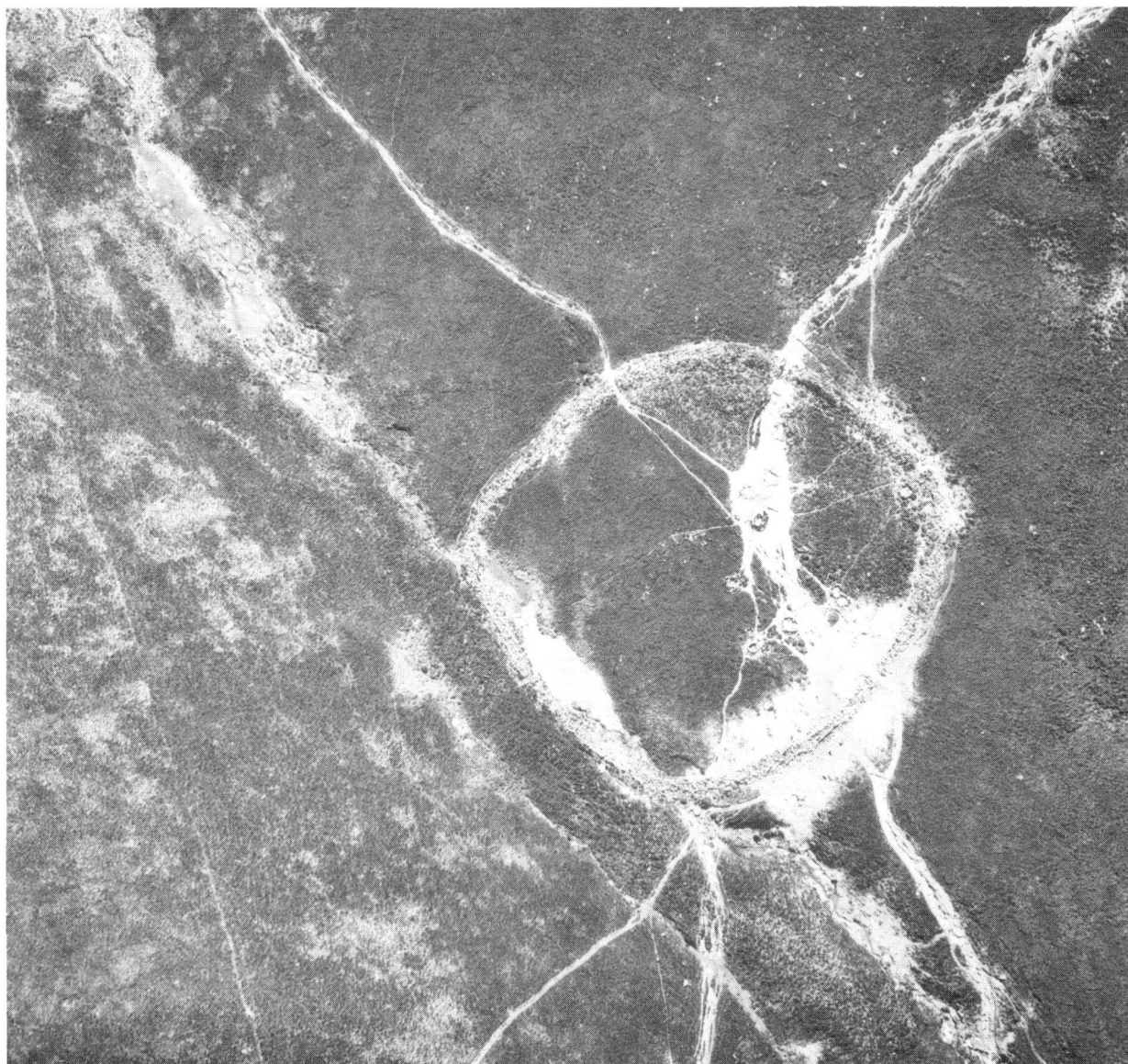

Fig 39 Grimspound, Dartmoor (Devon): visitor erosion in and around the popular Bronze Age enclosure. The enclosure is at the crossing point of several paths and bridle ways which show clearly as vegetation free areas. A number of hut circles can be seen within the enclosure (photo National Monuments Record, Crown copyright reserved)

ditches of this once well preserved Iron Age site. Long stretches of bank are now in danger of collapse. On the summit visitors have constructed a large cairn by pulling stones out of a nearby Bronze Age burial mound (Fig 40). Similar problems affect other hillforts in the Clwydian range. At another hillfort, Moel-y-Gaer on Llantysilio Mountain, erosion has been exacerbated by motorbike scrambling (Grenter 1984). Scrambling is also a major problem at Carlton Bank in North Yorkshire. Among other leisure pursuits that can be damaging to the archaeological heritage is caving, especially where deposits in the entrances to caves and fissures are disturbed in order to gain entry to deeper parts (see Barrington & Stanton 1976, 9).

Visitor erosion often stimulates natural erosion, as in the case of the Blackstone Edge ancient road where trial bike riding, walkers and natural erosion have all contributed to the present poor state of the exposed surface (Walker 1984). Standing stones and stone circles on exposed moorland present yet another problem. The upright stones naturally attract animals and people and the area immediately round the stones suffers heavy attrition to the detriment of any surviving archaeological deposits. A good example of this is at the Altarnun Nine Stones circle on Bodmin Moor (Fig 41).

Public utilities

The impact upon archaeology of road widening, waste disposal and the construction of reservoirs and pipelines should not be underestimated: seven counties reported them as serious threats (Fig 42). Some large pipeline projects, such as the north Wales oil pipeline, are of sufficient scale to attract proper archaeological attention (Barnie & Robinson 1973). But unless public utilities have a system of consultation, as some do, local

work by water authorities, gas and electricity boards usually escapes attention and is not subject to planning legislation. The construction of large reservoirs has mostly ceased. The archaeological input on such projects as the Brenig Valley (Lynch 1974, 1975) and Keilder reservoir schemes was considerable. Water erosion round the edges of large reservoirs through fluctuating water levels is a constant source of damage (see Savory 1978), and occasional enlargement of some existing reservoirs takes place.

Vandalism

As with visitor erosion, this threat is particularly noticeable at sites near urban centres. The use of metal detectors and indiscriminate "excavations" in the name of archaeology are a source of some concern in many areas. Use of metal detectors on Scheduled Ancient Monuments without the permission of the Secretary of State for the Environment is a criminal offence. Graffiti are a problem on some sites, especially post-medieval structures, and less commonly rubbish dumping and stone robbing. Neolithic stone axe factory sites in the Lake District and North Wales have suffered particularly badly from visitors collecting and removing unfinished axes and samples. The incentive to do this comes largely from unintentional publicity generated by guidebooks and television programmes which, by drawing attention to the sites, have rendered them attractive to indiscriminate collectors.

Military

Heavy use of parts of the uplands for military training is a current, although unquantifiable, threat to archaeological remains, especially on open moorland where no other threats, such as agriculture, yet present them-

Fig 40   Visitor cairn on the top of Moel Fenlli (Clwyd). The stones used to build this cairn were mostly robbed from a Bronze Age barrow nearby. Erosion of the soil cover on the hilltop is also visible (photo Stephen Grenter for Clwyd County Council)

Fig 41   Altarnun Nine Stones, Bodmin Moor (Cornwall). The ground surface around the stones has been eroded through a combination of natural and visitor erosion. Any archaeological deposits around the stones have probably been lost or badly disturbed (photo Mick Sharp)

Fig 42   (A) Hunterleigh Crags (Northumberland) in 1981. A Romano-British field-wall can be seen in the foreground leading from the camera to the towards the medieval (ridge and furrow) cultivation in the field with sheep in. A pipeline is under construction across the area (photo Tim Gates)

selves. Although not included in the five most serious threats for any county, areas such as the Brecon Beacons are used by large numbers of troops who unwittingly pound footpaths and sites while on exercises. The use of impact explosive devices minimizes surface damage, but areas used for live firing must be regarded as archaeologically sterilized because of the likely presence of unexploded ammunition and of explosive devices above and below ground.

5.3 The geography of destruction

Destruction does not take place evenly over upland landscapes. Areas subject to multiple land use (eg grazing and water catchment) tend to be at less risk, as do areas in communal ownership. Other areas are relatively safe because they are beyond the reach of modern machines, are too exposed or are covered in peat. These areas largely take care of themselves except for damage by visitors and other intermittent threats. Detailed surveys of marginal lands in Pembrokeshire and Cardiganshire by the Dyfed Archaeological Trust (nd.A; nd.B) and Bodmin Moor by the Cornwall Committee for Rescue Archaeology (Johnson 1983) allow the following types of area to be identified as zones at maximum risk:

Moorland fringes
The risks of archaeological destruction are greatest at the moorland edge, especially where it meets improved land, a zone where archaeological remains enjoy max-

Fig 42 (B) Mardale Reservoir (Cumbria) in 1984. Traces of ancient fields, roads, and enclosures can be seen below the usual water level (photo National Monuments Record, Crown copyright reserved)

imum preservation (ch 3.3). The processes of encroachment onto moorland are well illustrated by the situation on Bodmin Moor (Johnson 1983). Land improvement along the main river valleys that dissect the uplands has fragmented the area of moorland. As more land is improved, so the total length of moorland edge that faces threats increases. Farming, quarrying, mineral extraction and other works nibble away along these edges. In many upland areas this interface lies between 210 and 335 m (700 and 1100 ft), although it can be lower.

Pockets of upland

Small areas of upland surrounded by improved land are particularly at risk because modern technology makes their incorporation within existing farmland both desirable and possible. Large parts of the Mendips, the Cotswolds and the Welsh Marches have been lost in recent centuries, and south-west Wales is currently undergoing a similar change.

Company landholdings

Land held in company ownership is most at risk through high capital investment for maximum financial return. The natural forces of conservatism inherent in many privately owned farming enterprises, which allow much of the landscape to be preserved by default, do not apply.

Changes of ownership

Land which changes hand is at high risk since new landlords may have access to sources of capital (including grants) previously unavailable and often have "new" ideas on how to make improvements. If they are unfamiliar with the farm they may not even realize that the land contains archaeological monuments.

5.4 Future threats

Predicting future threats in upland areas is not easy. Water schemes, hydroelectric power projects, disposal of radioactive waste and the reworking of mining spoil to extract remaining minerals and metals left behind by earlier generations are all likely to affect the uplands over the next few decades. The increase in private forestry predicted for the next few years has been touched upon above. In addition, certain present threats will undoubtedly continue for many years to come.

6 Legislation, planning controls and resources

Threats to the archaeological heritage will only be averted within the context of effective legislation, and a professional ability to implement it. This chapter presents a summary of existing arrangements.

6.1 Legislation

Legislation that touches archaeology is scattered widely through the Statute Book. Apart from the aspects covered by the Ancient Monuments and Archaeological Areas Act 1979, there is no closely integrated antiquities legislation. The main provisions are as follows:

A. Ancient Monuments and Archaeological Areas Act 1979 (amended in England by the National Heritage Act 1983)

This is the single most powerful piece of antiquities legislation and represents the consolidation and amendment of a series of earlier Acts that originated in 1882. It applies to England and Wales alike. Appendix B summarizes the main provisions of the 1979 Act. Protection of archaeological remains is offered in two ways: through guardianship and scheduling. Table 4 summarizes the conditions relevant to each. Areas designated as of "archaeological importance" are designed to facilitate archaeological access, for the purpose of recording evidence that would otherwise be destroyed by development. The archaeological advice on these provisions is given principally by regional Inspectors operating from London or Cardiff. About 29 upland monuments are in State Guardianship, maintained by HBMC or Cadw (see below 7.3). At present no Areas of Archaeological Importance have been designated in the uplands or for that matter anywhere outside towns, or in Wales, and it is widely understood that none will be so designated in the foreseeable future.

Scheduling is the form of statutory protection offered that is most widely used (see Appendix B). Today approximately 3098 (9.7%) out of the 31881 recorded upland sites are scheduled. Overall, this percentage is higher than the national average for England of 4.2% scheduled (HBMC 1984, 36) which reflects the better preservation of monuments in upland areas. Even so, the proportion of sites protected by scheduling is low, and within the average of 9.7% there is great regional variation. This is shown graphically on Figure 43. Some areas have as few as 1.6% of monuments scheduled, whereas other areas possess over 30%. To complicate matters further, prehistoric monuments tend to be better covered than sites of later periods, although within certain areas Roman sites are well served. Table 5 summarizes the distribution. At a still more detailed level, a greater proportion of Bronze Age round barrows enjoy protection than other Bronze Age features such as field systems or settlements. Similar biases exist in the protection offered to monu-ments of other periods, and reflect national trends (HBMC 1984, 5.2 and 5.3). It is now being proposed that the list of scheduled monuments in England should be heavily revised and extended over the next few years, but until this is achieved the realities and consequences of unrepresentative protection must be appreciated. Moreover, as we have seen (above 3.3), it is not so much the number of scheduled sites that should concern us, as the area of archaeological land that is involved.

Does scheduling protect? The legislation existing before the 1979 Act did not necessarily preserve monuments effectively. Where monuments are under little or no immediate threat the efficacy of scheduling is difficult to determine. In order to assess the past protective value of scheduling one must turn to areas of high risk. On the Cotswolds, where ploughing is widespread (see 5.2), a survey of the condition of monuments by Alan Saville in 1979 showed that 55% of unscheduled sites were unploughed whereas only 53% of scheduled monuments were unploughed (Saville 1980, 37). In a study of Bronze Age burial monuments in Cleveland it was found that 14 out of 50 scheduled monuments (28%) had been badly damaged or des-troyed when they were checked in 1978 (Crawford 1980).

The 1979 Act (which did not receive Royal Assent until 1981) recognized the weaknesses of the previous legislation and introduced the requirement for sche-duled monument consent to be obtained prior to any works on a protected site. It should, however, be noted that consent is not required if the works involved are the same as those carried out during the previous five years. Hence, sites can continue to be ploughed, although the depth of ploughing may not be increased without consent.

In addition, the 1979 Act replaced the old system of acknowledgement payments to owners of scheduled monuments with a provision for positive management agreements (Sections 17 and 24) to ensure continued preservation.

The promising – but in the archaeological situation largely untested – potential of management agreements should not obscure the strong need to schedule large *areas* of historic landscape (perhaps areas of 100 hectares (250 acres) or more where necessary). This was seldom done in the past. Arguably, it is an approach which is particularly called for in the up-lands. That it can be done is illustrated by the fact that area schedulings have been undertaken recently, or are in progress, in the Plym Valley, Isles of Scilly, and West Penwith (Cornwall).

Table 4 Powers available under the Ancient Monuments and Archaeological Areas Act 1979

Situation	Must monument be scheduled?	Secretary of State power	Local authority power
1 Scheduled Monument Consent for work may be refused, granted subject to conditions, revoked, amended. A class consent may be withdrawn (eg to prevent ploughing). It will be an offence not to have consent for work to a Scheduled Ancient Monument.	yes	yes	
2 An agreement with the owner/occupier of a monument can provide for maintenance, public access, protection.		yes	yes
3 Money can be given to a person to acquire a monument, do works to it, manage it etc.		yes	yes
4 Advice can be given to a person on how to treat the monument, the work can be superintended (*and in the case of a SAM, whether the owner likes it or not).	yes*	yes	
5 Archaeological excavation may be undertaken, financed etc.		yes	yes
6 A power of entry will enable excavation of and search for monuments.		yes	
7 The public are normally to have access to monuments in care. Facilities may be provided.		yes	yes
8 A monument (and associated land) may be acquired by agreement.		yes	yes
9 A monument (and associated land) may be taken into guardianship by agreement.		yes	yes
10 A monument (and associated land) may be compulsorily purchased.		yes	
11 Preservation works may be carried out without owner's consent.	yes	yes	
12 It will be an offence to unlawfully damage or destroy a protected monument (*one that is scheduled and/or owned or in guardianship).	yes*	yes	
13 The unauthorized use of a metal detector in a protected place will be an offence (*any place which is either the site of a SAM, a monument in the ownership or guardianship of the Secretary of State or a local authority or a place within an AAI).	yes*	yes	

(Taken from Appendix A, DoE Advisory Note 28 [March 1981])

National Heritage Act 1983
The definition of "ancient monument" is extended to cover "any structure, work, site, garden or area which in HBMC's opinion is of historic, architectural, traditional, artistic or archaeological interest" (section 33(8)). This gives the Commission wider interests than the range of monuments which may be considered for scheduling (Appendix B).

Wildlife and Countryside Act 1981
This contains a number of provisions relevant to archaeology. Section 39 provides for the establishment of local authority management agreements for the purposes of conserving or enhancing the natural beauty or amenity of land in their area. Under section 43, National Parks are required to prepare and periodically revise maps showing areas of moor or heath, the natural

60

1 NORTHUMBERLAND
2 CUMBRIA
3 DURHAM
4 CLEVELAND
5 NORTH YORKSHIRE
6 LANCASHIRE
7 WEST YORKSHIRE
8 GREATER MANCHESTER
9 SOUTH YORKSHIRE
10 DERBYSHIRE
11 CHESHIRE
12 CLWYD
13 GWYNEDD
14 STAFFORDSHIRE
15 SHROPSHIRE
16 POWYS
17 HEREFORD & WORCESTER
18 DYFED
19 & 20 WEST & MID GLAMORGAN
21 GWENT
22 GLOUCESTERSHIRE
23 SOMERSET
24 DEVON
25 CORNWALL

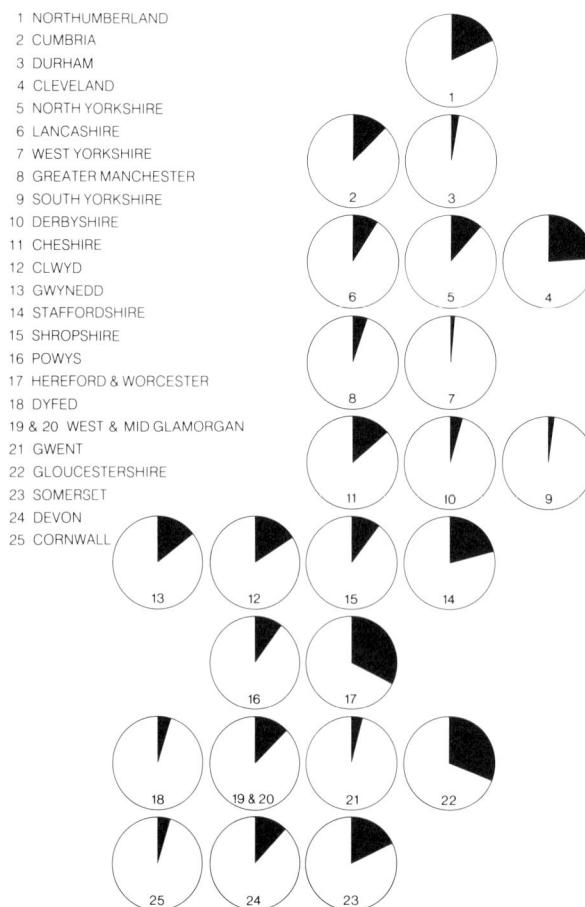

Fig 43   Pie-charts showing the percentage of recorded upland sites which are currently scheduled in each county

beauty of which is, in the opinion of the Park Authority, of particular importance and deserving of conservation. Although no formal protection is offered to areas so defined, they tend to coincide with areas particularly rich in archaeological remains. The North York Moors National Park Board includes archaeological factors among the criteria for judging the importance of such areas.

Section 48 of the Act (which replaces section 22 of the 1973 Water Act) requires Water Authorities to have regard to the desirability of protecting buildings or other objects of archaeological, architectural or historic interest on their land. In response to this, the North West Water Authority, for example, has produced a survey of the historic resource on its landholdings to provide the basis for conservation and management policies (NWWA 1979).

Town and Country Planning Act 1971
This contains several important provisions which relate both directly and indirectly to archaeology. Local authorities are given the power to grant conditional planning permission, or even to refuse planning permission on archaeological grounds. These powers have recently been clarified (DoE Circular 1/85), and may be applied to land in an area which is considered to be of archaeological interest but which has not been formally designated as such under section 33 of the 1979 Act. The Act also requires local authorities to produce Structure plans which in many cases include archaeological policies. The Local Government Act 1972 re-

quires National Parks to produce Park Plans which, like the County Structure Plans, cover strategies for future development and may include archaeological policies. These are dealt with in more detail below (6.2).

National Parks and Access to the Countryside Act 1949
Section 87 of this Act, in addition to establishing the National Parks, provides for the designation of Areas of Outstanding National Beauty (AONBs). The main purpose of these is to conserve and enhance "natural beauty" through the protection of flora, fauna, and geological as well as landscape features. This affects archaeology, firstly by limiting development in designated areas, and secondly by promoting the use of management plans (see Countryside Commission 1983).

Countryside Act 1968
The Countryside Commission was established under the 1949 Act (above). This act extended the functions of the Commission in order to promote the provision of educational and study facilities in National Parks. Archaeological interests are specifically included (section 12).

Capital Transfer Tax 1984
Conditional exemption from Capital Transfer tax may be given for land of outstanding scenic, historic or scientific interest, including created landscapes. The conditions of exemption require that reasonable steps will be taken for

Table 5 Percentage of recorded sites with scheduled status, by period and area

County	Prehist. (%)	Roman (%)	Medieval (%)	Post-medieval (%)	Unknown date (%)	All (%)
1 Northumberland	31.0	30.5	5.6	2.9	5.3	18.3
2 Cumbria	18.0	36.2	9.2	2.9	4.5	12.6
3 Durham	5.8	35.0	4.3	0.0	0.0	3.3
4 Cleveland	47.5	0.0	15.3	0.0	0.0	23.9
5 North Yorkshire (M)	17.3	0.0	10.6	0.0	1.6	11.4
North Yorkshire (D)	–	–	–	–	–	
6 Lancashire	18.7	7.6	4.5	11.4	0.9	9.1
7 West Yorkshire	2.6	0.8	0.7	2.9	0.0	1.6
8 Greater Manchester	3.9	12.5	0.0	0.0	0.0	4.7
9 South Yorkshire	3.5	0.0	0.7	0.0	100.0	1.7
10 Derbyshire	5.1	1.1	4.1	3.4	3.2	4.1
11 Cheshire	20.9	0.0	14.2	0.0	15.3	13.3
12 Clwyd	20.8	0.0	11.9	0.0	0.0	16.0
13 Gwynedd	25.7	50.0	3.5	0.0	2.1	14.6
14 Staffordshire	36.0	0.0	16.6	1.0	6.0	21.9
15 Shropshire	11.0	3.7	15.4	2.6	7.2	10.0
16 Powys	15.4	21.9	10.9	0.5	0.0	10.2
17 Hereford & Worcester	18.6	0.0	63.0	0.0	0.0	32.8
18 Dyfed	22.0	31.0	0.7	0.1	1.0	5.0
19 West Glamorgan	17.2	60.0	5.7	2.3	4.4	12.8
20 Mid Glamorgan						
21 Gwent	25.0	0.0	6.1	0.6	0.0	3.7
22 Gloucestershire	48.0	8.3	10.0	12.5	2.3	31.3
23 Somerset	39.0	3.7	1.6	0.2	0.0	18.0
24 Devon	24.0	12.9	4.2	0.7	0.7	11.2
25 Cornwall	5.7	0.0	8.4	0.1	0.0	4.4

(M) Moors
(D) Dales
– No data available

the maintenance of the land and the preservation of its character, and for securing reasonable public access. This is normally achieved through implementing a detailed management plan. Capital Transfer Tax is not normally payable on gifts of land or buildings of outstanding scenic, historic or scientific value made over to a body not established or conducted for profit, which includes HBMC, the National Trust, and any Local Authority. Exemption of Bransdale Moor (North Yorkshire) included recognition of the rich archaeological heritage (Stratham 1982).

Other Acts
A number of other acts give protection to monuments in the context of specific activities. Thus section 44(3) of the Electricity (Supply) Act 1926 provides protection against the effects of placing electricity lines above ground; section 9(1) of the Coal Mining Subsidence Act 1957 makes special provision for subsidence damage to scheduled ancient monuments; and section 6(4)b of the Land Powers (Defence) Act 1958 contains restrictions on the use for training purposes of land that contains scheduled ancient monuments.

6.2 Planning controls

A number of statutes devolve powers to local authorities for planning purposes (see above and Appendix B). Most of the power in planning matters rests with District Councils, but County Councils have the responsibility of formulating the Structure Plan within which development and Local Plans are construed, and they also provide back-up services to assist in decision-making at the local level. Although archaeological considerations are not mandatory in any part of the planning procedure, considerable safeguards exist and are effective in some cases, especially in National Parks. Where scheduled monuments are involved, applications for Scheduled Monument Consent will be addressed to the Secretary of State, not to the local planning authority. However, the informality of approach towards archaeology which is inherent in current planning regulations, especially in the definition of terms such as "natural beauty", "landscape value" and even "historic interest" can make the treatment of archaeological issues rather arbitrary, and in some cases highly subjective. The failure of the Porchester Inquiry to recognize the archaeological value of the preserved remains on Exmoor and the archaeological contribution to the form of the landscape provides an example of such subjectivity (Porchester 1977).

All the counties with upland, and all the National Parks, include archaeological policies and/or intentions in their current Structure/Park Plans. These provisions are summarized in Tables 6 and 7. It is immediately clear that National Parks include a greater range of more specific and more powerful policies than do County Councils, but that among both groups there is great variety in the topics covered. As the various plans become due for review, the archaeological contribution has tended to be broadened, following the recognition that scheduled monuments represent only a fraction of the archaeological heritage and that, in upland areas at least, the earmarking of individual features for protection falls short of the need to apprehend such remains as part of the substance of the landscape as a whole.

In recognition of the importance of archaeological remains, and the limitations of the 1979 Act (for example, the inappropriateness of the Area of Archaeological Importance, as defined by the Act, as a weapon for conservation), at least five local authorities

Table 6 Archaeological provisions in National Park Plans

Policy/Intentions	1	2	3	4	5	6	7	8	9	10
Protection of important sites (whatever status) through planning controls	★	★	★	★	★	★	★	★	★	★
Seek and promote management or guardianship agreements	★	★	★	★	★	★		★	★	★
Increase public appreciation/awareness of archaeological heritage	★	★	★	★		★		★	★	★
Define areas of archaeological interest on local criteria	★	★				★		★	★	★
Recommend sites to HBMC for scheduling	★	★		★	★	★		★		
Undertake interpretative/educational work at monuments/areas of interest			★	★		★	★	★		★
Establish archaeological liaison/coordinating committee	★	★	★							★
Purchase sites where other protection unsuccessful	★	★				★				★
Ensure sites faced with destruction are fully investigated/recorded		★			★	★			★	
Maintain SMR or hold copy of county SMR extracts		★	★			★				★
Pay special attention to industrial archaeology		★	★		★					
Assist other bodies compiling SMR			★	★	★					
Undertake 'stock-taking' surveys			★			★		★		
Provide advice on site management			★			★				★
Impose archaeological planning constraints on afforestation and agricultural improvements									★	★
Encourage study and research on archaeological heritage	★				★					★
Undertake remedial work on sites threatened by erosion				★						
Prohibit use of metal detectors and unscientific excavation	★									
Mark archaeological sites	★									

Parks:
1 North York Moors (First Review 1984)
2 Brecon Beacons (Draft First Review and 1979 Plan)
3 Pembrokeshire coast (1972 Plan)
4 Northumberland (First Review 1984)
5 Lake District (Draft First Review 1985)
6 Yorkshire Dales (First Review 1984 and 1977 Plan)
7 Dartmoor (First Review 1983)
8 Exmoor (First Review 1982)
9 Peak District (Plan 1977)
10 Snowdonia (Draft First Review 1985)

Table 7 Archaeological provisions in County Structure Plans

Counties		1	2	3	4	5	6	7	8	9	10
						Policy (see below)					
1	Northumberland	★			★						
2	Cumbria	★		★		★					
3	Durham		★								
4	Cleveland	★		★	★	★					
5	North Yorkshire	★									
6	Lancashire	★							★		
7	West Yorkshire	★									
8	Greater Manchester				no information supplied						
9	South Yorkshire	★									
10	Derbyshire	★					★				
11	Cheshire	★		★							
12	Clwyd				no information supplied						
13	Gwynedd	★									
14	Staffordshire	★		★	★			★			
15	Shropshire	★		★	★						
16	Powys	★		★	★						
17	Hereford and Worcester				no information supplied						
18	Dyfed		★				★				
19	West Glamorgan	★		★	★					★	
20	Mid Glamorgan	★			★			★			
21	Gwent	★							★		
22	Gloucestershire	★		★	★	★		★			
23	Somerset	★		★		★	★				
24	Devon	★		★	★						
25	Cornwall	★		★	★		★				★

Policy:
1 Protection for all types of site through planning controls
2 Protection of SAMs only through planning controls
3 Ensure sites faced with destruction are recorded/excavated
4 Support for interpretation of monuments and educational work
5 Maintain SMR
6 Define and protect areas of archaeological/historic/amenity value
7 Give special mention of industrial archaeology
8 Undertake environmental improvement/enhancement at heritage sites
9 Increase public appreciation of archaeological heritage
10 Recommend sites for scheduling to HBMC

in upland areas have started to define their own areas of special archaeological significance. These areas are called by various names. North York Moors National Park, for example, has 29 "Areas of Special Archaeological Significance" and the Peak Park has "Park Treasures". Delineation is determined on the basis of importance as perceived locally. It does not affect normal agricultural activities, but introduces additional controls on any proposed development in these areas, or changes to existing practices.

A comprehensive Sites and Monuments Record (SMR) is a prerequisite for the effective assimilation of archaeology to the planning process. The reluctance of some County Councils to support such records has been partly overcome by HBMC- and Cadw- funded projects (for practical purposes, fixed-term posts), although it is anticipated that in due course the responsibilities for maintaining these records will pass to local authorities. Of the 23 County Councils who returned questionnaires, 16 operate an SMR. The remainder draw upon records maintained by other organizations (see 6.3 below). Planning constraint maps are held by many District Councils. The value of SMRs for day-to-day planning purposes hinges upon the ability of those who run them to recognize a relatively small number of threats amid a large number of planning applications. Seventeen out of 23 SMRs visited for this survey (representing the major records covering all 25 counties) are regularly used to scrutinize all or most applications. Various systems have been developed for monitoring and imposing appropriate controls and conditions. One of the most thorough is run by the Glamorgan-Gwent Archaeological Trust and has recently been described in detail (Dobbins 1983). Experience with that system shows that between 0.3 and 2.4% of all planning applications involving substantial ground disturbance require an active archaeological response (information from GGAT).

It should be emphasized that in 40% of the uplands many of the most severe threats to archaeological remains lie outside existing planning controls (see 5.2). Twenty out of 23 SMRs have formal or informal relationships with service industries, and most report that, assuming they are informed of prospective work, archaeological implications can be monitored. Thirteen SMRs out of 23 have relationships with various warden services which can often provide information on remains endangered through erosion of various sorts. The Forestry Commission report that all new land acquisitions are referred to the Inspectorate of Ancient Monuments who mark up details of scheduled and unscheduled monuments on appropriate maps and advise on the need for reconnaissance work. The most disturbing exclusion from planning controls, however, is that which covers agricultural improvements. Retrospective claim procedures and the confidentiality between grant recipient and MAFF together preclude any planning input to the award of discretionary grants.

In National Parks, which represent nearly 60% of the uplands, the position is better and planning controls are tighter. Prior notification is still needed for agricultural grant work, and the Park Authorities have to assess the conservation implications of all projects. However, only three National Parks employ archaeological officers who evaluate applications. More have the

work done for them by the appropriate County Council archaeologist. The number of grant applications affecting recorded archaeological remains in National Parks is rather higher than the percentage of conventional applications (Table 8), and this can probably be taken as a reflection of the unmonitored situation in areas outside the Parks.

6.3 Resources and manpower

No single organization controls or oversees archaeological work, and there is considerable overlap between the roles of different organizations. Given such diversity it is useful, though difficult, to classify existing manpower and resources.

Commissions

Four separate Commissions are directly concerned with archaeology: the Royal Commission on the Historical Monuments of England, the Royal Commission on Ancient and Historical Monuments in Wales, the Historic Buildings and Monuments Commission (English Heritage), and Cadw, the Welsh Historic Monuments department of the Welsh Office. Countryside aspects of archaeological work fall at least partly within the remit of the Countryside Commission, although they do not at present have any archaeological officers.

The primary role of the two Royal Commissions lies in recording the archaeological heritage. RCHME has published inventories covering all, or part, of three upland areas, as well as a discussion of the bastles and shielings of the north. Five survey projects in upland areas are currently in progress: on Bodmin Moor, the Cheviots, Dartmoor, Peak District National Park, and the Clee Hills (Shropshire), the first three having been supported jointly by RCHME and HBMC. A thematic survey of Roman camps and signal stations in northern England is also in progress, and up to 7 aerial reconnaissance flights per year have been undertaken in upland areas since 1980. RCAHMW has, since its foundation in 1908, published 14 inventories covering

Table 8 Summary of planning applications with archaeological considerations in National Parks (1983/84) – effects known to authorities only

	% of conventional applications with archaeological considerations	% of grant applications with archaeological considerations
Snowdonia	<1%	not known
Peak District	c 2%	not known
Exmoor	<1%	10–15%
Dartmoor	<6%	not known
YorkshireDales	<1%	2% affect SAMs
Lake District	<1%	not known
Northumberland	<1%	not known
Pembrokeshire Coast	<1%	not known
Brecon Beacons	<1%	not known
North York Moors	<2%	c 2%

10 (old) Welsh counties, although some will be resurveyed in due course. Inventory research is currently focused on Brecknockshire. The National Archaeological Survey, the "field arm" of RCAHMW, is working on a survey of the uplands in south Brecknockshire and west Carmarthenshire. RCAHMW has not in the past undertaken aerial reconnaissance, although it does hold a large collection of pictures taken by other organizations and individuals. Both Commissions maintain their respective National Monuments Records, supply information to the Ordnance Survey for inclusion on published maps, and to members of the public.

The Historic Buildings and Monuments Commission (HBMC) has three important spheres of activity. Firstly it is responsible for the day-to-day running of monuments in State Guardianship (see below 7.3). Secondly, it acts as adviser to the Secretary of State on the scheduling of ancient monuments, their selection and management. Field Monument Wardens assist the regional Inspectors in monitoring the condition of Scheduled Ancient Monuments. Thirdly, it apportions funds – the "rescue budget" – to recognized archaeological organizations. The cash limit for this expenditure in 1984/5 was £5.3 million, a 4% increase on that for 1983/4 (HBMC 1984a,1). Funds are allocated to projects. Bids for projects are submitted for consideration by local organizations and a proportion of these projects is then selected for support on the basis of national priorities (it is understood that projects commissioned by HBMC will become a more important area of its grant support). Examples of excavation projects funded by DoE/HBMC in upland areas over the last four years include Cow Gill Reservoir (Durham), Lismore Fields (Derbyshire), Mount Pleasant (Derbyshire) and Hazleton (Gloucestershire). Aerial photography and survey projects have been widespread, but include Cheviots, Lake District, Exmoor, Bodmin Moor and Dartmoor. The "rescue budget" has also been used to fund the compilation of sites and monuments records in the counties of Northumberland, Cumbria, North Yorkshire, Derbyshire, Staffordshire, Shropshire, Gloucestershire, Somerset, Devon and Cornwall. In addition the Central Excavation Unit, operated by HBMC for emergency excavations which cannot be undertaken by other bodies, has worked in upland areas in the north of England, and undertook a major project on Shaugh Moor, Dartmoor between 1976 and 1980. The Ancient Monuments Laboratory provides specialist technical advice and services and has worked on material from a number of upland sites in recent years.

Cadw's role in Wales is very similar to that of HBMC in England, except it does not support a central excavation unit or an ancient monuments laboratory. Because Cadw came into being during the preparation of this report no details of recent work can be given.

County Councils
Twenty-three out of 25 County Councils returned questionnaires. Of these, sixteen have professional archaeological staff, some of them in England supported through project funding from HBMC. A total equivalent to 22 full-time posts is represented. In most cases these posts relate to sites and monuments records and associated work. In ten out of sixteen counties the

posts are within County Planning Departments, the remainder are in various other departments. The County Council-funded work undertaken by museums and museum services is described below (6.3G).

Twelve out of 23 County Councils operate some sort of warden/ranger service, including AONB wardens, FWAG advisors, and County Rangers. Of these, eight include archaeology within their remit (see Countryside Commission 1979, 3). Other County Councils support National Park warden services.

National Parks
Out of ten National Parks only three – Dartmoor, Peak District and Snowdonia – have archaeological officers. Only the Dartmoor post deals with site management and conservation on a full-time basis. The Peak Park archaeologist is shared with Derbyshire County Council, and Snowdonia Park has an archaeologist as a lecturer at the park study centre. North Yorkshire's County Archaeologist also serves the Dales and North York Moors National Park, and similar arrangements exist in other areas too. National Parks grant-aid archaeological work by other bodies, for example the Cumbria and Lancashire Unit in the Lake District. Seven out of ten Parks maintain a sites and monuments record, often consisting of copies of relevant portions from county-based SMRs. Six out of ten Park Ranger services include archaeology within their remits.

County-based trusts and units
Thirteen out of 25 counties containing uplands are served by eight archaeological trusts or units. Somerset and Gloucestershire were served by a ninth trust until March 1985, but lack of project support forced it into voluntary liquidation. All the Welsh Counties are served by Trusts. The role of these organizations is varied (see Musson 1983, 1984), but includes surveys and excavations, maintaining sites and monuments records, responding to threats to known archaeological sites, and providing services of information, education and advice. Increasingly, these organizations are becoming recognized as the focus for archaeological activity at county level. But funding is always difficult and largely unpredictable. Support from the Manpower Services Commission for a wide range of projects over recent years has enabled many units and trusts to achieve an impressive amount of work (see Musson 1981 for breakdown of support in Wales).

Sites and monuments records
All 25 counties with upland areas are served by at least one principal sites and monuments record (within 23 separate organizations), although in the case of Durham no one of the three existing records can claim to be comprehensive. Ten counties are covered by records in County Planning Departments, six by records in other County Council departments and nine by records run by units or trusts. Seven records are complete for upland areas as far as sources allow, the remainder range from only just begun to 90% complete. Approximately 31881 sites have been catalogued from upland areas, and this has taken a total of about 63 man-years. In 1984 approximately eleven man-years were spent working on the compilation, management and deployment of the sites and monuments records for upland areas.

66

Since 1980, 19 out of 23 organizations responsible for maintaining SMRs have undertaken approximately 105 projects in connection with SMR work. These include field surveys, excavations, record enhancement surveys, watching briefs, visitor surveys and erosion surveys. Fig 44b shows a changing emphasis in this work, with marked increases in field and aerial surveys in recent years.

University departments
Twenty three out of 26 universities which teach

archaeology replied to the questionnaire. Of these, sixteen have undertaken fieldwork of a rescue/research nature in the uplands in the past five years, and the overall number of projects undertaken has risen sharply since 1980 (Fig 44a). Field survey projects in particular are on the increase. In addition, 44 students spread among the 23 departments who replied are currently preparing theses or dissertations, at various levels, on upland-related topics. Seven research assistants/research fellows are working on upland-related topics.

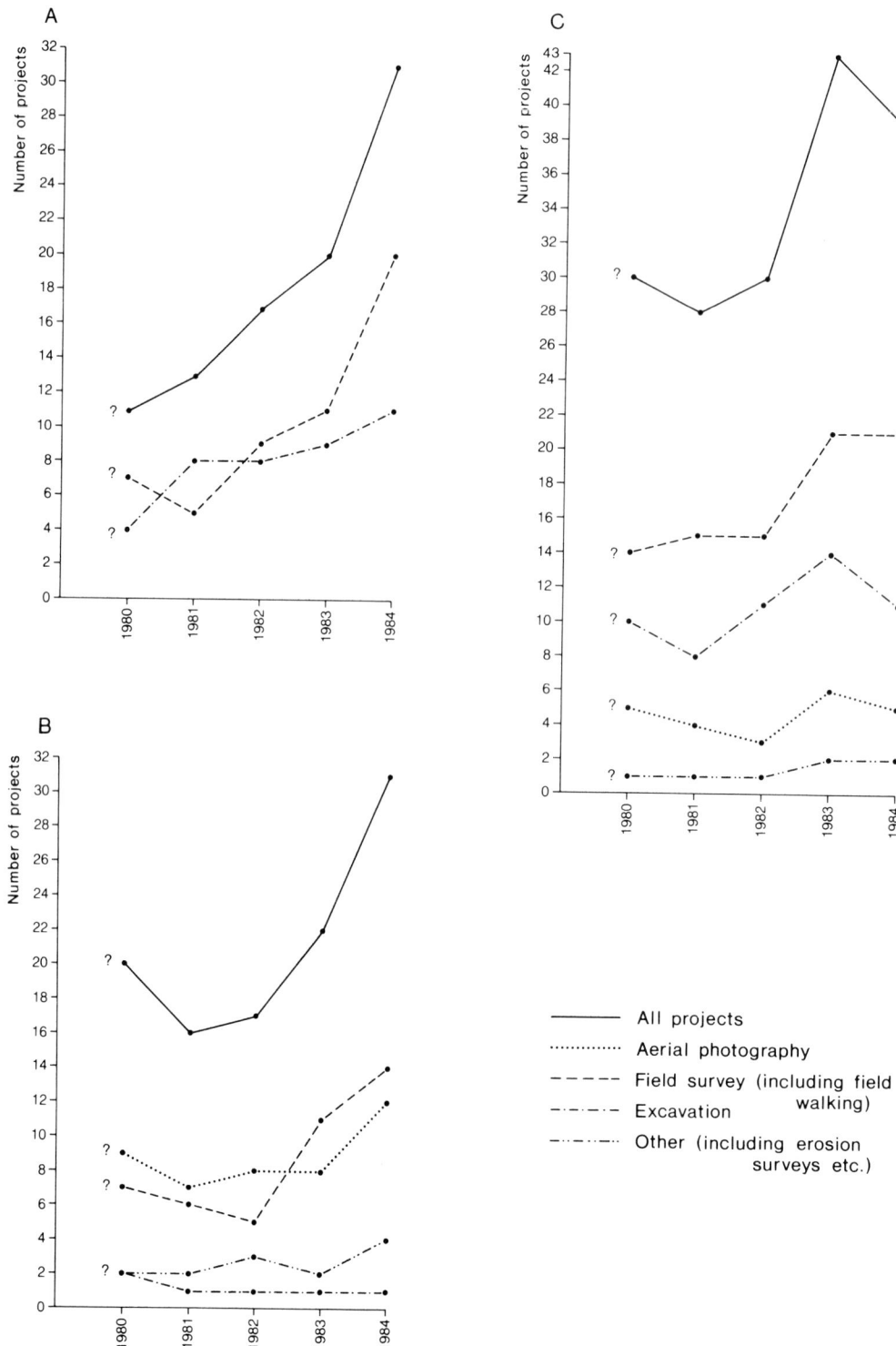

Fig 44 Frequency curves showing the number and type of archaeological projects undertaken 1980–4 in upland areas: (A) projects by university departments; (B) projects by SMRs; (C) all projects recorded by SMRs excluding their own.

Museums

Fifty-one out of 63 museums with archaeological
collections within or adjacent to upland areas replied to
the questionnaire. Of these, twenty have professional
archaeological staff who carry out fieldwork. Six out of
the twenty report that the amount of fieldwork undertaken in upland areas over the last five years has
increased, three reported that it decreased, for the rest
it remained stable. Fifteen out of 51 museums sponsor
archaeological work either directly or indirectly,
although the extent of this varies enormously. Four
museums undertake their own excavations or survey
projects, some give specialist support such as conservation to other projects, and many give practical help and
guidance to local societies. Several museums are
funded by bodies which also contribute to other
archaeological work.

Twenty out of the 51 museums which supplied
information operate some sort of SMR. In one case
(Cleveland) this is the principal county record, and in
others one of the main records. District Councils and
County Councils are reported as the main users of
museum SMRs, but in four cases the records appear to
be solely for the use of the museum. Thirty-two out of
the 51 museums reported that they regularly exchanged information with the county-based SMR.

Museums also provide the major repositories for
finds and records from upland sites. Forty-eight out of
51 have current collecting policies which include
upland sources. The other three have upland collections, but local government boundary changes prevent
them from acquiring further upland material.

Local societies

Local archaeological societies are active in all the
counties containing uplands. In some cases more than
one society exists in an area. Many have long and
distinguished histories as supporters of archaeology.
Most publish journals or proceedings containing reports on archaeological projects. Some of the more
active ones undertake surveys and/or excavations.
Parish by parish surveys are underway in some counties, including Devon, Cornwall and Dyfed. Membership of many societies is currently at an all-time
high, and is still rising. For example, the Cambrian
Archaeological Association has a membership of about
900, and the Devon Archaeological Society about 500.

Other bodies

A number of other bodies can call upon some
archaeological expertise. The National Trust employs
one full-time archaeological officer and a number of
others on a contract basis (some with funds from the
Manpower Services Commission). At present the Trust
is establishing a record of archaeological remains on its
extensive landholdings, including many upland areas,
as an aid to evolving management strategies. Three out
of five Water Authorities covering upland areas maintain records of known archaeological remains on their
property, although none of those who replied to the
questionnaire at present employ archaeological staff.
Other major landowners have arrangements for the
provision of archaeological advice. The Duchy of
Cornwall, for example, has an Archaeological Advisory
Group under the chairmanship of Professor Glyn
Daniel, and the Ministry of Defence has set up a series
of voluntary conservation groups, many of which
include an archaeologist, to advise on management
issues. Independent archaeological organizations are
also active in the uplands, for example, the Search
Archaeological Group, which works in the Lake District (Dickinson 1984).

7 Archaeology and the public

This chapter examines ways in which members of the public come into contact with the archaeological heritage in the uplands.

7.1 The public and the past

In order to communicate information about the past to the general public it is necessary to address a wide range of interests and backgrounds, each of which may require a slightly different approach. Landowners and farmers with sites on their land, local inhabitants, tourists and casual visitors should all be catered for; at present these groups do not always receive the attention they deserve.

In recent years tourists and visitors have been singled out for special attention. This is not surprising, given that tourism is still a growth industry in many upland areas (Countryside Commission 1984, 21). Available statistics suggest that between 7% and 10% of tourists consider heritage interests to be high on the list of attractions which draw them to holiday areas (eg NTB 1983, 13; EMTB 1983, 13). Facilities for tourists are also widely used by local people for day-trips and to fill leisure time.

Very little rigorous survey work has been undertaken to ascertain consumer attitudes to the heritage "products" that are currently being offered. It is known that stately homes attract the largest single section of heritage visitors, but it is not clear to what extent the general public may differentiate between the antiquity of heritage attractions, and to what extent advertisement-induced fashion dictates its interests. The surveys which have been carried out focus almost exclusively on users of the services as they are (eg museum visitor surveys), without taking control samples of a wider cross-section of the community who represent potential users. An extension of the work of the Cambridge Research Co-operative (Hodder 1984; CRC 1983) to include tourists might shed some light on public attitudes to existing arrangements.

The promotion of archaeological attractions in the uplands tends to be on a small scale and *ad hoc*. Some District and County Councils have their own outlets, while English Heritage (HBMC), the National Trust and other major landowners such as the Forestry Commission and the Nature Conservancy Council produce a wide range of leaflets advertising their properties. The largest suppliers of information on heritage topics are the regional Tourist Boards which produce high quality leaflets and information packs, regularly updated. These cover a wide range of attractions over an equally wide area, but they can only promote attractions operated by member organizations.

In the following sections attention is focused not simply on tourism, but on a wide range of links between archaeology and the public.

7.2 Museums

Traditionally, museums have provided the main point of contact between archaeologists and the public. In many areas they still do, but the emergence of archaeological trusts and other organizations has begun to encroach upon the monopoly, leaving many museums with the specialized roles of display, curation and education. There are about 63 museums with archaeological collections within or close to upland areas, and of these 51 (81%) returned questionnaires. This sample includes museums of all sizes from small establishments of a single room that may be open for only a few months of the year up to the large city museums with many galleries and substantial professional support services.

Upland archaeological material is currently on display in 43 out of the 51 museums for which information is available. New displays which will include upland archaeology are planned in a further four. Currently, over 300 display units are involved, although many displays ignore the purely altitudinal division of the evidence in favour of a more traditional chronological or thematic approach. Fifteen out of the 43 museums with upland material on display said they had increased the display area in recent years; one had decreased it; in the remainder it had been stable.

Details of visitor figures were given by 44 museums. In 1983 these collectively recorded 3.08 million person-visits (some individuals undoubtedly visited more than one museum). As Fig 45a & b here shows, the average attendance figures show a slight decrease from 1981 visitor levels which represent the peak of museum attendance in recent decades. However, it should also be noted that a number of medium-sized museums with outgoing, innovative policies towards display have continued to increase attendances while figures are falling elsewhere.

Among the facilities which museums provide, 46 out of 51 (90%) offer identification or information services. Usage ranges from 5 up to 1500 requests per year, mostly relating to artefacts found locally or in the possession of local people. Some museums charge for this service. School rooms and/or lecture rooms are provided by 39 out of 51 museums (76%), and the same proportion have school/college loan facilities including artefact packs or illustrative material to the uplands. Many museums give active support to the work of local archaeological societies.

7.3 Countryside attractions

Sites on private land, including scheduled monuments, are not accessible without the landowner's permission. Even public landowners sometimes restrict access to such sites for logistical reasons. However, many archaeological sites in the uplands lie on common land and can be freely visited by anyone (freedom of access

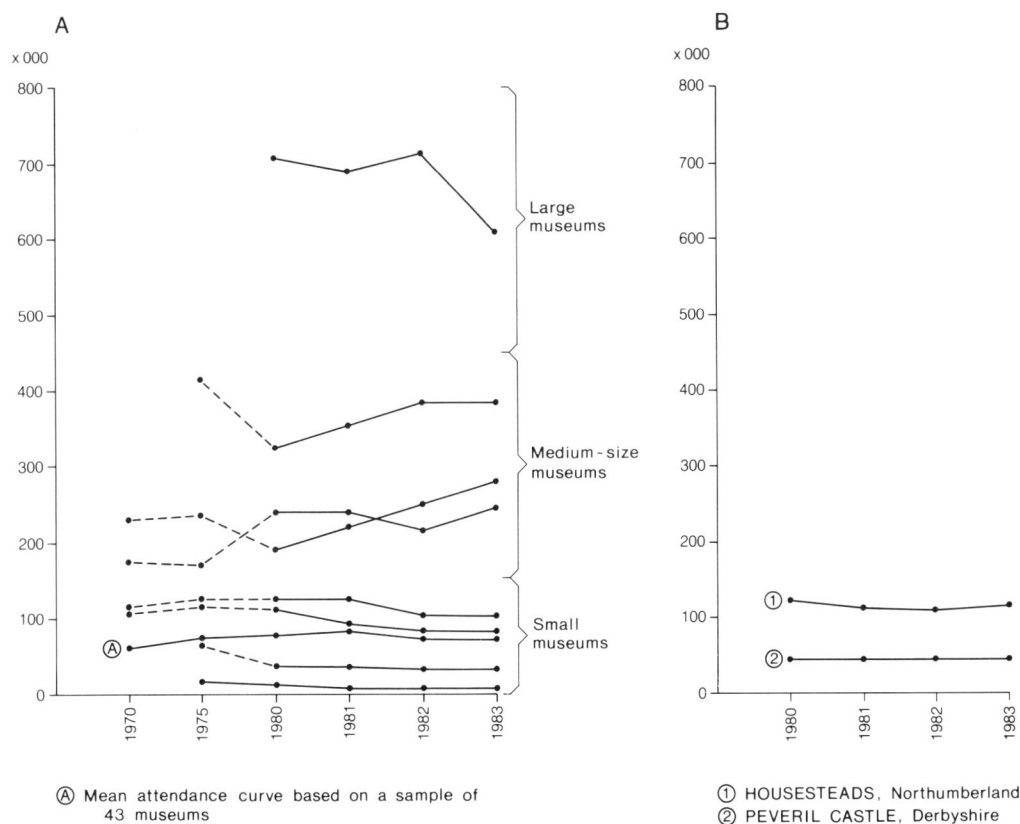

A
x 000

Large museums

Medium-size museums

Small museums

Ⓐ Mean attendance curve based on a sample of 43 museums

B
x 000

① HOUSESTEADS, Northumberland
② PEVERIL CASTLE, Derbyshire

Fig 45 Visitor numbers for: (A) upland area museums 1970–83; (B) HBMC upland Guardianship monuments 1980–3.

to common land is, however, *de facto* rather than *de jure*; the Dartmoor Commons Bill is seeking to establish legal right). In recent years numerous useful guidebooks have been published which lead the visitor round the sites while explaining something of their background and function.

Some visitors find the guidebook-and-map approach too casual and prefer greater structuring of visits. The following set out to provide such facilities.

Guardianship sites

All sites (about 29 in the uplands) in this class are ultimately the responsibility of the State, being managed by HBMC and Cadw on behalf of the Secretary of State for the Environment in England and the Secretary of State for Wales respectively. They tend to be the most upstanding and spectacular sites, although their impact has usually been enhanced by careful restoration (Fig 46). Concentrations of uplands guardianship sites occur along Hadrian's Wall, in Northumberland and Cumbria, in Derbyshire, on Dartmoor and in north Wales (Fig 47).

Upland Guardianship sites represent about 5% of all sites in state care, although there are more within the immediate vicinity of upland areas. In general, such sites are laid out for visitors and guidebooks and leaflets are available. In upland areas, however, only a fraction of the *c* 29 sites have any visitor facilities at all. Many lack even an up-to-date information board. Guidebooks are difficult to obtain. The overall situation is well summarized in a recent report on the state of historic monuments in Wales by John Brown (1984, 4) in which he says "the Welsh Office's Ancient Monuments are suffering from the effects of a long period of inadequate investment of money and skilled manpow-

er, in facilities for the public, in interpretative presentation and in marketing. They are in a serious decline which shows evidence of continuing".

For most monuments there are no reliable visitor figures, not even estimates of the magnitude of use based upon random samples. But for two sites where figures are available a slight decline in the number of visitors over recent years is evident (Fig 45b above). Both Cadw and HBMC are committed to improving the presentation of monuments in general, although no firm plans have yet been made public.

Four out of the ten National Parks own archaeological sites; all are promoted as visitor attractions. The National Trust and some County Councils also maintain upland monuments in their care.

Guided walks

These are becoming increasingly popular, especially in National Parks and areas where countryside interpretation has become a significant aspect of the work of statutory and voluntary agencies. The Countryside Commission (1978a, 1980) has published detailed studies and guidelines on the scope, organization, and popularity of guided walks. Three National Parks said they run archaeologically-based walks, as do several County Councils through ranger volunteers and warden services. A survey of guided walks on Dartmoor over the period 1973–77 revealed that archaeologically-based walks were very popular. Approximately 12% of the walks during the study period were archaeologically-based, and these attracted about 12% of the total attendance, with parties averaging 8 persons. Industrial archaeology proved especially popular (Countryside Commission 1980, 53). In upland Durham, archaeological walks attracted the high-

Fig 46   Housesteads Roman fort and Hadrian's Wall (Northumberland). The fort and wall are Guardianship monuments and attract large numbers of visitors. Outside the fort are traces of a Roman civilian settlement; and underlying the fort and on both sides of the wall can be seen traces of prehistoric fields (photo National Monuments Record, Crown copyright reserved)

est average number of participants (nineteen) of all types of walks organized over the period April 1983 to December 1984 (information from Durham County Planning Department).

Self-guided trails

As with guided walks, this is an area of public involvement which is currently increasing and is favoured by many as a compromise between the guidebook-and-map approach and the more formal visitor arrangements. The Countryside Commission has again provided a useful summary of the range and organization of such trails (1980a; Binks 1978), although it is only proposed to consider the longer (landscape appreciation) walks here. English Heritage (HBMC) and Cadw make great use of short self-guided trails on their larger Guardianship monuments, but have not, as yet at least, established any trails which link monuments in care or relate monuments with the landscape in upland areas.

The aim of all self-guided trails is to explain the

meaning and relationship of features rather than simply present facts about an individual site. Appendix C lists the upland trails with a high archaeological content which have been recorded by this survey. With only a few exceptions, National Parks, AONBs and Country Parks provide the setting for these trails. Three out of ten National Parks have established trails with specific archaeological content, and several other Park authorities are planning them in the near future. The Roystone Grange Trail set up jointly by the Peak National Park and the Department of Archaeology at Sheffield University covers a wide range of archaeological interests and is able to draw on the results of excavation and survey work (Hodges 1984). Out of the 23 County Councils who responded to the questionnaire, six operate between them a total of fourteen upland trails and two drives with archaeological content, sometimes in cooperation with other organizations. West Glamorgan, Lancashire and Gloucestershire in particular have been quick to set up trails with good guidebooks. The longest-running, and possibly

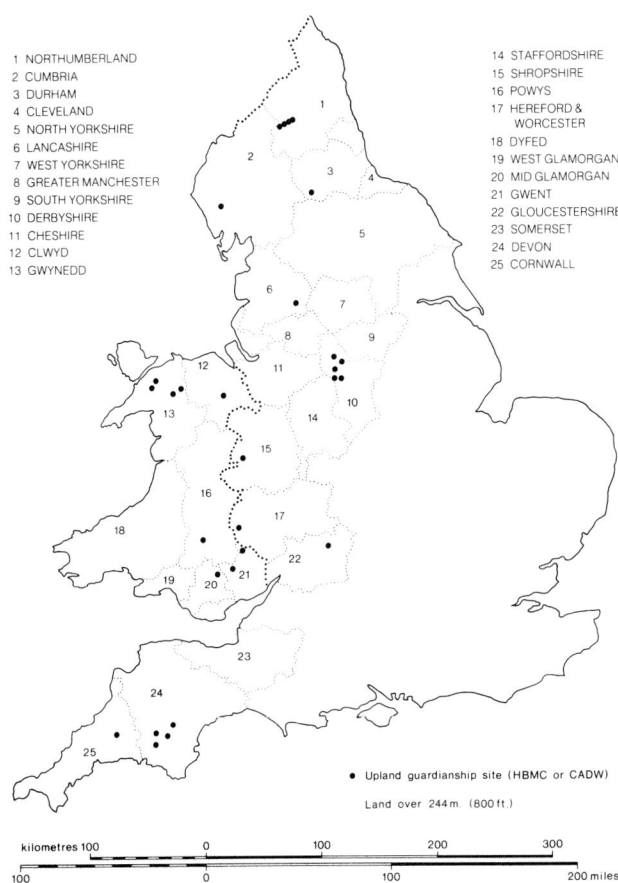

Fig 47   Distribution of upland Guardianship monuments

the most impressive archaeological trail was set up by Welsh Water around the shore of Llyn Brenig, a reservoir in Clwyd. Here several excavated sites, including Bronze Age barrows of various sorts (see Fig 48) and a medieval hafod have been restored and conserved for visitors to see (Lynch 1974; 1975). It is very difficult to assess the use of these trails, but estimates for Roystone Grange suggest that between 4000 and 5000 people walked the route in its first six months (June to December 1984). Once established, an annual visitor rate of 1000–2000 is expected (information from Dr R Hodges).

Long-distance footpaths
All the existing long distance footpaths in upland areas – Offa's Dyke Path, Pennine Way and Cotswold Way – pass by or through archaeological sites, many of which are described for walkers in the numerous guidebooks available. The first mentioned route owes its existence to an archaeological monument. In the Countryside Commission's survey (1973) of the Pennine way in 1973, 1% of all walkers questioned cited archaeological/ historical interests as the main reason for undertaking the walk, and a further 8% said these things were contributory. A recent footpath venture between the Forestry Commission and West Glamorgan County Council, the Coed Morgannwy Way, has been publicized as featuring a number of archaeological sites along its route.

Interpretation centres and signboards
Many major owners of amenity land in the uplands, including the Forestry Commission and Water Author-

ities, have information centres with displays that outline the history of the local landscape. Signboarding is also becoming used at sites, such as country parks and picnic areas with high numbers of visitors (Fig 49). In such places signs are relatively unobtrusive and can provide pertinent information which inspires in the visitor a more responsible attitude to the sites, promotes a sense of discovery, and is altogether more positive than notices merely forbidding damage to monuments.

Problems
As indicated above (ch 5.2), there is a negative aspect to popular interest. In some areas (eg Dartmoor) it has been found that where site-specific/trail orientated guidebooks become popular, erosion of sites by visitor pressure may follow.

7.4 Information and warden services

All the sites and monuments records visited are able to provide information about particular sites or areas on written request, subject to the relevant part of the record being complete, and several anticipate being able to provide a walk-in information service in the near future. The National Monuments Records, held by RCHME and RCAHMW are also available for public use, although until computerization is complete, access to information can be laborious.

Rangers and wardens of various sorts provide a valuable link with both the public and landowners. Six

72

Fig 48   Reconstructed Bronze Age ring-cairn at Llyn Brenig (Clwyd). The reservoir and a second reconstructed Bronze Age monument can be seen in the background. This reconstruction is one of the sites on the archaeological trail at Brenig. Excavations revealed that burial pits were dug within the ring defined by the stone wall. The monument was first built about 1650 BC (photo Mick Sharp)

Fig 49   Signboards and visitor facilities at the Iron Age hillfort on Crickley Hill (Gloucestershire). The hilltop attracts many visitors during the year and a wooden platform has been built as a viewing point to protect the rampart from erosion (photo Tim Darvill)

out of the ten National Parks have warden services which include archaeological roles within their brief. Much of course depends on the skills of individual rangers, but the lack of professional archaeological staff in some Parks is critical here since in such cases there is no easily available source of advice for the rangers. Twelve out of the 23 responding County Councils also operate ranger services of various sorts, mostly as part of their responsibilities for public relations. Of these, eight include archaeological matters within the brief of the ranger/warden service.

The Field Monument Wardens of HBMC are concerned only with scheduled ancient monuments. They have a systematic work programme which ensures that each monument is visited every few years (see Paterson 1984). The Field Monument Wardens recently appointed by Cadw to cover Wales have broadly the same role.

Leaflets and publicity material are now widely used for the rapid and cheap dissemination of information. Guidebooks apart, however, they have not often been used by archaeologists. No leaflet specifically covers the problems relating to upland archaeology and land-use. Considerable use has been made of *Protecting Ancient Monuments and historical features* published by the Countryside Commission (1980b) jointly with the Forestry Commission, MAFF and the NCC in 1980 and also *Farming on Ancient Monuments* published by MAFF/ADAS in 1979. But both leaflets require updating to take account of new legislation. Seven out of ten National Park Authorities produce some sort of guidebook outlining the archaeology of their area, and some have topic publications. The newspapers produced by most Park Authorities carry archaeological articles from time to time. Eleven out of 23 County Councils produce some archaeological leaflets, mostly guidebooks to specific sites or areas. Six counties produce more substantial publications of archaeological relevance, including management plans (Stratham 1982), archaeological surveys (Crawford 1980; Haynes 1983a; Faull & Moorhouse 1980; Staffordshire County Planning and Development Department 1984)), annual archaeological reviews (Manley ed) and county archaeologies (Aston & Burrow 1982). With the aid of a Manpower Services Scheme, the Clwyd Powys Archaeological Trust produced a series of leaflets on recent work within their area (CPAT 1983, 2). Twenty-seven out of 51 museums sell or distribute leaflets containing information about upland archaeology. HBMC issues a leaflet on the use of metal detectors on Ancient Monuments.

7.5 Teaching and training

Archaeological teaching and training for the general public (as opposed to university level vocational courses) is widespread and varied in upland areas. The facilities offered by museums have been mentioned above. In addition to these most museums, archaeological trusts and other archaeological bodies regularly send staff to give talks in schools and colleges. Some museums and trusts have established projects funded by the Manpower Services Commission which are specifically orientated to the needs of education. North Yorkshire County Council publishes a very comprehensive Education Resources Handbook (NYCC nd): an outline of the service provided by the archaeological division of the planning Department is among the topics covered.

For adults, extra-mural departments run by universities and Workers Education Association branches around the uplands, and the National Park Study Centres, provide a variety of formal and informal short courses in archaeology. Snowdonia National Park Study Centre and Peak District National Park Study Centre, in particular, run a range of weekend and residential courses, including practical work such as excavation and surveying. Local archaeological societies flourish throughout upland areas and collectively have a large and influential membership.

7.6 Outreach projects

It is widely recognized that the single most important aspect of public relations for archaeology is to visit landowners and farmers, in order to help them to recognize and understand the history of the landscape in their own area. Failure in this field is very clear from the results of Countryside Commission's survey of demonstration farms (Cobham 1984), and also from comments made at all three seminars organized in advance of this report. It is equally clear, however, that farmers and landowners take a good deal of interest in archaeological remains when someone takes the time to explain them (Cobham 1984, 46; Beeson and Masterman 1979, viii).

An illustration of what can be achieved is provided by the Clwyd Powys Archaeological Trust. As part of the work on its sites and monuments record between 1977 and 1981, the Trust established a programme of site visits throughout Powys and parts of Clwyd (Musson 1984, 69). This was funded by the Manpower Services Commission. There were three objectives: to record the present condition of known sites, to record new sites known only to local people through their familiarity with their own land, and to enlist the interest and concern of local people in the protection of sites in their area. A similar project is now being undertaken by the Dyfed Archaeological Trust; with the aid of its sites and monuments record the Trust produces a simple printed summary of the type and importance of known sites on the land of those visited. In both cases, these projects have proved to be valuable in achieving all the aims.

Such work is time-consuming and the resources to undertake it on a large scale do not yet exist (HBMC/Cadw Field Monuments Wardens deal only with scheduled sites). At present it cannot therefore be considered as a major part of the work undertaken by archaeologists in established posts, much as they would like to do so. However, in view of the clear benefits that flow from the positive provision of information, it is arguable that this is an area where additional investment would be well worthwhile.

III Upland archaeology in the future

"By all means let us scientifically study the landscape, let us have a well used landscape, managed efficiently and interpreted knowledgeably, but always mindful of the question to what end?"

(P Fowler 1978, 9)

8 An inheritance for tomorrow

This chapter examines some of the reasons for conserving archaeological features in the uplands for our own and future generations.

8.1 The value of the evidence

The archaeological importance of the uplands lies in the quantity and quality of the remains they preserve. The uplands may be justly described as the last great reserves of relatively undisturbed prehistoric and medieval landscape in Britain. Although the environment has changed since earlier times, where else in Britain do prehistoric fields still have standing gateposts, and ruined 14th century farmsteads still have walls up to 1.8 m (5 ft) high and complete field systems about them? With so many different types of site preserved, often within a limited area, these remains are important as records of *total* ancient landscapes – not just the special places but the complete neighbourhoods of the forgotten people of history.

The value of the archaeological remains lies not simply in aesthetics, but also in what society expects to derive from them. Wager (1981, 4) and Haynes (1983) have considered the purpose of historical landscape conservation in the context of National Parks, and the themes they raise can be developed and extended for the uplands as a whole.

8.2 The environment

The value of archaeology for today's upland environment is two-fold: firstly as a contribution to the environment as we know it, and secondly as an aid to understanding the environment in its long term context.

Archaeological features are an integral part of today's landscape. The barrows, standing stones, Roman camps and deserted villages are just as much part of the upland landscape as the open moors, granite tors, high cliffs and incised valleys. The respective contributions of nature and man are, however, different. Nature sculpts, man clothes and adapts the landscape. The landscape would not look the same without the skyline barrows, hillforts and industrial ruins (Fig 50). To remove archaeological features is to alter landscape appearances and visual amenity.

The realization that what many regard as natural and immutable is in fact partly man-made and constantly changing adds a new dynamic dimension to the landscape in popular perception. To expect to halt such change is futile, for change will always happen. The practical value of the archaeological evidence is as a record of those changes that have already occurred. This allows us to plot a trajectory of change for the past and possibly to project its consequences into the future.

8.3 An academic resource

The only source of information about the condition and development of society in Britain for most of its past is contained within the archaeological evidence. The upland evidence is notably valuable as such a resource: it is generally well preserved; so far only a limited amount of research has been carried out and, by lowland standards, the pressures of exploitation have not yet become overwhelming (Fig 51).

The academic value of the archaeological remains in the uplands may be appreciated at two distinct levels. At the regional level, the operation and organization of societies living, working and dying within a given range of environments, of which the uplands will be one, provide the basis for understanding the processes and mechanisms of change, the dynamics of adaptation and the impact of both indigenous and external social, economic, ideological and technological developments. At a rather more local level the uplands provide a relatively complete picture of the organization of the landscape at intervals through time: the distribution of population, the scale of investment in land management, and the relative value of resources. For those periods when environmental factors narrowed the differences between the uplands and the lowlands, the fine state of preservation of the upland evidence has obvious implications for our understanding of material which is less well preserved in the lowlands (Fleming 1983), and as an aid to the development of more comprehensive survey techniques and evaluation procedures.

Archaeological remains also have a contribution to make to other academic disciplines, for example geography, biology, palynology and anthropology.

8.4 Education

The sharp delineation and good preservation of archaeological remains in the uplands give them special

Fig 50   Lead mining hush at Nenthead (Durham) (photo Stafford Linsley)

Fig 51   Bronze Age house on Holne Moor, Dartmoor, during excavation. The doorway, marked by two upright stones, is on the far side, and there is partial paving inside it. The walls were lined with wood as is shown by the vertical packing stones to the left of the door. Note the ditch outside the wall, and the well coursed wall construction in the foreground (photo Andrew Fleming)

value as an educational resource for all types of study. The recovery and reinterpretation of man's past experience and creations is an indispensable counterpart to the teaching of natural or mathematical sciences, and a crucial part of education (Fig 52).

Within the school, the possibility of ready access to archaeological monuments is of great value for two reasons. Firstly, the remains are three-dimensional and by their very nature stimulate the imagination of children. Secondly, as an educational resource they are predictable in the sense that their visible existence is guaranteed; the teacher can therefore prepare lessons on the basis of what will be seen in the field rather than what might be seen, as in the case of plant or animal studies. The resources available to teachers from upland area museums and other organizations have been considered above (7.5). It has been estimated that some 70% of group visits to Exmoor comprise school children under 13 years of age (Haynes 1983, 8).

At university level too, upland archaeology provides a valuable teaching resource. Fifteen out of the 21 university departments with undergraduate courses for which information is available run regular field trips to upland areas as a routine part of undergraduate teaching. The remainder visit upland areas occasionally. Table 9 summarizes the use made of different upland areas. Again, it is quality of preservation and the density of evidence within small areas, thus minimizing travel time, as much as particular types of site, which attracts such heavy use of upland areas for field classes.

In adult education upland areas also prove very appealing. Formal courses such as those staged by National Park Study Centres and university extramural departments attract large numbers of students for much the same reasons as other university departments. The extent of informal and self-help study is unquantifiable, but if the popularity of guided walks and sales of archaeological guidebooks are anything to go by, upland areas are among the most popular in Britain (Fig 53).

8.5 Recreation

As an element of informal recreation, archaeological sites in the uplands have a greater value than is often realized. Some sites are marked on Ordnance Survey outdoor leisure maps and these frequently provide points of interest for walkers, hikers and even pony trekkers. For the more dedicated, walking may be incidental to the pursuit of visiting sites, perhaps for sheer enjoyment or perhaps as subjects for photography, painting or drawing. Again, the increase in the number of guidebooks, self-guided trails etc reflects the value which is placed upon an appreciation of historic landscapes, in the widest sense, by many individuals. With the aid of such publications the sense of discovery can be particularly rewarding in upland areas because the relationships between features within the landscape exist to be explored, and there is every likelihood that once one arrives at a site described in the guidebook there will be other things to see in the immediate vicinity.

Fig 52 Party visiting Merrivale standing stones and stone rows, Dartmoor (Devon) (photo Tim Darvill)

Table 9   Incidence of regular University Department field visits to upland areas in England and Wales* (1980 – 1984)

Area	No. of departments
Northumberland	7
North Wales	6
Dartmoor	5
South Wales	4
Pennines	4
Cornwall	3
Cheviots	3
North York Moors	3
Yorkshire Dales	2
Welsh Marches	2
Cotswolds	1
Lake District	1

*Note: some departments use more than one area either in parallel or on a rotation

8.6 Economic value

The value of archaeological remains in hard cash is difficult to quantify, but may be reviewed in two contexts, the short-term returns and the longer-term investment.

Income from visitors is perhaps the most tangible economic attraction. Entrance fees, car parking charges and the sale of merchandise and souvenirs are immediately related to the exploitation of ancient monuments. But regional income and higher cash circulation through visitor use of other facilities such as accommodation and nearby shops is no less important. These matters have been covered by the Countryside Commission's upland study (Sinclair & Bell 1983).

Economic gains may also be derived from using the empirical experience of past generations in planning for the future. Earlier users of the uplands were no less conscious of the peculiarities of the landscape in which they lived than are present landowners. Some might argue that earlier populations lived closer to the landscape than today. Whether or not this was so, cairns were not built on the best land, settlements were not focused on the most exposed hillsides and tracks were not laid along the steepest routes. A careful study of the way individual pieces of land were used in the past may lead to a more profitable management of the landscape today. For example, were field walls built on a particular axis to stop movement of soil downslope ? If so, would the removal of such features cause, over a period of perhaps a few decades, erosion of the soil ? At the very least a second look at development proposals with an eye to the archaeological remains may improve details of design.

Fig 53   Guided tour of a Neolithic chambered tomb for members of the Prehistoric Society during their autumn meeting in the Cotswolds in 1979 (photo Tim Darvill)

An exceptional example of the value of archaeological research comes from the uplands of Gwynedd. Excavations by the Gwynedd Archaeological Trust at Cefn Graenog Clynnog in advance of gravel extraction revealed a substantial 12th to 13th century AD farmstead situated in a small valley below Mynydd Craig Goch. The economy of this farmstead included cultivation of spelt wheat. Experiments revealed that this particular strain could still be grown under the harsh upland conditions of this part of Wales, whereas the modern wheats which were grown alongside the spelt as a control perished during growth (in Kelly 1982, 902). The investigation of other crops used in the past, with a view to their reintroduction in selected upland areas, may well repay research costs.

One further point should be considered. It is impossible to predict how attitudes to the landscape will change in the future, even within the next few decades, and it is not beyond the bounds of possibility that future generations will ascribe higher value to land which retains archaeological features than land where such features have been erased (Fig 54). Beeson &

Masterman (1979, ix), for instance, found that on Dartmoor many farmers and landowners considered it highly prestigious to have archaeological remains on their land.

8.7 Human and social value

To many people the remains of the past give a sense of security and continuity in an uncertain world. People are, in general, interested in the cultural and aesthetic achievements of past generations. There is an urgent need for further research into these aspects of psychology for it is far from clear exactly how an interest in the distant past affects people. Appleton (1975) suggests that the experience of landscape is significant in satisfying certain "basic human needs" which can be summarized as "identity", "security" and "stimulation". All these can be provided by historic landscapes. Visitor figures to museums and archaeological attractions, and the media coverage of spectacular finds speak for themselves as indicators of public interest.

Fig 54 Moorland fringe on the northern side of Bodmin Moor (Cornwall). The modern fields are laid out on the pattern of ancient fields whose boundaries can be seen still standing in the unimproved areas (photo National Monuments Record, Crown copyright reserved)

9 Archaeological resource management

This chapter assesses the options and policies available for the management of the archaeological resource.

9.1 Management options

Since archaeological features are a product of the evolution of the landscape, their future preservation can only be assured within the context of a dynamic landscape. Hitherto, archaeological remains have survived largely by default; traditional land-use practices have been kind to them, and indeed it is not so long ago that some sites were protected by superstition and folklore. Only in recent decades has the technical capacity and economic incentive become available to clear (perhaps unknowingly) archaeologically rich areas. A certain amount has already been lost, but much remains and, in comparison to lowland areas, the rapid attrition of the archaeological heritage has only just begun. But our heritage can no longer be left to chance: proper management is needed.

Archaeologists have talked about landscape management often over the last few years (Fowler 1977a; Fowler & Ellison 1977; Swanwick 1982; Cleere 1984), but only relatively recently has much been achieved. This survey revealed that among many archaeologists the doctrines of the "rescue" era in British archaeology (see Fowler 1977, 176; Jones 1984) still prevail in decision-making processes: the choice is seen as being between excavation and preservation by averting a threat. But the countryside equation has become much more complicated. Long-term strategic planning and the formulation of multi-option management policies represent a way forward which archaeologists have been slow to take up. *Doing nothing is not a sensible management option.*

It is perhaps useful to consider again the model of archaeological decay which was described in Chapter 5.1. In graphical terms, management can be visualized as the interception of the decay path in order to lessen its downward steepness. Such intervention can take several forms, which may be implemented in isolation or in parallel. Conservation and protection are the most obvious, but given that various demands are placed upon the archaeological heritage (see 8.2–6) management of exploitation is important too (Fig 55). Also,

Fig 55   Stone row on open moorland at Merrivale, Dartmoor (Devon) (photo Tim Darvill)

there will, inevitably, be occasions when the only option available is to remove the archaeological evidence from its site. The usual method for this is excavation since no technique exists to remove sites wholesale to safety. All of these options are considered in detail in the following sections; they have implications which extend beyond the uplands.

9.2 Conservation

Conservation has a variety of meanings today. Arguably it is not a technique or a methodology as such but a philosophy, a set of aims establishing a positive relationship between preservation and change (Green 1981). With reference to archaeology alone this means arresting the processes of decay so as to extend the life of a site for as long as possible. In achieving this it is axiomatic that those landscapes which preserve the relationships between individual features, and which incorporate the widest possible range of evidence, are given priority.

Some aspects of archaeological conservation will overlap with the needs of other conservation interests in countryside disciplines, for example nature conservation (Lambrick 1985), and sometimes both can be served by common policies and joint ventures. The area over which conservation schemes can operate depends on the extent of the authority responsible, and here the question of scale and land-use intensity arises. A generalized approach to conservation can be immensely valuable in ensuring the well-being of archaeological sites on open moorland where land-use is not intensive. Monitoring the condition of sites and taking immediate remedial action if problems arise (for example if a footpath starts to cut into a site) can be achieved by relatively few staff who may well have other duties besides archaeology. The National Parks in particular have developed considerable experience and skill in this aspect of conservation.

In areas of enclosed land where land-use is more intensive the picture is rather different, and although the National Parks and other authorities have a role to play in conservation in these areas, much of the responsibility must rest with individual landowners/landusers. Archaeological conservation here requires total commitment on the part of the landowner/landuser. No provision is made in advance for specific eventualities; rather day-to-day management is undertaken with the purposes of conservation to the fore (Fig 56). Thus if a new track is needed its route is devised to avoid known remains; if land/pasture needs improving only those areas known to be free of remains are reseeded; if some accidental surface damage is noted (eg turf missing) remedial action is immediately taken. If conservation is undertaken seriously, direct threats never arise; before a problem becomes a threat it has been identified and averted. The initiative is essentially in the hands of the landowner/landuser, and experience suggests that such work need not cost very much (Cobham 1984, 49).

Naturally, conservation cannot be effective unless the nature and extent of the resource being conserved is known and understood, which may necessitate intensive field survey. With this information to hand, however, the starting point for successful archaeological conservation is the development of management plans which deal firstly with any outstanding threats to the surviving heritage, and secondly allow for the direct input of archaeological considerations at an early stage of all decision-making. At the general level of low-intensity conservation this sort of forward planning is covered by Structure Plans and Park Plans. At the more specific level this means having a comprehensive farm/estate management plan.

The application of appropriate management techniques is essential. Such techniques will of course vary according to the circumstances of individual cases – land-use, vegetation cover and so on. Particularly sensitive areas may perhaps be laid to pasture with mixed species flora and a careful watch on grazing levels. In other cases rotavation and sod-sowing may provide a suitable method of cultivation where minimal ground disturbance is desirable. On rough grazing areas the control of bracken may be important. Lambrick (1977) has assessed the advantages and disadvantages of different agricultural practices.

Within this rather narrow definition there is little true archaeological conservation being undertaken in upland areas. Some lands owned by organizations conscious of landscape conservation are managed in this way, and a few examples are given later in this chapter (9.7). Until the introduction of the 1979 Ancient Monuments Act, however, scheduling did not provide for conservation at all. With the introduction of management agreements under sections 17 and 24 of the 1979 Act some progress may be possible, but the existing experience is that such agreements apply to individual sites or small groups of sites and that until block scheduling of some sort is widely implemented the limited areas involved hardly justify the use of the term conservation. Furthermore, as shown in Chapter 6, only a fraction of known sites are scheduled, and in a statement to National Parks in January 1982, the Ancient Monuments Secretariat make it clear that "The Department will not wish to be involved in management agreement negotiations in respect of unscheduled sites" (DoE 1982, vi). The value of management agreements in the context of conservation of the sort proposed here may also be questioned on the basis of financial and legal problems inherent in their very structure (see Feist 1978, 62).

9.3 Protection

In contrast to conservation, protection as a management option does not rely on internal initiative but is imposed by an outside authority. It has the aim of preservation, but rather than being a philosophy it is essentially a set of procedures which recognize or anticipate one or more threats. By its very nature protection requires careful definition both of the area and the eventualities to which it applies.

Protection is most commonly achieved by direct negotiation. Where a threat is posed to a given area the protecting authority attempts to avert it either by discussion and persuasion or through payment of some kind. In other instances specific threats can be anticipated and preventative action taken, perhaps by declaring a buffer zone round a monument, or by erecting bollards or by marking sites in some way. Sites deliberately left on unploughed "islands" in arable or

Fig 56   Deserted medieval settlement and fields on Brown Willey, Bodmin Moor (Cornwall). A farm track runs through the settlement. Minor changes in its line would have prevented damage to the archaeological deposits (photo National Monuments Record, Crown copyright reserved)

on unplanted ground in a forest are obvious examples of such protection (Fig 57).

Scheduling is at present the method most commonly used for protection. The need for Scheduled Monument Consent for change to existing land-use allows the option of refusal, or conditional refusal when threats arise. It is hoped that the use of management agreements under the terms of the 1979 Act will afford some protection against long-term threats such as ploughing and erosion. But the small and unrepresentative fraction of sites currently scheduled (6.1) severely limits the value of this form of protection.

One major disadvantage of protection as a management option is that landowners and tenants may feel, rightly or wrongly, that the authorities are only interested in their sites when they are under threat. Naturally this causes some resentment, although it may be hoped that visits from Field Monument Wardens will help to alleviate this.

9.4 Resource exploitation: striking the balance

Any exploitation of the archaeological heritage – for example by encouraging numerous visitors, and thereby increasing erosion, or excavation to increase knowledge – will accelerate decay. It is essential to control exploitation and also minimize damage by means of recognized management techniques.

Fortunately, upland sites are usually fairly robust and able to withstand a measure of visitor attention without serious damage. Informal management such as guided walks and self-guided trails, with carefully positioned signboards, are economical ways of controlling visitors and directing them around sites. Access and management agreements granting access rights over private land have also proved useful and may be particularly valuable where they enable by-laws to be introduced to assist in the management of visitors.

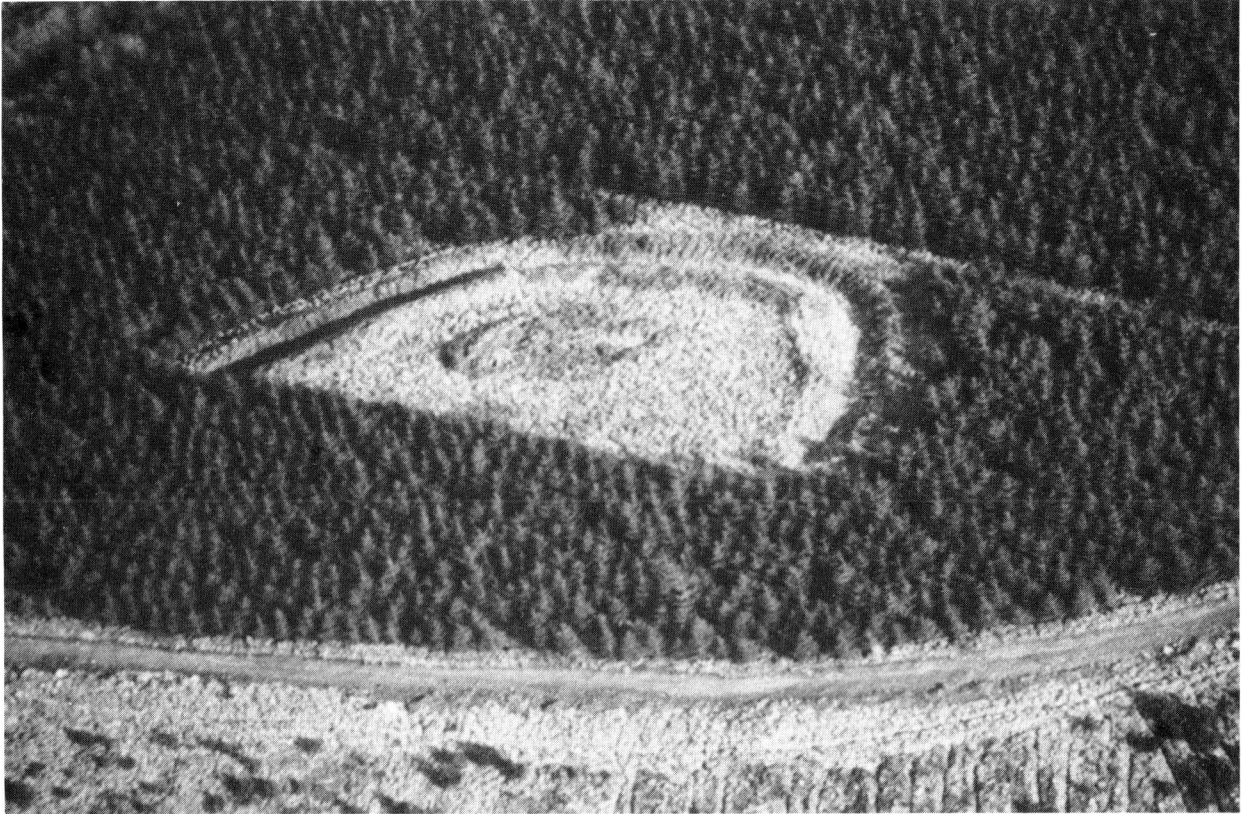

Fig 57 Gwersyll hillfort (Mid Glamorgan) respected as an archaeological monument during afforestation and left on an "island" of unplanted ground (photo Glamorgan Gwent Archaeological Trust)

Intensive exploitation of monuments for display is rather more complicated and more difficult to reconcile with preservation. Visitors expect a certain level of information which may necessitate excavation and reconstruction to make the remains intelligible. It is important to make interpretative exhibitions effective (Stanfield 1982), but expectations must not be raised beyond the capacity to satisfy them. Two recent reports (Brown 1984; HWCC 1984), which have addressed the problems and potentials of exploiting the archaeological heritage of upland areas, show that effective display can only be achieved at the cost of losing some features of the site. Management must therefore be concerned with balancing the needs of display with the wish to protect and conserve the site and its landscape context.

Exploitation of the academic resource through destructive techniques such as excavation require management in two respects: first the loss of sites selected for excavation should be justified in terms of the potential increase in knowledge; and second during the process of excavation the maximum amount of information must be recovered.

9.5 Rescue excavation

Excavation is expensive and can only be justified as a management option as a last resort, if neither preservation nor conservation is possible. It is imperative that academic demands are integrated with management possibilities.

In the case of localized threats the excavation option is relatively easy to define in terms of the scale and cost of the task involved. However, many threats in upland areas are extensive and it is very difficult to judge when the excavation option is the only solution. There is apparently little or no money available for evaluation work in this field and projects cannot be properly formulated on the basis of inadequate information. When weighed against the potential results from, say, a large-scale urban excavation, the results of upland excavations can appear negligible, and for this reason it is essential that bids for upland projects are measured against bids for similar projects.

9.6 Management selection

The existence of a range of management options means that choices have to be made: which sites or areas should receive attention, and what form that attention should take. In November 1983, the Secretary of State for the Environment announced the criteria approved for the identification and selection of monuments for inclusion in the Schedule of Ancient Monuments (DoE 1983). They were (not in rank order):

i   **Survival/condition** the archaeological potential of a monument, both above and below ground, is a crucial consideration and must be assessed in terms of its present condition and surviving features.

ii   **Period** it is important to consider for preservation all types of monuments that are representative of a category or period.

iii **Rarity** some categories of monuments are so scarce that all of those with archaeological potential should be preserved. In general, however, a selection must be made which portrays the typical and commonplace as well as the rare. For this, account should be taken of all aspects of the distribution of a particular class of monument not only in the broad national context but also in its region.

iv **Fragility/vulnerability** highly important archaeological evidence can be destroyed by a single ploughing or other unsympathetic treatment of some field monuments. They would benefit particularly from the statutory protection which scheduling confers. Similarly, the value of buildings and other standing structures can be severely reduced by neglect or careless treatment, and they too are well suited to protection by this legislation even though they may also be listed buildings.

v **Diversity** some monuments have a combination of high quality features, others are chosen for a single important attribute.

vi **Documentation** the significance of a monument may be given greater weight by the existence of records of previous investigation or, in the case of more recent monuments, by the support of contemporary written records.

vii **Group value** the value of a single monument (such as a field system) is greatly enhanced by association with related contemporary monuments (such as a settlement and cemetery) or with those of other periods. In some instances it is preferable to protect the whole including the associated and adjacent land rather than to protect isolated monuments within the group.

viii **Potential** on occasion the nature of the evidence cannot be precisely specified but it is possible to document reasons for anticipating probable existence and importance and so demonstrate the justification for scheduling. This is usually confined to sites rather than upstanding monuments.

These criteria are broadly similar to those used by the NCC for the selection of SSSIs (Green 1981, 196) and are in essence subjective, which makes comparative study very difficult. Moreover, directing selection criteria towards one eventuality, in this case scheduling, hardly does justice to the problem in hand which involves selecting between a range of management options. A development of Groube's (Groube & Bowden 1982) priority scale may offer one solution, although a rather more straightforward attribute scoring system may be preferable. Such a system is currently being developed by Wiltshire County Council for assessing management priorities on Salisbury Plain (information supplied by Mr R Canham).

There is a clear need for other levels of designation than those offered by the 1979 Act, and, as documented in ch 6, some local authorities have begun to use their planning powers to such ends in upland areas. Definition of Areas of Archaeological Importance under part II of the 1979 Act does not help in the field of conservation or protection, as the main provisions are for access to record and excavate threatened remains.

The controls offered by the 1979 Act are mostly negative in their effect, operating as a "safety valve" in the promotion of conservation of the type advocated in section 9.2 above. Planning controls in the sphere of extensive (but low intensity) conservation have an important, although rarely acknowledged, role. What would seem to be needed at both national and local levels is the capacity to define areas in which conservation is positively encouraged by means of grant-aid and, perhaps, certain tax concessions. Such areas might be integrated with the provision of protection considered below. Any management agreements for effective conservation need to be tied to the land rather than be of short-term duration. Revision of the approach to guardianship may prove of value in promoting conservation of highly sensitive areas.

The option of protection requires more than the existing scheduled category at a national level. Four generalized categories may be proposed (*cf* Morgan Evans 1985, 92) as a way of grading sites for management purposes:

1 Sites/Areas of National importance (Scheduled Ancient Monuments).
2 Sites/Areas of county or regional importance (County Heritage sites or similar).
3 Sites/Areas of district or local importance.
4 Sites which are not authentic antiquities or are so badly damaged that nothing now remains.

The protection offered at each grade would come from authorities at the appropriate level, and for maximum effect they could be linked with positive conservation schemes. A standardized nomenclature and quantitatively based selection criteria are essential if more than one authority is to be involved in providing protection. The National Monuments Records, once computerized, will play key roles in assessing nationally important areas and monuments. For the county/regional and district/local level information held by county based or National Park based SMRs will provide the yardstick for selection criteria.

A possible fifth category comprises areas with high archaeological potential. In parts of the uplands blanks exist on distribution maps either because peat cover masks archaeological remains or because no detailed survey work has been carried out. Such a designation would not offer protection so much as a means of finding out what is there when an opportunity arises. Later, such areas might merit more specific protection.

Criteria for the selection of monuments for exploitation represents yet another dimension which needs to be cross-referenced with the demands of conservation and protection. At present sites appear to be selected for display on the basis of their visible remains, whereas in fact accessibility and scope for visitor amenities should perhaps be accorded higher priority, with greater use of excavation and reconstruction to enhance the display value. Rethinking of the guardianship provisions to distinguish between those sites in guardianship for display and those in guardianship for conservation reasons should be considered as an alternative to the present rather noncommittal approach where neither management option is satisfactorily achieved. Comments on the use of the academic resource and on the selection of sites for excavation have been made above (9.4 and 9.5 and see Mercer 1982, 93).

In summary, management of the archaeological resource requires an integrated approach to the selection of options, with clearer distinctions between the roles of national and local authorities.

9.7 Towards an integrated approach

Widespread and successful management of the archaeological resource is not imminent. Progress has been made in a few areas, but this results largely from the enthusiasm of a few individuals. Much, too, depends on the attitudes of those outside the discipline, especially farmers and landowners.

A prerequisite for the selection and use of any management option is the availability of information. The compilation of county-based SMRs is now well advanced for many upland areas and the information they contain will provide a sound basis for decision making. Compiling such records is, however, only the first stage. The information within each record requires analysis to allow the identification of recurrent patterns within the evidence, to weigh the advantages of one site against another, to perceive optimal points for attention and to select and justify possible management options. But there is no need to wait in some upland areas, clear cut cases pertinent to all levels of management are identifiable from existing information.

It would be naïve in the extreme to think that archaeological management can, or should, exist in isolation. There are many other factors to be weighed, and this should ideally be done at the level of individual land holdings, involving owners, occupiers, local authorities, and even, if necessary, national bodies. Each farm or estate requires a management plan (and see MacEwen & Sinclair 1983, 37) that includes archaeological provisions. Some large amenity landowners such as the National Trust and Water Authorities have already established such plans for some or all of their landholdings. The Anglezarke Recreation Area Local Plan by Lancashire County Council is an example. Private owners too have had such plans prepared, for example Bransdale Moor (North Yorkshire) (Stratham 1982), Huccaby Farm (Devon) (MAFF 1984) and under the Demonstration Farm Scheme (Cobham 1984). Such plans will take into account not only the options of archaeological management (what is conserved, what protected, what exploited) but also integrate them with the needs of agriculture, forestry, recreation, water catchment, nature conservation etc. as necessary. Preparing such plans is sometimes costly and at present there are few incentives and even fewer qualified staff available to do the work. Six-year farm development plans are needed for some agricultural grant applications, but these do not cover such aspects as archaeology. Exemption from Capital Transfer Tax is normally conditional upon preparation of a management plan (6.1) and the Bransdale Moor Plan already referred to is an example of this. Clearly there is a need for grants to be made available to individual farms to enable the purchase of specialist advice and surveys. There is also scope for the preparation of a handbook, similar to that used by the NCC (1983) outlining the nature of archaeological contributions to management plans.

Management agreements are likely to increase in importance as a means of implementing management options. Experience of such agreements in other fields inspires little confidence in their long-term value because of difficulties in renegotiation and the uncertainty of government willingness to support them on anything more than a year-to-year basis (Feist 1978). It is, however, crucial to distinguish between the different aims of management agreements and to balance these against the form of an agreement and its duration.

The cost of conservation on an extensive and low-intensity basis such as many upland areas require need not be high. Many of the threats illustrated in ch 5 could have been averted with a little thought and understanding (Fig 58). Central to the success of conservation is local initiative and local decision making. The upland management experiments undertaken by the Countryside Commission (1976, 1979a) demonstrate how valuable relatively modest investment in a local project can be. Advice to users of the land is a major component of successful management, and as the number of organizations seeking advice increases so too does the need for an archaeological countryside advisory service, perhaps allied or even linked with existing ADAS or FWAG services.

Management will only work if there is public support for its aims and practice. This is an area where archaeologists have again fallen seriously behind in their approach, mostly because appropriate funds have not been available. The contributions from MAFF/ADAS and the Countryside Commission for the preparation of leaflets and publicity have been most welcome. Informing by example is perhaps the most valuable way forward, however, and this means greater involvement with demonstration farms and similar projects. Upland farms within the existing Countryside Commission project, Ottercops and Raechester (Northumberland) and Tynllan (Powys) are not especially rich in archaeological remains (Cobham 1984, 45). In contrast, the Huccaby Demonstration Farm on the Duchy of Cornwall's land on Dartmoor is more typical of many upland farms in terms of its archaeology. To demonstrate that management of the archaeological resource can be integrated with other needs of landscape management is the first step towards ensuring that adequate conservation, effective protection, meaningful exploitation and minimum rescue excavation takes place in upland areas.

Fig 58   Moel Goedog stone circle near Harlech (Gwynedd). Excavated and restored in 1978 after being disturbed by stone clearance connected with a land improvement project (photo Mick Sharp)

10 Summary, conclusions and recommendations

10.1 Summary

The uplands of England and Wales, because of their relative isolation and lack of development, are extremely rich in upstanding archaeological remains of most periods, from earliest times to the Industrial Revolution. Recent investigations, especially by field survey and aerial photography, have emphasized both the quality and the quantity of those remains. Over 31,000 sites have been recorded so far, but many areas have yet to be surveyed, and the final figure may well be over half a million.

Counting sites does not do justice to the evidence. Rather than a scatter of isolated features, upland archaeology comprises large tracts of relict landscape containing settlements, fields, paddocks, quarries, burial sites and ritual centres left by many generations (Fig 59).

Such landscapes are exciting and their study over the last two decades or so has done much to enhance our understanding of the development of the uplands. The traditional view that the uplands were a cultural backwater for much of the prehistoric and historic period is not supported by the evidence. Neither is the idea that the uplands are virgin countryside unspoilt by Man.

Although different areas experienced differences in the cycle of settlement advance and retreat, the general picture is as follows. The uplands were first exploited by hunters and gatherers as long ago as 10,000 BC. At that time they were wooded and provided ideal hunting grounds. During the period when early farming communities were becoming established in Britain the uplands continued to be used as hunting grounds, for grazing animals and as a source of high quality stone for making tools. The warmer climate of the Bronze Age gave rise to the first major phase of forest clearance, as agriculture became possible on land up to and above the 300 m (1000 ft) contour. Portions of the uplands were by now densely populated, but by the 1st millennium BC the soils were becoming less fertile, the climate was deteriorating, and a retreat was in progress. During the Roman period the uplands were a major source of wealth in the form of natural resources and, some of them being frontier areas of the Empire, were heavily occupied by the army. In the 5th to 9th

Fig 59 Main entrance to the Bronze Age enclosure at Grimspound, Dartmoor. The gate stones are still standing and a rough cobbled path can be seen exposed by erosion (photo Tim Darvill)

centuries the uplands appear to have been little used but from the 10th century AD an ameliorating climate, the restored fertility of the soil after a period of rest, and a growing population encouraged settlement once more to extend well into the hills. Abandonment and retreat began again in the 13th century and thereafter the uplands mainly provided natural resources.

These rich archaeological resources currently face a wide range of threats. Most disturbing is the damage being done by intensive agriculture and by agricultural improvement schemes promoted by national government and EEC incentives. The archaeological remains on the moorland fringes in particular face obliteration as agricultural improvement schemes convert open moorland into rough grazing and rough grazing into arable.

The manpower to cope with these threats is grossly inadequate. Archaeological organizations do not have the financial resources, or the necessary support from grant-giving authorities to deal with these threats. The legislation, too, has been found wanting by present circumstances. Far too few sites are protected by scheduling to preserve anything like a representative sample of the known archaeological resource, and, in any case, protected sites often appear to be as much at risk as unprotected ones. Existing legislation is unequal to the task of preserving and protecting the wide tracts of archaeological remains that abound in the uplands.

The needs of conservation in upland areas are not matched by available resources to promote effective management strategies at a local level. Some local authorities, recognizing the problem, have initiated conservation and protection measures using their planning controls but these lack mandatory backing from central government.

Public interest in the archaeology of the uplands is high. Traditional attractions such as museums and guardianship monuments draw large numbers of visitors, although over the last few years attendances have been falling. Interest in guided walks, self-guided trails and other informal uses of archaeological resources has increased. Use of the uplands for practical teaching of archaeology and landscape studies at all levels from school to university and adult education is high.

Archaeologists themselves are not without blame for some of what is happening. There has been a general failure to communicate the findings of recent work to the general public and more particularly to interest landowners and farmers in the remains that survive on their land. But again, lack of funding and sparse resources underlie much of this failure.

10.2 Conclusions and recommendations

Many conclusions can be drawn from the information and analyses presented in this report, but it is not the intention here to provide an exhaustive set of conclusions. Rather countryside interests such as the Countryside Commission, the various farmer's Unions, the Country Landowners Association, the Council for National Parks, MAFF, WOAD and ADAS must draw their own conclusions in the light of their particular present and future policies. Nevertheless, their are certain topics which merit emphasis.

Approaches and philosophy

In the past a lop-sided emphasis has been given to the visual and scenic aspects of upland landscapes as an indicator of their value. Archaeology is very much a part of such landscapes and should be integral in their evaluation. In some areas there would be little scenic or visual interest were it not for the archaeology.

Current and future threats

Threats to upland archaeology are constantly changing. Hence it is not practical to suggest controls for what might in some cases be short-lived (although by no means trivial) problems. The key is for archaeologists to anticipate and avert future threats by being involved formally in any discussion of proposals that might otherwise inadvertently endanger archaeological heritage. Long-term threats require more fundamental solutions, involving changes in legislation and the introduction of management strategies outlined below.

It is recommended that:

Greater cooperation between existing archaeological organizations and the Ministry of Agriculture Fisheries and Food, the Welsh Office Agricultural Department, the Countryside Commission, the Nature Conservancy Council and the Forestry Commission be promoted by the appointment of qualified archaeological advisers within these bodies to assimilate the needs of archaeological management to policy formulation at an early stage.

Greater control be exercised over the provision of agricultural grants by submitting schemes to county archaeological officers for comment and consultation before implementation.

A campaign be launched to increase public awareness of the need to respect archaeological monuments. The surprising absence of an appropriate clause in the Country Code in support of this aspect must be rectified.

Gaps in the distribution of known archaeological remains should be identified, recorded, and recommended for future upland development, other circumstances permitting.

Legislation

Existing ancient monuments legislation is rapidly becoming outdated and inappropriate to the needs of conserving and protecting the types of archaeological remains encountered in the uplands. Future legislation must build on the strengths of the present system. Clarification of the role of local authorities, and a thorough overhaul of the categories of protection, and the criteria for their selection, are urgently needed. Planning legislation requires tightening to include mandatory reponsibilities for regional categories of monuments, and there is a need for more specific reference to archaeology in existing countryside legislation. Some wider application of the powers available in National Parks would prove useful.

It is recommended that:

Existing antiquities legislation be reviewed in the light of changing perceptions of the archaeological heritage.

Section 43 of the Wildlife and Countryside Act be extended to specifically include archaeological remains as one of the factors for selecting areas for conservation.

Account be taken of archaeological remains in the drafting of management plans for Sites of Special Scientific Interest and National Nature Reserves.

The time limits placed on the expiry of planning permissions for mineral extraction be reduced so that changing awareness of archaeological constraints can be taken into account.

Organisation and workforce

Trained archaeological staff in employment are relatively few. Much valuable work is currently funded by the Manpower Services Commission, but this does not provide the continuity which is necessary for many of the tasks outlined in this document. Archaeology is over-centralized. There is insufficient support for local organizations; project funding on an annual basis does not assist long-term planning, nor can it be used to underpin involvement in a wider range of activities, such as the provision of management advice. At present many counties do not have the financial capacity to respond to local threats or to initiate pilot surveys to appraise what should be done.

It is recommended that:

Central government funding to regional and county-based archaeological organizations for field survey, monument management and public relations work be increased, with long-term projects involving a wide range of countryside interests being given priority.

Full-time permanent posts be created in those county councils and National Parks currently lacking archaeological officers to advise on planning and management matters.

Database

Cost-effective management of the archaeological resource depends upon the existence of reliable and accessible information. In the uplands, where sites generally survive in a better state of preservation than elsewhere, techniques of air and ground survey should be employed as methods of primary data collection, since it is only in this way that the full extent of the archaeological landscapes will become apparent. Field survey in the uplands is labour-intensive. It must be emphasized that the evidence at present recorded is only the *known* resource, not the existing resource.

It is recommended that:

Compilation of sites and monuments records in upland areas be given high priority because of the

quality of the information recoverable and of the threats to it.

Maximum use be made of all relevant survey techniques as the primary method of data acquisition.

Public relations

This has been one of the weakest areas of archaeologistical proformance in recent years. Yet there is a considerable demand for information, at all levels. People who understand the history of the landscape they live in are more likely to care for it. For farmers demonstration farms offer one way of drawing attention to what can be achieved.

It is recommended that:

The possibility of an archaeological countryside advisory service within existing services, such as the Agricultural Development Advisory Service, be investigated, perhaps by setting up a trial scheme in one or two areas.

Publicity projects be instigated more regularly by both archaeological and countryside organizations, and informative and attractive leaflets presenting the case for the conservation and preservation of archaeological remains be prepared and distributed to generate greater awareness of archaeology as a conservation issue.

A programme for the positive provision of information to farmers and landowners' projects be established as a part of the services provided by regional archaeological bodies, in association with the National Farmers' Union, the County Landowners' Association, and the Agricultural Development Advisory Service.

Tourism and leisure

The large numbers of tourists visiting upland areas require to be catered for through more carefully managed attractions (Fig 60).

It is recommended that:

Money for the development of the tourist industry available through Article 10(2) of the European Economic Community Less Favoured Area directives be freed for use in the British uplands.

More research be undertaken by the Historic Buildings and Monuments Commission and Cadw to provide information on public use of and interest in different types of archaeological attractions.

Greater attention be given by local authorities and regional tourist boards, action in consultation to the selection and presentation of monuments and landscapes as visitor attractions.

Resource management

In proportion to the size of the resource, past public

Fig 60 Prehistoric houses, enclosures, land boundaries, and fieldsystems visible over a large area on Rough Tor, Bodmin Moor (Cornwall). Such remains scattered throughout the uplands are part of the last great reserve of well preserved relict landscapes in Britain (photo National Monuments Record, Crown copyright reserved)

expenditure on archaeology has been small. Now that active management of the archaeological resource has been shown to be necessary it is going to cost more. Research into effective and appropriate management options is needed for all areas, especially upland areas; the fundamental importance of management plans and selection criteria is alrcady clear.

It is recommended that:

Grants be made available to cover the specialist costs of preparing management plans.

A handbook be produced by one or more archaeological organizations setting out clearly the archaeological considerations relevant to the preparation of management plans, and courses be established to give training on the management of archaeological sites and landscapes.

Tighter controls be introduced at national and local level to ensure the efficient use of archaeological resources.

Capital Transfer Tax exemption be extended to encourage the implementation of management plans over wider areas.

Grants be made available from central government under the new EEC Agricultural Structures Regulation for the preservation of archaeological monuments, farm buildings and ancient field boundaries.

Further ways of supporting conservation schemes through grant aid and tax concessions be investigated by central government.

Contacts be established with other conservation interests, notably the Nature Conservancy Council and county naturalist trusts, to enhance protection

and sympathetic management of areas of mutual
interest, and to discuss the selection and protection
of areas wherein the interaction of human activity
and the natural environment are outstandingly demonstrated.

91

Appendix A Uplands project data collection procedure

The researching and preparation of this report were carried out between 1 October 1984 and 1 April 1985. In this short time no original fieldwork was possible. Information was collected in three ways.

A Questionnaires

A set of eight different questionnaires was prepared and distributed to organizations involved with archaeological work in the uplands. The questions were structured to provide quantifiable data as well as providing scope for general comment and subjective views. The questionnaires directed to the Sites and Monuments Records were delivered and explained by the Project Officer in person between November and December 1984. The other seven sets of questionnaires were sent out by post in mid November, accompanied by a letter explaining the project and a copy of the leaflet (see B below). A deadline of 15 February 1985 was set for the return of the questionnaires; reminders were sent out in late January 1985. Table 10 summarizes the returns, which were generally very high. The following organizations and institutions received questionnaires:

Sites and monuments records
Archaeological Unit for north-east England, University of Newcastle Upon Tyne (Northumberland & Durham)
County Planning Department, Cumbria County Council, Kendal
Cleveland County Archaeology Section, Middlesborough
County Planning Department, North Yorkshire County Council, Northallerton
Cumbria and Lancashire Archaeological Unit, University of Lancaster (Lancashire)
County Archaeology Department, West Yorkshire County Council, Wakefield
County Archaeology Department, South Yorkshire County Council, Sheffield
Greater Manchester Archaeological Unit, University of Manchester
County Planning Department, Derbyshire County Council, Matlock
County Planning Department, Cheshire County Council, Chester
County Planning Department, Clwyd County Council, Mold
Gwynedd Archaeological Trust, Bangor
County Planning Department, Staffordshire County Council, Stafford
County Planning Department, Shropshire County Council, Shrewsbury
Clwyd Powys Archaeological Trust, Welshpool (Powys)
Dyfed Archaeological Trust, Carmarthen
County Archaeology Department, Hereford and Worcester County Council, Worcester
County Planning Department, Gloucestershire County Council, Gloucester
Glamorgan Gwent Archaeological Trust, Swansea (Mid Glamorgan, West Glamorgan & Gwent)
County Planning Department, Somerset County Council, Taunton
County Sites and Monuments Record, Devon County Council, Exeter
Cornwall Committee for Rescue Archaeology, Truro

County Planning Officers
Northumberland County Council, Morpeth
Cumbria County Council, Kendal
Durham County Council, Durham
Cleveland County Council, Middlesborough
North Yorkshire County Council, Northallerton
Lancashire County Council, Preston
West Yorkshire County Council, Wakefield
South Yorkshire County Council, Barnsley
Greater Manchester County Council, Manchester
Derbyshire County Council, Matlock
Cheshire County Council, Chester
Clwyd County Council, Mold *

Table 10 Summary of responses to questionnaires

Questionnaire		Number issued	Number returned	% returned
1	Sites and monuments records	24	24	100
2	County Planning Departments	25	23	92
3	National Park Offices	10	10	100
4	Upland area museums	63	51	81
5	Tourist boards	12	6	50
6	University departments	26	23	88
7	Selected major landowners	11	10	91
8	Other organizations	4	4	100
Totals		175	151	86.2

Gwynedd County Council, Caernarvon
Staffordshire County Council, Stafford
Shropshire County Council, Shrewsbury
Powys County Council, Llandrindod Wells
Dyfed County Council, Carmarthen
Hereford and Worcester County Council, Worcester ⋆
Gloucestershire County Council, Gloucester
Gwent County Council, Cwmbran
Somerset County Council, Taunton
Devon County Council, Exeter
Cornwall County Council, Truro
West Glamorgan County Council, Swansea
Mid Glamorgan County Council, Cardiff

National Parks
Dartmoor National Park, Newton Abbott, Devon
Lake District National Park, Kendal, Cumbria
Snowdonia National Park, Penrhyndeudraeth, Gwynedd
Brecon Beacons National Park, Brecon, Powys
Pembrokeshire Coast National Park, Haverfordwest, Dyfed
Exmoor National Park, Dulverton, Somerset
Peak District National Park, Bakewell, Derbyshire
North York Moors National Park, Helmsley, North Yorkshire
Northumberland National Park, Hexham, Northumberland
Yorkshire Dales National Park, Leyburn, North Yorkshire

Museums within and adjacent to upland areas
Ceredigion Museum, Aberystwyth, Dyfed
Tameside Museum Service, Ashton under Lyne, Greater Manchester
Museum of Welsh Antiquities, Bangor, Gwynedd
The Bowes Museum, Barnard Castle, Durham
Cannon Hall Museum, Cawthorne, South Yorkshire⋆
Barnstaple Museum, Barnstaple, Devon⋆
County Museum Service, Preston, Lancashire
The Furness Museum, Barrow in Furness, Cumbria
Bagshaw Museum, Batley, West Yorkshire
Torfaen Museum Service, Blaenafon, Gwent
Bolton Museum, Bolton, Greater Manchester
Bradford Museum, Bradford, West Yorkshire (incl Ilkely Museum and Keighley Museum)
Brecknock Museum, Brecon, Powys
Bristol City Museum, Bristol, Avon
Towneley Hall Museum, Burnley, Lancashire
Burton-on-Trent Museum, Burton-on-Trent, Staffordshire⋆
Bury Art Gallery and Museum, Greater Manchester
Buxton Museum, Buxton, Derbyshire
National Museum of Wales, Cardiff, Glamorgan
Carlisle Museum, Carlisle, Cumbria
Carmarthen Museum, Carmarthen, Dyfed
Cheddar Museum, Cheddar, Somerset
Cheltenham Museum and Art Gallery, Cheltenham, Gloucestershire
Chesterfield Museum, Chesterfield, Derbyshire⋆
Corinium Museum, Cirencester, Gloucestershire
Clun Town Museum, Clun, Shropshire
Derby Museum, Derby, Derbyshire
Royal Albert Memorial Museum, Exeter, Devon
Gloucester City Museum, Gloucester, Gloucestershire

Upper Wharfedale Museum, Grassington, North Yorkshire⋆
Bankfield Museum, Halifax, West Yorkshire
Royal Pump Room Museum, Harrogate, North Yorkshire
Haverfordwest Museum, Haverfordwest, Dyfed
Tolson Memorial Museum, Huddersfield, West Yorkshire
Ilfracombe Museum, Ilfracombe, Devon
Kendal Museum, Kendal, Cumbria
Fitz Park Museum, Keswick, Cumbria
Lancaster City Museum, Lancaster, Lancashire
Leeds City Museum, Leeds, West Yorkshire⋆
Llandrindod Wells Museum, Llandrindod Wells, Powys
The Buttercross Museum, Ludlow, Shropshire
West Park Museum, Macclesfield, Cheshire
Manchester City Museum, Greater Manchester
Manchester Museum, University of Manchester, Greater Manchester
Cleveland County Museum Service, Middlesborough, Cleveland
Much Wenlock Museum, Much Wenlock, Shropshire
Museum of Antiquities, University of Newcastle upon Tyne, Tyne and Wear
Oldham Museum, Oldham, Greater Manchester⋆
Plymouth City Museum, Plymouth, Devon
Rochdale Museum, Rochdale, Greater Manchester
Sheffield City Museum, Sheffield, South Yorkshire
Rowley's House Museum, Shrewsbury, Shropshire
Scarborough Museums, Scarborough, North Yorkshire
Craven Museum, Skipton, North Yorkshire
South Molton Museum, South Molton, Devon
Woodbank Hall Museum, Stockport, Greater Manchester⋆
City Museum, Stoke-on-Trent, Staffordshire
Stroud District Museum, Stroud, Gloucestershire
Totnes Museum, Totnes, Devon
Wakefield Museum, Wakefield, West Yorkshire
Wells Museum, Wells, Somerset
Powysland Museum, Welshpool, Powys

Tourist Boards
Cumbria Tourist Board, Windermere, Cumbria⋆
East Midlands Tourist Board, Lincoln, Lincolnshire
Heart of England Tourist Board, Worcester, Hereford and Worcester⋆
Northumbria Tourist Board, Newcastle upon Tyne, Tyne and Wear
North West Tourist Board, Bolton, Greater Manchester
West Country Tourist Board, Exeter, Devon
Yorkshire and Humberside Tourist Board, York, North Yorkshire
Wales Tourist Board, Cardiff, South Glamorgan⋆
North Wales Tourist Council, Colwyn Bay, Clwyd⋆
Mid Wales Tourist Council, Machynlleth, Powys
South Wales Tourist Board, Swansea, West Glamorgan⋆
English Tourist Board, London⋆

University Archaeology Departments
University College of Wales, Aberystwyth
University College of North Wales, Bangor

University of Birmingham
University of Bradford★
University of Bristol
University of Cambridge
University College Cardiff
University of Durham★
University of Edinburgh
University of Exeter
University of Glasgow
University College, Lampeter
University of Lancaster★
University of Leeds
University of Leicester
University of Liverpool
University College, London
University of London, Institute of Archaeology
University of Manchester
University of Newcastle upon Tyne
University of Nottingham
University of Oxford, Institute of Archaeology
University of Reading
University of Sheffield
University of Southampton
University of York

Selected major landowners and land owning authorities
Forestry Commission
Ministry of Defence
National Trust
Nature Conservancy Council
The Duchy of Cornwall
Northumbrian Water Authority, Newcastle upon Tyne★
North-west Water Authority, Warrington
Severn–Trent Water Authority, Birmingham
South-west Water Authority, Exeter
Yorkshire Water Authority, Leeds
Welsh Water Authority, Brecon

Other organizations
Royal Commission on Historic Monuments (England), London
Royal Commission on Ancient and Historic Monuments Wales, Aberystwyth
Historic Buildings and Monuments Commission, London
Cadw, Cardiff

(★ Questionnaire not returned)

B Leaflets

A leaflet outlining the scope and background of the project was printed and distributed widely in October and November 1984. This was primarily intended to inform individuals and organizations who could not be contacted personally in the time available. The leaflet invited comments and advertised the seminars (see below). About fifteen written reponses were received. Extracts from the leaflet appeared in the CBA Calendar (January 1985), Countryside Commission News (November 1984), and many other countryside interest periodicals. Leaflets were sent by post to many institutions for distribution.

C Seminars

A series of three seminars was organized, in Leeds on 15 January, in Newtown (Powys) on 16 January and in Bristol on 17 January. Informal papers were presented at each, and in all cases discussion was lively and wide-ranging. A total of about 120 individuals participated over the three days. Heavy snow falls prevented some attending, but it was disappointing that more countryside interests were not represented, especially after sending out invitations to more than 50 non-archaeological organizations.

The Uplands Project was carried out under the aegis of the CBA's Countryside Committee. The project panel comprised: Desmond Bonney (RCHME), Mike Feist (Countryside Commission), Peter Clack (CBA Countryside Committee), Richard Morris (CBA Research Officer) and Tim Darvill (Project Officer).

Appendix B Summary of the Ancient Monuments and Archaeological Areas Act 1979

The Act was made law on 4 April 1979, and came into force in stages. In England the Act is amended by the National Heritage Act 1983.

Part I

Section 1
The Secretary of State (for the Environment, for Wales, for Scotland) is empowered to "compile and maintain...a schedule of monuments".

Monuments for inclusion on the schedule are required to be "of national importance" (see Part III for definitions). A structure occupied as a dwelling house (except where the sole occupier is a caretaker), or an ecclesiastical building in use for ecclesiastical purposes, may not be included in the schedule.

The Secretary of State is required to notify the owner and occupier (where not the owner) and the local authority in which the monument is situated when it is added to the schedule.

Lists of scheduled monuments are to be published periodically.

Entry in the schedule is a local land charge.

Sections 2–4
It is an offence to carry out work resulting in the demolition or destruction of, or damage to, a monument, to remove, repair or add to any part of it, or to carry out flooding or tipping without the prior written consent of the Secretary of State.

Scheduled Monument Consent (SMC) may be granted subject to conditions, eg the opportunity for archaeological excavation.

Certain works of a specified nature under the Act are covered by "class consents": eg the continued ploughing of monuments, although not an increase in the depth of ploughing.

SMC is normally granted for a specified period of up to five years, after which the consent expires.

Sections 5–6
The Secretary of State is empowered to carry out urgent works after giving the owner 7 days' notice.

Persons authorised by the Secretary of State may enter land to inspect scheduled monuments at any reasonable time.

Section 7–9
Compensation may be payable where expenditure or loss is incurred by any person with an interest in a monument as a result of refusal of SMC, conditional consent, or revocation of consent.

Sections 10-16
The Secretary of State may acquire a monument compulsorily to secure its preservation. The provisions of the Acquisition of Land (Authorisation Procedure) Act 1946 apply in respect of compensation.

The Secretary of State or any local authority may acquire a monument by agreement or gift.

The Secretary of State or a local authority may be constituted guardian of a monument by deed.

The Secretary of State or the local authority have a duty to maintain any monument under their guardianship and in their full control and management.

Land adjoining or in the vicinity of a monument may be compulsorily acquired to facilitate maintenance of the monument, provide access, etc. There is provision for the acquisition of easements for similar purposes.

Section 17
The Secretary of State or a local authority may enter into management agreements with occupiers of scheduled monuments in connexion with their maintenance and preservation.

Section 19–20
The public shall have access to any monument under the guardianship of the Secretary of State or a local authority, who may provide facilities and services for the public. Scheduling does *not* imply public access.

Section 26–27
A person authorised by the Secretary of State may at any reasonable time enter land believed to contain an ancient monument to inspect or record it.

Sections 28–29
It is an offence to destroy or damage any monument (this applies to owners, occupiers, or any other persons).

Part II

Sections 33–41
The Secretary of State or a local authority, may designate any area as "an area of archaeological importance" (AAI).

Archaeological bodies will be appointed as investigating authorities in respect of AAIs.

A notice detailing any operations which disturb the ground or involve flooding or tipping within an AAI must be served on the relevant local authority.

The investigating authority then has the right to enter the site in order to inspect it during a period of six weeks from the serving of the notice.

If archaeological excavations are to be carried out, a further period not exceeding four months two weeks is available for their completion without compensation being payable, provided that notice is served in due form on the developer.

Part II

Section 42

It is an offence to use a metal detector in a protected place (scheduled or guardianship monument or AAI) without the prior written consent of the Secretary of State.

It is an offence to remove any object of archaeological or historical interest discovered by the use of a metal detector in a protected place without the prior written consent of the Secretary of State.

Section 50

A monument on Crown Land may be included in the schedule but no powers are exercizable under the Act without the consent of the appropriate authority.

Crown Land is defined as that owned by the sovereign, belonging to a government department, or forming part of the estates of the Duchies of Lancaster or Cornwall.

Section 61

A "monument" is defined as:

(a) Any building, structure, or work, whether above or below the surface of the land, and any cave or building;

(b) Any site comprising the remains of any such building, structure or work or any cave or excavation; and

(c) Any site comprising, or comprising the remains of, any vehicle, vessel, aircraft ot the movable structure or part thereof which neither constitutes nor forms part of any work which is a monument within (a) above.

And any machinery attached to a monument is regarded as part of the monument if it cannot be detached without being dismantled.

In the 1983 Act (Section 33(8)) an ancient monument is defined as "Any structure, work, site, garden or area which in the Commission's (ie HBMC) opinion is of historic, architectural, traditional, artistic or archaeological interest".

Appendix C Gazetteer of Upland self-guided trails and drives with archaeological interest

Trails

1 Blaenrhondda Walk, Mid Glamorgan
A circular trail established by Mid Glamorgan County Council. Approximately 3.2 km (2 miles) long, archaeological interests include prehistoric settlement (reconstruction in guidebook) and industrial remains

2 Brenig Valley, Clwyd
A circular trail established by Welsh Water Authority on the north east shore of Llyn Brenig. Approximately 3.2 km (2 miles) long. Visitor centre. Content specifically archaeological; includes reconstructed Bronze Age barrows and medieval hafod

3 Calf Hey Trail, Lancashire
A circular trail established by Lancashire County Council. Approximately 2.4 km (1.5 miles) long. Not specifically archaeological, but includes some industrial archaeology

4 Clydach Gorge, Gwent
Three separate trails in and around the Gorge established by Brecon Beacons National Park. Approximately 4–5 km (2.5–3.2 miles) long. All focus on industrial archaeology

5 Coaley Peak, Gloucestershire
A circular trail established by Gloucestershire County Council from the Coaley Peak Picnic Area. Approximately 9.5 km (6 miles). Not specifically archaeological, but sites visited and explained in the guide include two Neolithic long barrows and an Iron Age hillfort

6 Coopers Hill Trail, Gloucestershire
A circular trail established by Gloucestershire County Council in a local nature reserve. Approximately 3.2 km (2 miles) long. Not specifically archaeological, but includes a number of sites which are described in the guidebook

7 Creswell Crags, Derbyshire
Short circular trail established by Derbyshire County Council and Nottinghamshire County Council. Approximately 1.6 km (1 mile) long. Visitor centre. Specifically geology/archaeology

8 Crickley Hill, Gloucestershire
Two circular trails starting from Crickley Hill Country Park established by Gloucestershire County Council. A short trail (c 0.8 kilometre (0.5 mile)) within the Park takes in the multi-period prehistoric hillfort and associated features. The longer trail (up to 13.6 km (8.5 miles)), not specifically archaeological but takes in several prehistoric and later sites in the area.

9 Hambleton Drove Road, North Yorkshire
Linear trail, following the line of an ancient track, established by North York Moors National Park. Approximately 24 km (15 miles). Sites of many periods can be seen on or beside the trail, and are explained in chronological order in the guidebook

10 High Peak Trail, Derbyshire
Linear trail established by Derbyshire County Council and Peak Park Planning Board. Approximately 28 km (17.5 miles) long. Focus is industrial archaeology

11 Lead Mines Clough, Lancashire
Short trail established by Lancashire County Council. Approximately 1.6 km (1 mile) long. Specifically industrial archaeology (lead mining industry)

12 Ravenscar Geological Trail, North Yorkshire
Circular trail established by the North York Moors National Park. Approximately 7.2 km (4.5 miles) long. Specifically geological, but includes industrial archaeology

13 Roystone Grange Trail, Derbyshire
Circular trail established by Peak District National Park and University of Sheffield. Approximately 6.5 km (4 miles) long. Specifically archaeological; includes sites of many periods

14 Rudry Common, Mid Glamorgan
Circular trail established by Mid Glamorgan County Council. Approximately 3.2 km (2 miles) long. Not specifically archaeological, but includes industrial archaeology

15 Sywd Gwladys Walk, West Glamorgan
Linear trail established by West Glamorgan County Council. Approximately 4.0 km (2.5 miles) long. Not specifically archaeological, but includes sites to visit along the route

16 Wycollier, Lancashire
Series of three separate trails established by Lancashire County Council. Range in length from 3.2 to 11 km (2 to 7 miles). Not specifically archaeological, but all include some sites of archaeological interest

Drives

1 Lliw Upland drive, West Glamorgan
A circular drive established by West Glamorgan County Council. Approximately 24 km (15 miles). Not specifically archaeological, but includes sites to visit along the route.

2 Rheola Forest Drive, West Glamorgan
A circular drive established by West Glamorgan County Council. Approximately 56 km (35 miles) long. Not specifically archaeological, but includes sites to visit along the route

Abbreviations

AAI	Area of Archaeological Importance
AD	*Anno Domini*
ADAS	Agricultural Development Advisory Service
BC	Before Christ (uncalibrated radiocarbon years used throughout this report)
CBA	Council for British Archaeology
CCRA	Cornwall Committee for Rescue Archaeology
CPAT	Clwyd Powys Archaeological Trust
CRC	Cambridge Research Co-operative DoE Department of the Environment (now HBMC)
EEC	European Economic Community
EFG	English Forestry Group
EMTB	East Midlands Tourist Board
FMW	Field Monument Warden
FWAG	Farming and Wildlife Advisory Group
GGAT	Glamorgan Gwent Archaeological Trust
HBMC	Historic Buildings and Monuments Commission (English Heritage)
HWCC	Hadrian's Wall Consultative Committee
LFA	Less Favoured Area
MAFF	Ministry of Agriculture, Fisheries and Food
NCC	Nature Conservancy Council
NTB	Northumbria Tourist Board
NWWA	North-West Water Authority
NYCC	North Yorkshire County Council
OD	Ordnance Datum (=Height above sea level)
RCHME	Royal Commission on the Historical Monuments of England
RCAHMW	Royal Commission on Ancient and Historic Monuments Wales
SAM	Scheduled Ancient Monument
SMC	Scheduled Monument Concent
SMR	Sites and Monuments Record
SSSI	Site of Special Scientific Interest
WOAD	Welsh Office Agriculture Department

Glossary of terms used

Anglian Anglo-Saxon culture represented in northern England before the Viking age

Blowing house furnace used for smelting tin in the south west

Bronze Age Period of prehistory traditionally characterized by the extensive use of bronze for tools; c 2000–800 BC

Clearance cairn pile of stones built up from clearing fields or grazing areas

Dendrochronology technique to date pieces of timber by counting back the number of annual rings developed during growth

Honour area of special jurisdiction based on the court of a lord

Iron Age period of prehistory traditionally defined by the common use of iron; c 800 BC to AD 43. Terminated in many areas by the arrival of the Romans in AD 43, but in some upland zones Iron-Age lifestyles continued unchanged well into the first millennium AD

Marginal (land) land on the edge of intensively used areas, with the overtone that its quality is not compatible with intensive use under the prevailing circumstances. The limits of this land change over time so that what might be regarded as marginal now was not always so

Mesolithic period of prehistory after the last ice age and before the introduction of farming; c 8000–3500 BC

Neolithic period of prehistory characterized by the early farming economies, before the use of metal; c 3500–2000 BC

Neutron activation analysis technique of analysis to determine the chemical composition of a substance. This in turn may lead to information on its origin

Optical emission spectrometry technique of analysis to determine the nature of trace elements in a substance. This in turn may lead to information on its origin

Palaeolithic earliest period of prehistory extending back through the last ice age. During this time man evolved from early hominid species to modern man, Before c 8000 BC

Palaeo– prefix meaning old or ancient; thus palaeoenvironment (ancient environment), palaeoeconomy, (ancient economy) etc

Petrology study of the origin and structure of rocks. Used in archaeology to characterize stone and determine its source

Pillow mounds low oblong mounds of earth and stones, often with a shallow ditch round them, constructed as rabbit warrens in the Middle Ages

Radiocarbon dating method of determining an absolute date for preserved organic matter (eg charcoal, bone, wood etc) by measuring the level of the radioactive isotope 14C remaining in a sample, and comparing this with both the level of the non-radioactive isotope 12C and the expected ratio between the two. The date so obtained relates to the time of death of the organic matter tested. Radiocarbon dates are given here as dates BC, but due to fluctuations in the level of 14C in the atmosphere, and a number of other factors, radiocarbon years do not correspond exactly with calendar years

Scanning electron microscopy detailed study of the topography of the surface of materials (eg pottery, metal) with a special microscope which uses high energy electrons rather than light.

Shieling northern term for a seasonal hut for shepherds or herdsmen. Sometimes with enclosures for stock

Stone row upright stones set in a single line or in parallel lines. Purpose unknown, presumed to be some sort of ritual monument. Mostly Late Neolithic or Bronze Age in date

Stratification superimposition of one deposit over an earlier one

Transhumance seasonal moving of livestock (and section of the population) to take advantage of short-lived grazing away from the home farmstead

Bibliography

Allaby, M, 1983 *The changing uplands*, Cheltenham, Countryside Commission

Allcroft, A H, 1908 *Earthwork of England*, London, Macmillan & Co

Appleton, J H, 1975 *The experience of landscape*, London, Wiley

Aston, M, 1983 "Deserted farmsteads on Exmoor and the Lay Subsidy of 1327 in west Somerset", *Proc Somerset Archaeol Natur Hist Soc*, **127**, 71–104

Aston, M & Burrow, I (eds), 1982 *The archaeology of Somerset*, Taunton, Somerset County Council

Barker, P, 1977 *Techniques of archaeological excavation*, London, Batsford

Bakhevig, S, 1980 "Phosphate analysis in archaeology: problems and recent progress", *Norwegian Archaeol Rev*, **13**, 73–100

Balaam, N D & Porter, H M, 1982 "The phosphate surveys" in N Balaam, K Smith & G J Wainwright, "The Shaugh Moor project: fourth report – environment, context and conclusion", *Proc Prehist Soc*, **48**, 203–278

Balaam, N D, Smith, K & Wainwright, G J, 1982 "The Shaugh Moor project: fourth report – environment, context and conclusion", *Proc Prehist Soc*, **48**, 203–278

Barnie, H & Robinson, D, 1973 *North Wales Shell pipeline – an archaeological survey* (Rescue Publication no 3) Worcester, Rescue

Barrington, N & Stanton, W, 1976 *Mendip: the complete caves and a view of the hills*, Cheddar, Barton

Beeson, E B & Masterman, M C H, 1979 *Archaeological survey of enclosed land in Widecombe-in-the-Moor parish* (Devon Archaeol Society Occ Paper no 7), Exeter, DAS

Berridge, P, 1979 "Waun Fignen Felin, Breconshire", *Archaeol in Wales*, **19**, 11

Binks, G, 1978 *Self-guided trails*, Cheltenham, Countryside Commission

Birks, H J B, Deacon, J & Pegler, S, 1975 "Pollen maps for the British Isles 5000 years ago", *Proc Roy Soc London*, B, **189**, 87–105

Bradley, R & Hart, C, 1983 "Prehistoric settlement in the Peak District during the third and second millennium bc: a preliminary analysis in the light of recent fieldwork", *Proc Prehist Soc*, **49**, 177–193

Briggs, S, 1984 "An eroding asset: archaeology on the Beacons", *Brecon Beacons Nat Park Newsletter*, **35**, 3

Brown, J, 1984 *Historic monuments of Wales: ways of making them more enjoyable, more enlightening, more profitable*, Worcester, John Brown Tourism Marketing

Charlton, D B & Day, J C, 1978 "Excavation and field survey in Upper Redesdale", *Archaeol Aeliana*, (ns 5), **6**, 61–86

Cleere, H (ed), 1984 *Approaches to the archaeological heritage*, Cambridge, At the University Press

Cobham, R, 1984 *Agricultural landscapes demonstration farms*, Cheltenham, Countryside Commission

Coggins, D, Fairless, K J & Batey, C E, 1983 "Simy Folds: an early medieval settlement in upper Teesdale", *Medieval Archaeol*, **27**, 1–26

Council for British Archaeology, 1948 *A survey and policy of field research in the archaeology of Great Britain: I prehistoric and early historic ages to the seventh century AD*, London, CBA

Countryside Commission, 1973 *Pennine way survey*, Cheltenham, Countryside Commission

Countryside Commission, 1976 *The Lake District upland management experiment*, Cheltenham, Countryside Commission

Countryside Commission, 1978 *Upland land use*, Cheltenham, Countryside Commission

Countryside Commission, 1978a *Guided walks*, (Advisory Series no 4), Cheltenham, Countryside Commission

Countryside Commission, 1979 *Countryside rangers and related staff*, (Advisory Series no 7), Cheltenham, Countryside Commission

Countryside Commission, 1979a *The Snowdonia upland management experiment*, Cheltenham, Countryside Commission

Countryside Commission, 1980 *Guided walks*, Cheltenham, Countryside Commission

Countryside Commission, 1980a *Self-guided trails*, (Advisory Series no 9) Cheltenham, Countryside Commission

Countryside Commission, 1980b *Protecting historic monuments and ancient features*, (Leaflet no 8 in *Countryside Conservation Handbook*), Cheltenham, Countryside Commission

Countryside Commission, 1983 *Areas of Outstanding Natural Beauty: Policy statement 1983*, Cheltenham, Countryside Commission

Countryside Commission, 1984 *A better future for the uplands*, Cheltenham, Countryside Commission

Countryside Commission, 1984a *Bibliography No 5: The uplands*, Cheltenham, Countryside Commission

CPAT (Clwyd Powys Archaeological Trust), 1983 *Review of projects*, Welshpool, CPAT

Crawford, G M, 1980 *Bronze Age burial mounds in Cleveland*, Middlesborough, Cleveland County Council

Crawford, O G S & Keiller, A, 1928 *Wessex from the air*, Oxford

CRC (Cambridge Research Co-Operative), 1983 "The national survey of public opinion towards archaeology", *Archaeol Rev Cambridge*, **2**, (1), 24–26

Cummins, W A, 1979 "Neolithic stone axes – distribution and trade in England and Wales" in T H McK Clough & W A Cummins (eds), *Stone axe studies* (CBA Res Rep 23), London, CBA, 5–12,

Daniel, G E, 1975 *A hundred and fifty years of archaeology*, London, Duckworth

DOE (Department of the Environment), 1982 "The 1979 AM Act and National Parks", Circular issued by DoE (Ancient Monuments Secretariat), January 1982

DOE, 1983 *Criteria for the selection of Ancient Monuments*, Press Notice, **523**, London, DoE

Darvill, T C, 1984 *Birdlip bypass project – first report: field survey and archaeological assessment*, Bristol, Western Archaeological Trust

DAT (Dyfed Archaeological Trust), nd, A *Marginal land survey – Cardiganshire*, (typescript report) Carmarthen, DAT

DAT, nd, B *Marginal land survey – Pembrokeshire*, (typescript report) Carmarthen, DAT

Dickinson, S, 1984 *The Kentmere Archaeological Project: a brief description*, Barrow in Furness, Search

Dobbins, C M, 1983 "Planning controls", *Glamorgan Gwent Archaeological Trust Annual Report 1982–3*, Swansea, GGAT 92–98

EMTB (East Midlands Tourist Board), 1983 *Tourism fact sheets – East Midlands 1982*, Lincoln, EMTB

Evans, J G, Limbrey, S & Cleere, H (eds), 1975 *The effect of man on the landscape: the Highland Zone*, (CBA Res Rep 11), London, CBA

Faull, M L & Moorhouse, S A, 1981 *West Yorkshire: an archaeological survey*, Wakefield, West Yorkshire County Council

Feist, M J, 1978 *A study of management agreements*, Cheltenham, Countryside Commission

Fell, C & Hildyard, E J, 1953 "Prehistoric Weardale – a new survey", *Archaeol Aeliana*, **31**, 98–115

Ferguson, R S, 1890 *A history of Cumberland*

Fleming, A, 1975 "Prehistoric land boundaries in upland Britain – an appeal", *Antiquity*, **49**, 215–6

Fleming, A, 1982 "Social boundaries and land boundaries", in C Renfrew & S Shennan (eds), *Ranking, resource and exchange*, Cambridge, At the University Press, 52–55

Fleming, A, 1983 "Upland settlement in Britain: the second millennium and after", *Scottish Archaeol Rev*, **2**, 171–79

Fleming, A, 1983a "The prehistoric landscape of Dartmoor Part 2: north and east Dartmoor", *Proc Prehist Soc*, **49**, 195–241

Fleming, A & Ralph, N, 1982 "Medieval settlement and land use on Holne Moor, Dartmoor: the landscape evidence", *Medieval Archaeol*, **26**, 101–137

Fowler, P J, 1977 *Approaches to archaeology*, London, Black

Fowler, P J, 1977a "Land management and the cultural resource", in T Rowley & M Breakell (eds), *Planning and the historic environment II*, Oxford, Oxford University Department of External Studies, 131–142

Fowler, P J, 1978 "Lowland landscapes: culture, time and personality", in S Limbrey & J G Evans (eds), *The effect of man on the landscape: the lowland zone*, (CBA Res Rep 21), London, 1–11, CBA

Fowler, P J, 1980 "Traditions and objectives in British field archaeology, 1953–78", *Archaeol J*, **137**, 1–21

Fowler, P J & Ellison, A B, 1977 "Archaeology on Exmoor: its nature, assessment and management", *Exmoor Review*, **18**, 78–84

Fox, C, 1932 *The personality of Britain*, Cardiff, National Museum of Wales. (1947 = 4th Edition)

Fry, G L A, Cooke A S, 1984 *Acid deposition and its implications for nature conservation in Britain*, (Focus on nature conservation no 7), Shrewsbury, Nature Conservancy Council

Garton, D & Beswick, P, 1983 "The survey and excavation of a neolithic settlement area at Mount Pleasant, Kenslow, 1980–3", *Derbyshire Archaeol J*, **103**, 7–40

Gates, T, 1983 "Unenclosed settlements in Northumberland", in J C Chapman & H C Mytum (eds), *Settlement in North Britain*

1000 BC – AD 1000, (British Archaeological Reports 118), Oxford, BAR, 103–148

Godwin, H, 1975 *History of the British flora*, (2nd ed), Cambridge, At the University Press

Green, B, 1981 *Countryside conservation: the protection and management of amenity ecosystems*, London, Allen & Unwin

Grenter, S, 1984 "The erosion of the past", *Archaeol in Clwyd*, **6**, 28–29

Grimes, W F, 1946 "Prehistoric period", in V E Nash-Williams (ed), *A hundred years of Welsh archaeology*, Cardiff, Cambrian Archaeol Association, 24–79

Grinsell, L V, 1964 "The Royce collection at Stow-on-the-Wold", *Trans Bristol Gloucestershire Archaeol Soc*, **83**, 5–33

Groube, L M, 1978 "Priorities and problems in Dorset archaeology" in T C Darvill, M Parker Pearson, R W Smith and R Thomas (eds), *New approaches to our past: an archaeological forum*, Southampton, University of Southampton Archaeological Society, 29–52

Groube, L M & Bowden, M C B, 1982 *The archaeology of rural Dorset, past present and future*, (Dorset Natur Hist Archaeol Soc Monograph Series no 4), Dorchester, DNHAS

Guilbert, G, 1975 "Ratlinghope/Still Hill Shropshire: earthworks, enclosures and cross dykes", *Bull Board Celtic Stud*, **26**, 363–373

Harbottle, B & Newman, T G, 1973 "Excavation and survey on the Starsley Burn, North Tynedale 1972", *Archaeol Aeliana*, (ns 5), **1**, 136–175

Harding, A, 1984 *Archaeological survey on Danby Rigg – 1984*, (typescript report) Durham, University of Durham, Department of Archaeology

Hayfield, C (ed), 1980 *Fieldwalking as a method of archaeological research*, (Directorate of Ancient Monuments and Historic Buildings Occasional Papers no 2), London, DoE

Haynes, J S, 1983 *Historic landscape conservation*, (Gloucestershire Papers in Local and Rural Planning no 20), Gloucester, Gloucestershire College of Arts and Technology

Haynes, J S, 1983a *Levisham Moor: Archaeological investigations 1957–1978*, Helmsley, North York Moors National Park

HBMC (Historic Buildings and Monuments Commission), 1984 *England's archaeological resource: a rapid quantification of the national archaeological resource and a comparison with the schedule of ancient monuments*, London, HBMC

HBMC, 1984a *An analysis of support from Central Government (DAMHB) and the Historic Buildings and Monuments Commission (HBMC) for the recording of archaeological sites and landscapes in advance of their destruction between 1982 and 1984*, London, HBMC

Henderson, A H, 1979 "Mesolithic material from the surface of Stanage Barrows", *Trans Hunter Archaeol Soc*, **10**, 365–369

Higham, N J, 1978 "Dyke systems in northern Cumbria", *Bull Board Celtic Stud*, **28**, 142–156

Hinchcliffe, J & Schadla-Hall, T (eds), 1980 *The past under the plough*, (Directorate of Ancient Monuments and Historic Buildings Occasional Papers no 3), London, DoE

Hodder, I 1984 "Archaeology in 1984", *Antiquity*, **58**, 25–32

Hodges, R, 1984 "The Roystone Grange Archaeological Trail", *Antiquity* **58**, 206–208

Hoskins, W G, 1955 *The making of the English landscape*, London Hodder and Stoughton

HWCC (Hadrian's Wall Consultative Committee), 1984 *The strategy for Hadrian's Wall*, Newcastle upon Tyne, Countryside Commission

Jackson, A, 1978 *Forestry and Archaeology: a study in survival of field monuments in south west Scotland*, Hertford, Rescue

Jobey, G, 1973 "A Romano-British settlement at Tower Knowe, Wellhaugh, Northumberland", *Archaeol Aeliana*, (ns 5) **1**, 55–79

Jobey, G, 1974 "Notes on some population problems in the area between the two Roman walls", *Archaeol Aeliana*, (ns 5) **2**, 17–26

Jobey, G, 1977 "Iron Age and later farmsteads on Belling Law, Northumberland", *Archaeol Aeliana*, (ns 5), **5**, 1–38

Jobey, G, 1978 "Iron Age and Romano-British settlement on Kennel Hall Knowe, N Tynedale, Northumberland", *Archaeol Aeliana*, (ns 5), **6**, 1–28

Jobey, G, 1981 "Groups of small cairns and the excavation of a cairnfield on Millstone Hill, Northumberland", *Archaeol Aeliana*, (ns 5) **9**, 23–44

Johnson, N, 1983 "The result of air and ground survey of Bodmin Moor, Cornwall" in G S Maxwell (ed), *The impact of aerial reconnaissance on archaeology*, (CBA Res Rep no 49), London, 5–13, CBA

Johnson, N & Rose, P, 1983 *Archaeological survey and conservation in West Penwith, Cornwall*, Truro, Cornwall Committee for Rescue Archaeology

Jones, B, 1984 *Past imperfect: the story of rescue archaeology*, London, Heinemann

Jones, B, 1985 "Introduction" in MacReady, S & Thompson, F M (eds), *Archaeological field survey in Britain and abroad*, London, Society of Antiquaries

Keeley, H C M (ed), 1984 *Environmental archaeology – a regional review*, (Directorate of Ancient Monuments and Historic Buildings Occasional Papers no 6) London, DoE

Kelly, R, 1982 "The excavation of a medieval farmstead at Cefn Graenog Clynnog, Gwynedd", *Bull Board Celtic Stud*, **29**, 859–908

Kelly, R, 1982a "The Ardudwy survey: fieldwork in western Merioneth 1971–81", *J Merioneth Hist Record Soc*, **9**, 121–162

Kelly, R, 1983 "A pre-afforestation survey at Cynfannedd, Arthog, Gwynedd", *Bull Board Celtic Stud*, **30**, 441–452

Lambrick, G, 1977 *Archaeology and agriculture*, (Oxfordshire Archaeological Unit Survey no 4), London, CBA and OAU

Lambrick, G (ed), 1985 *Archaeology and nature conservation*, Oxford, Oxford University Department for External Studies

Leech, R, 1983 "Settlements and groups of small cairns on Birkby and Birker Fells, Eskdale, Cumbria – survey undertaken in 1982", *Trans Cumberland Westmorland Antiq Archaeol Soc*, **83**, 15–23

Lhwyd, E, 1699 [Letter] *Phil Trans Roy Soc London*, (1713), **97**

Limbrey, S & Evans, J G, 1978 *The effect of man on the landscape: the Lowland Zone*, (CBA Res Rep 21) London, CBA

Lynch, F M 1974 "Brenig Valley excavations 1973: interim report", *Trans Denbighshire Hist Soc*, **23**, 9–64

Lynch, F M, 1975 "Brenig Valley excavations 1974", *Trans Denbighshire Hist Soc*, **24**, 13–37

Lynch, F M, 1978 "Moel Goedog Circle I, Merionethshire", *Archaeol in Wales*, **18**, 37–39

Lynch, F M, 1983 "Tir Mostyn, Nantglyn", *Archaeol in Wales*, **23**, 14

Macewen, M & Sinclair, G, 1983 *New life for the hills*, London, Council for National Parks

MAFF (Ministry of Agriculture Fisheries and Food), 1979 *Farming on Ancient Monuments*, (Leaflet 764), London, MAFF

MAFF, 1984 *Huccaby Demonstration Farm: draft management plan*, (Typescript report), Leeds and Exeter

Manley, J, 1984 "Archaeological survey of Ffridd Brynhelen, Pentre-llyn-Cymmer", *Archaeol in Clwyd*, **6**, 5–7

Manley, J (ed), *Archaeology in Clwyd* [annual publication 1978 –]

Mercer, R J, 1980 *Archaeological field survey in northern Scotland Volume I*, (University of Edinburgh Department of Archaeology Occasional Papers no 4), Edinburgh, University of Edinburgh

Mercer, R J, 1982 "Field survey: a route to research strategies", *Scottish Archaeol Rev*, **1**, 91–97

Morgan Evans, D, 1985 "The management of historic landscapes", in G Lambrick (ed), *Archaeology and nature conservation*, Oxford, Oxford University Department of External Studies, 89–94

Musson, C R, 1981 "Rescue archaeology in Wales: how, where, when and who pays?", *Archaeol in Wales*, **21**, 6–16

Musson, C R, 1983 "From Rhondda to Rhuddlan: the Welsh Archaeological Trusts at work", *Popular Archaeology*, **5**, 6–10

Musson, C R, 1984 "Clwyd Powys Archaeological Trust: an introduction", *Montgomeryshire Coll*, **72**, 69–78

Musson, C R, 1984a "Aerial survey", *Archaeol in Clwyd*, **6**, 24–28

NCC (Nature Conservancy Council), 1983 *Handbook for the preparation of management plans*, Shrewsbury, NCC

Netting, R, 1981 *Balancing on an Alp*, Cambridge, At the University Press

NTB (Northumbria Tourist Board), 1983 *Tourism fact sheets – Northumbria 1982*, Newcastle upon Tyne, NTB

NWWA (North West Water Authority), 1979 *Historic conservation*, Warrington, NWWA

North Yorkshire County Planning Department, nd, *Environmental Education resource directory*, Northallerton, NYCC

Palmer, R, 1977 "A computer method for transcribing information graphically from oblique aerial photographs to maps", *J Archaeol Sci*, **4**, 283–290

Paterson, H, 1984 "Preserving the cultural resource – why have Field Monument Wardens?", *Fld Archaeol*, **2**, 14–15

Piggott, S, 1950 *William Stukeley: an eighteenth century antiquary*, Oxford, At the University Press

Piggott, S, 1968 *The Druids*, London, Thames & Hudson

Piggott, S, 1976 *Ruins in a Landscape: essays on antiquarianism*, Edinburgh, At the University Press

Porchester, Lord H, 1977 *A study of Exmoor*, London, HMSO

Quest, P, 1982 "Capital transfer tax and historic landscapes", in C Swainwick (ed), *Conserving historic landscapes*, Castleton, Peak National Park, 33–36

RCHME (Royal Commission on the Historical Monuments of England), 1978 *Survey of surveys*, London, RCHME

Robinson, G R, 1948 "The prehistoric occupation of Cefn Hill near Craswell", *Trans Woolhope Natur Fld Club*, **34**, 32–37

Rollinson, W, 1967 *A history of man in the Lake District*, London, Dent & Sons

Saville, A, 1980, *Archaeological sites in the Avon and Gloucestershire Cotswolds: an extensive survey of a rural archaeological resource with special reference to plough damage*, (Committee for Rescue Archaeology in Avon, Gloucestershire and Somerset Survey no 5), Bristol, CRAAGS

Savory, H N, 1978 "Lluest Wen Reservoir", *Morgannwg*, **22**, 82

Sawyer, P H, 1978 *From Roman Britain to Norman England*, London, Methuen

Selkirk, A, 1978 "Otterburn", *Current Archaeol*, **6**, 152–155

Sell, S, 1983 "Coelbren Roman fort", *Glamorgan Gwent Archaeological Trust Annual Report 1982–3*, 65–66

Sinclair, G & Bell, S, 1983 *The uplands landscape study*, London, Environmental Information Services

Smith, C A 1977 "Late prehistoric and Romano-British enclosed homesteads in north-west Wales: an interpretation of their morphology", *Archaeol Cambrensis*, **126**, 38–52

Staffordshire County Planning and Development Department, 1984, *The Manifold Valley Survey*, Stafford, County Planning and Development Department

Stansfield, G 1982 *Effective interpretive exhibitions*, Cheltenham, Countryside Commission

Stevenson, J B, 1975 "Survival and discovery", in J G Evans, S Limbrey and H Cleere (eds), *The effect of man on the landscape: the Highland Zone*, (CBA Res Rep 11), London, CBA, 104–108,

Stratham, D C, 1982 *The Bransdale Moor Management Plan*, Helmsley, North York Moors National Park

Swanwick, C (ed), 1982 *Conserving historic landscapes*, Castleton, Peak National Park

Taylor, C, 1983 *Village and farmstead: a history of rural settlement in England*, London, George Philip

Taylor, J A, 1976 "Upland climates", in T J Chandler & S Gregory (eds), *The climate of the British Isles*, London, Longman, 264–87

Wager, J F, 1981 *Conservation of historical landscapes in the Peak District National Park*, Bakewell, Peak Park Joint Planning Board

Walker, J S F (ed), 1984, *Blackstone Edge Roman Road*, (typescript report) Manchester, Greater Manchester Archaeological Unit

Wheeler, R E M, 1925 *Prehistoric and Roman Wales*, Oxford, At the University Press

Wilson, D R, 1975 "The evidence of air-photography", in J G Evans, S Limbrey & H Cleere (eds), *The effect of man on the landscape: the Highland Zone*, (CBA Res Rep 11), London, CBA, 108–111,

Wingerson, L, 1979 "Heritage under siege", *New Scientist*, **83**, 962

Wood, E S, 1963 *A field guide to archaeology*, London, Collins